Bitchin' Bodies

young women talk about body dissatisfaction

Bitchin' Bodies

young women talk about body dissatisfaction

Terri L. Russ
images by Karin E. Lekan

StepSister Press, LLC
Chicago, Illinois

ISBN 978-0-9802300-1-7

Library of Congress Control Number 2008932594

Printed in the United States of America by Publishers' Graphics, Carol Stream, Illinois

First edition printed for release on September 25, 2008

Different formats of books or book excerpts can be created to fit special needs. For details, write StepSister Press, 4064 N. Lincoln Ave #426, Chicago, Illinois 60618, USA, or email StepSisterPress@gmail.com.

Publisher's Cataloging-in-Publication Data

Russ, Terri L.

Bitchin' bodies : young women talk about body dissatisfaction / Terri L. Russ; with images by Karin E. Lekan.

p. cm.

ISBN 978-0-9802300-1-7

1. Body image in women. 2. Self-perception in women. 3. Feminism.

HQ1206.R87 2008

305.42—dc22   2008932594

Published by StepSister Press

StepSister Press, LLC

4064 N. Lincoln Ave. #426, Chicago, Illinois 60618, USA

StepSisterPress@gmail.com, StepSisterPress.com

While the publisher has made every effort to provide accurate telephone numbers and internet addresses at the time of publication, neither the publisher nor the author assumes any responsibility for errors or for changes that occur after publication. Further, the publisher does not have any control over and does not assume any responsibility for author or third-party websites or their content. This book contains the author's interpretations of No part of this book should be used as an instructional guide.

Contents

advance praise for Bitchin' Bodies

"Terri Russ masterfully depicts the depths of women's body dissatisfaction as a 'post-modern plague' in *Bitchin' Bodies*. Few can dispute the veracity of this plague after reading the multitude of disturbing body dissatisfaction discourse examples young women shared with her. However, Russ's greatest contribution is providing women with the language and tools to use as an antidote to battle the body dissatisfaction plague rather than each other. By recognizing how much we contribute daily to our own body dissatisfaction plight, Russ has empowered us to once again concentrate on internal rather than external substance."

—Dr. Jennifer Kramer
Assistant Professor of Communication,
The College of St. Benedict / St. John's University

"*Bitchin' Bodies* is simply the best book I have read about the cultural power of everyday talk, mediated images, the cult of celebrity, and even taken-for-granted advisories disguised as 'helpful messages' and 'advice' to create unrealistic expectations for beauty in women of all ages, literally from the cradle to the grave. Unlike other notable feminist perspectives on this subject, Dr. Russ doesn't stop at the corner of Power and Hegemony to simply rail against what's wrong, but instead offers sound communicative prescriptions for how all of us—women and men—may learn how to talk, write, argue, and discuss our way forward, understanding that while some aspects of this pervasive cultural surround will no doubt continue to seek influence over us, it need not dominate women's lives, women's bodies, and/or a woman's sense of self worth. Written in an accessible style and chock full of powerful examples drawn from the research and popular literature, I recommend this book to anyone interested in women's health and wellness, but especially to parents of teenage girls, classroom teachers, and college students."

—H.L. (Bud) Goodall, Jr., PhD
author of *A Need to Know: The Clandestine History of a CIA Family*
and *Writing Qualitative Inquiry: Self, Stories, and Academic Life*

"When I first glanced at *Bitchin' Bodies: young women talk about body dissatisfaction*, I must admit that the first thought than ran through my head was, 'Great! A book about women's bodies as rhetoric! I've been a fan of the female torso since I was about 13.' However, upon a more serious read of the work—which was hard to put down—I found myself feeling guilty for all of my stereotypical preconceptions and misconceptions of what beauty, per se, is. I, myself, weigh about 275 pounds from two decades of Mountain Dew abuse and a nasty computer programming and word-processing addiction. So, who am I to hold to these stereotypes? Yet, still, the tilted gaze inherent in my ideals of what a pretty woman is, clearly, warrants sober checking at the door. Russ and StepSister Press are about to do the communication discipline writ large and women in general a world of honest good. Russ slyly dispels many of the myths of 'beauty' by demonstrating the insidious havoc caused upon the female human pysche due to our prevailing beauty culture, and how it insidiously seeps into the female psyche—sometimes not only at the detriment of one's mental health, but also at their physiological health, as well. Bravo to Terri Russ for bringing a quality feminist critique to market …."

—Tyrone L. Adams, PhD
editor of *Electronic Tribes: The Virtual Worlds of Geeks, Gamers, Shamans, and Scammers* with Stephen A. Smith

Acknowledgments

Putting down into words the depth of appreciation I feel for all who have helped with this book is a daunting proposal at best and a potential disaster at worst. Knowing that I run the risk of leaving some out or offending others by not being effusive enough, I will attempt to tackle, with an economy of words, the challenge of memorializing my appreciation to those pivotal individuals who have made this project possible. I apologize now for any errors, omissions, or offenses.

Starting with the end, I want to extend my profuse thanks to Annie. I never could have imagined that a random bathroom conversation would lead to the publication of this book. Just when I was beginning to give up hope of finding a publisher who would share my vision for what this book can and should be, you wandered in. Thanks for continually believing in both me and the project, and big thanks for pushing me to make the final product even better than I thought possible. I'm looking forward to our friendship continuing to grow and to all the future bitchin' projects we'll tackle. I wish to also thank Jacqueline U. Heckman and Christina M. Heckman for their dedicated commitment and work in putting together the semblance of a manuscript I presented them into top shape form. Equally important, thanks to Karin E. Lekan for translating my theoretical ramblings into the awe-inspiring images that help bring my words to life. You are truly a master artist.

Of course this project would not have come to final fruition without the gracious participation of the many women who took time to talk to me. I am eternally indebted to all of you for the time and care you dedicated to this project. More importantly, I thank you for being so forthcoming with me and sharing your intensely personal stories, frustrations, and victories with me and my readers.

In a related vein, thanks to all my students who have dared to challenge me and tell me when I was just flat out wrong. This project began as a class project that morphed into my dissertation. As such, I would like to extend my profuse thanks to my dissertation committee: Myrdene Anderson, Don Burks, Geri Friedman, Bill Rawlins, and Amardo Rodriguez. Not only did they inspire me in their classes and personal discussions, but they also believed in this project when many others did not.

On a more personal level, I would like to thank all of the friends and colleagues over the years who have listened to my incessant ranting about these issues. I would like to extend a cornucopia of special thanks to my new SMC colleagues for sparking the light that allowed me to make it through the homestretch of this assignment. Jaclyn, what can I say? I am forever grateful for your helping me to see my theories come alive through dance and for always making me feel like a rock star. Keep dancing for now, but please come back to the Bend soon. Thanks to Lesley Long and Danielle Nuzzo for their dedicated and thorough research efforts. Special thanks to Jen Kramer for the many ways she has lived our friendship: From taking my middle of the night frantic phone calls, to constantly encouraging me when I wanted to quit, to forcing me to think in new directions, her friendship has helped me continue with this project and push it in new directions. My husband Jerry Crabbe's importance to this project cannot ever be accounted for in a few words. The best I can do is thank him for reminding me that even in academic theorizing, what the head makes cloudy, the heart makes clear. All of my love to Ginny, Mom, and John and thanks for putting up with me. Finally I would like to acknowledge my memories of Margaret Bennett, Cocoa Essig, Virginia Daugherty, RLD, Robert Lenick and big Desi. Thoughts of you always provide just the right inspiration for those middle of the night writing jags when words won't come.

Introduction

Bitchin' bodies bitchin'

Bitchin' bodies bitchin'

Driving to the interview I had the usual questions running through my mind: Would they show up? What did they look like? Would this be a helpful interview or another exercise in wasted time? For a few months, I had been talking to women of all different sizes as I conducted interviews about body dissatisfaction. The women, most in college, ranged in age from eighteen to twenty-four. When I walked into the coffee shop, I recognized them immediately. They had the fresh, preppy, skinny look of many sorority girls. I ordered a soy latte, introduced myself, and after some minor chit chat started the tape recorder. Approximately thirty minutes into our session, I found myself listening to the following exchange:

> Caitlyn: We came back from somewhere and we were like I wear a size two now.
>
> Isabelle: Yeah, we were admitting to each other that we weren't a size zero anymore.
>
> Caitlyn: Yeah.
>
> Isabelle: And then we both talked each other into feeling that it's ok. I mean a zero is what I always was. It's my base. But then all of a sudden you're like a size two.
>
> Caitlyn: I guess a size two is still small, but it's not what I am. It's not a …
>
> Isabelle: Zero …
>
> Caitlyn: Yeah …

They continued for a few more minutes before moving onto a different topic. When I asked them later why they were upset considering that by most standards a size two is still small, they gave a variety of reasons: Their friends still wore a size zero; their boyfriends made comments about their "fat stomachs" or the five pounds they could lose; they were afraid of what their parents think; they felt like "heifers."

Both women were close to graduating and leaving the sheltered life of college. At twenty-two, Caitlyn had one more semester to complete before finishing her degree in Special Education and moving on to a full-time teaching position. Twenty-three-year-old Isabelle was completing her last semester as an engineering major. She had already secured a job with a multi-national corporation and would be working in research and development within the food processing division. Despite these markers of apparent success, both repeatedly expressed concern and dissatisfaction with their bodies.

Caitlyn and Isabelle's concerns echoed the same things that I had heard in my other interviews. While most of the women I interviewed are not size two, there is a striking similarity to the concerns they have about their bodies and the ways they speak about them. Body dissatisfaction like this is everywhere and more rampant than we like to think. Pick up any entertainment or fashion magazine and you'll see articles about extreme diets or the latest weight loss story of a Hollywood star—perhaps twenty pounds in one month. Go to your bookstore and you'll see hundreds of books on diet and exercise. Talk to nearly any woman and she will tell you exactly which parts of her body "need work." Numerous studies have found that young women are more frightened of becoming fat than they are of getting cancer and that they would rather lose a leg or an arm than get fat.[1] According to one study, over 90% of all college age women are dissatisfied with some aspect of their body shape and size and have been on a diet in the last year.[2] I have talked to hundreds of college age women and have yet to meet one who is happy and satisfied with her body.

The title of this book, *Bitchin' Bodies,* encompasses both the presumed societal expectation that women have ideal bodies and the result of their trying to achieve that ideal. As adjective, *bitchin'* refers to the cultural mandate that women have ideal bodies that look sexy—bitchin' bodies. The current manifestation of this ideal body is ultra-thin with disproportionately large breasts—an impossibility for over 98% of the female population.[3] As verb, *bitchin'* refers to one of the results facing women who try to achieve this ideal. They turn into bodies that bitch about their bodies—bitchin' bodies. Young women quickly realize that within certain segments of society, no matter how much education they get, they are prized first for their bitchin' bodies. By listening to their bitchin' we can come to a greater understanding of how the lived experiences of body dissatisfaction impact all women.

As a woman, I understand their concerns. I have grown up immersed in a culture that is obsessed with the size and general appearance of my body. Like it or not, I have internalized this obsession and am constantly aware of my stomach that is no longer flat, my thighs that are covered with cellulite, and my upper arms that seem to jiggle at the slightest movement. Even though I am a feminist and a scholar who researches and teaches about these issues, I still find myself falling prey to that little voice which asks if I really need that piece of cake or reminds me that it's been three days since I worked out. In fact, part of the reason I became interested in studying body dissatisfaction was because of my fears and concerns about my own body.

Interweaving the public and the private

We are all private individuals living in a public world with our private lives intricately intertwined with the larger environment. Our actions are controlled by laws; our movements are restricted to designated areas—roads for driving, sidewalks for walking. Failure to control ourselves appropriately results in public reprimand ranging from the evil eye leveled by a fellow citizen to arrest and prosecution by government agents. For women, the public nature of our existence extends to the size and appearance of our bodies. Not only are female bodies put on display to sell items or attract sexual interest, but they are also on display every place we go. Every time we walk down the street, we may be judged. Are our clothes too sexy? Do we look too fat? Are we wearing too much make-up? Too little? Are we showing too much cleavage? The list seems to go on indefinitely. More troubling, though, is that a "yes" answer to any of these questions opens us up to possible criticism and scorn from others.

I am amazed at how often I hear complete strangers commenting on some aspect of a woman's appearance. Recently, while sitting in a hospital waiting room, I couldn't help but overhear the conversation of two older women sitting across the room. In the midst of their usual small talk I heard one say, "Those girls today and the way they dress, showing all that cleavage. They're just asking for trouble." The two then spent a few minutes discussing the problems with today's young women and their clothes. I found myself agreeing and disagreeing. Clothing is a form of expression. It does seem as if some clothing cuts today are extreme—low rider jeans that are just centimeters above being x-rated or shirts that have necklines plunging to the navel. I then looked down at my own shirt and my openly displayed cleavage. Looking back across the room, I realized that the women had been talking about me. I immediately pulled my jacket closed to cover the offending flesh. It wasn't until later that I began to question why these women felt entitled to comment, loudly, on my choice of clothes. I then wondered why I had cared.

With this public display of and commentary on female bodies, it's not surprising that so many women feel aware of and dissatisfied with their own bodies. What is surprising, though, is that despite the prevalence of body dissatisfaction amongst women of all ages, we don't know a lot about the daily experiences of living with body dissatisfaction. Certainly, there is a lot of research on the causes of and treatments for eating disorders and how negative body image leads to eating disorders, but eating disorders are only part of the problem. More women are dissatisfied with their bodies than suffer from eating disorders, yet their experiences are noticeably absent from the literature discussing these topics. Whenever I read these books and articles, I walk away wondering why we, as women, spend so much time thinking and talking about our bodies. Since so many of us think there is something wrong with our bodies, do we even have a clue what our bodies really look like? When we look in the mirror, do we see a whole person or just various body parts? As adult women, how do years of exposure to ultra-slim models, actresses, and dolls impact the way we view our bodies as well as those of other women?

Dissatisfaction stories

Keeping these questions in mind, I jumped into the scholarly fray. The problem is much too complex to be reduced to one simple cause. Most women are intimately aware of the multiple reasons they feel body dissatisfaction, but they don't feel comfortable talking about it openly. Despite the public interest in female bodies, discussion of the female body still carries with it a certain sense of stigma or taboo. Whenever I ask women what they think about body image and body dissatisfaction, floods of stories, frustrations, and concerns come pouring out. It seems that every woman has a story for every situation I ask about—either they've personally been involved in a similar incident or someone close to them has been. In this book I examine these stories in order to help illuminate what it is like to live with constant body dissatisfaction.

The role of stories in helping us understand the world and our place in it is multi-dimensional. Stories are more than entertainment; they are an integral part of life. We use stories to help structure and make sense of our world.[4] Communication scholar Art Bochner observes that "the stories people tell about their lives is both a means of 'knowing' and a way of 'telling' about the social world."[5] In other words, stories help us both understand the world and discuss it. When we meet someone new, we share stories as a way of getting to know each other. More importantly, though, through the stories that we share, we have the ability to change our lives while we simultaneously affect the lives of others. Through the telling of stories we bond with each other. We form communities of like-minded individuals.

The story that I am writing here is not a new story. The existing story is that which places a woman in the role of a sexualized body, a subjugation to all things male. Within this story, there are millions of characters and thousands of sub-plots. My story here is like one of those sub-plots. It is an interruption of the ongoing story, an interruption that changes the existing story line and sends it in a new direction. My hope is that this sub-plot will become the main plot.

Not quite the real world

Throughout this project, I have spoken with women of all ages—the youngest was eight years old and the oldest was "eighty-five, but I tell people that I'm eighty-two." However, I have chosen to focus on young women between the ages of eighteen and twenty-four: college age women. Whether they are heading for college or embarking on a new career, each fall thousands of young women leave the safety and security of the people and places they've known and enter this completely alien environment called "college" or the "real world." They're taken from a structured environment where they're surrounded by people they've grown up with and thrust into a free-form environment of strangers or near strangers where they are in a constant state of instability and adjustment. They must learn how to be responsible for themselves—wake up on time, make sure laundry is done fairly regularly, and eat a well-balanced diet. If they're college bound, they must learn how to function in college classes—what is the best way to get from one side of campus to the other in less than ten minutes, and how to complete 500 pages of reading in less than one week. They may be working part-time to defray expenses or holding an internship to gain practical work experience. They must figure out who to meet amongst the thousands of other students and how to meet them so that they can cobble together a social life. If the young women are entering the work world, they must get to know the daily ins and outs of both the company and their particular job, determine how to navigate the quagmire of internal politics, and figure out how to make friends without becoming the latest focus of break room gossip. Whether they're in college or working, these young women must learn to manage time and balance all the demands on their time. They may participate in organizations, join sports teams, or do volunteer work. They must choose what to eat and when in an environment with many choices, both healthy and unhealthy, and they must also find time to work out, sleep, relax, make friends, and have a social life.

For those women who enter college, life is a type of purgatory—this phase is about preparing for the rest of their lives. Overnight they've gone from being treated as children who needed rules and parents to control them to being adults who make their own rules. But while they are legally adults, they don't have much, if any, life experience as adults to guide them in making choices that will affect their future careers and family lives. They feel pressures from all sides, including those they put on themselves. All of this is happening at the same time in their lives that they're dealing with the final phases of adolescent maturation—the loss of baby fat and the end of being babied. And very often they are at the height of what society considers their physical perfection—or as close to it as one can get without the benefits of airbrushing, computer enhancement, or plastic surgery.

All these young women are faced with an ever-increasing (and often unrealistic) list of social and cultural demands. Be independent, but find a husband. Be assertive, but smile. Eat three healthy meals per day, but be super skinny. Be strong, but wear stiletto heels. To make sure that they're meeting these demands, everyone from parents to friends to boyfriends make comments—both directly and indirectly. The result is a tornado of social, cultural, and interpersonal pressures that assaults them every minute of every day.

Dissatisfaction interviews

Keeping these things in mind, since 2002 I've interviewed and spoken with college age women in both informal and formal interviews, resulting in over 2,000 single spaced pages of transcripts. Informal interviews include brief five-minute chats and extended conversations that seemingly occurred serendipitously. I conducted these informal interviews wherever I was at the moment the conversation developed—coffee shops, bookstores, department store dressing rooms, locker rooms, any place where women congregate.

Formal interviews were conducted on two separate college campuses with volunteers recruited from fliers and by word of mouth, a total of forty women interviewed with their friends—in pairs or groups of three and four. The examples included in this book are drawn from both the informal and the formal interviews. However, for specific conversational examples, I primarily use examples from the formal interviews to show how women talk with each other about body dissatisfaction and related issues. Since the project began as an academic study subject to the rigors and requirements of academic work, the women referenced throughout the book are referred to by pseudonyms of their choosing in order to preserve their confidentiality.

For most of the women interviewed, the interview was the first time that they were openly asked questions about how they feel about their bodies, the pressures they feel to look a certain way, what they are doing in response to these pressures and feelings, and what others say to them about their bodies. By participating in these interviews, transcribing them, and reading and analyzing them, I noticed a picture emerging of how body dissatisfaction is lived for many women.[6] Certain phrases, words, concepts, issues, and incidents appeared numerous times. Reading through the transcripts, I was amazed to see the number of similarities—not just in issues, but in the way these issues were discussed and the specific words chosen to illustrate the situations. Even though I conducted each interview, it was only by stepping back and looking at them as a whole that a picture began to form—the picture that is this book. For each individual topic, I have tried to choose the example or examples that most clearly illustrate it. For each example that made the cut, several others did not—enough to write a few more books. In making these decisions I focused on the story and not the storyteller. Therefore, some voices appear in every chapter and others may appear only once. This does not mean that only these women suffered from these issues. It merely means that their expression of their thoughts and feelings most clearly illuminates the issue under discussion.

The majority of the women who participated in the formal interviews are demographically similar—late teens to early twenties, white, heterosexual, middle class. Does this mean that these issues and experiences of body dissatisfaction are limited to women like them? These issues certainly impact women in different ways, but they are not in any sense limited to the demographic studied here.[7] The current standards for female beauty, including body size, seem to be primarily targeted at women who are similar to those who participated in my interviews. Women who do not meet these standards, however, do not realistically have the option of opting out because of cultural pressures. If they choose to celebrate their own body size, the best they can hope for is some sort of qualified beauty—the ethnic beauty, the older beauty, the plus-size beauty, etc. If they want to qualify as "truly" beautiful, apparently the best choice they have is to adopt the same standards discussed throughout this book.

When I talk with women from all demographic groups—lesbian, Hispanic, African American and others—I see vestiges of the same issues raised by the women I formally interviewed. The specifics may differ, but the substantive problems tend to remain the same. That said, what is presented in these pages is not a scientific treatise meant to generalize the experiences of a few to the experiences of the many. The specific experiences included in this book are not universal to all women—sharing a biological similarity does not mean that all women share a social similarity. Each woman's experience is unique based on her own circumstances. Nevertheless, there do tend to be aspects of experience that cross over or transcend individual differences. Through sharing and reading these stories of body dissatisfaction, certain meanings will emerge that help bind women to a common community created through discourse, through an ongoing conversation among women from many backgrounds. With this in mind, I cautiously use the word "woman" and its variants.

Although the word "woman" implies a common identity, myriad factors impact our individual development.[8] The suburban white heterosexual is faced with different expectations and demands than the urban Chicana lesbian, and both of these women face realities different from those encountered by the rural African American woman. Even women who appear to be similar will have different experiences, expectations, and identities. Each of us is unique. I could list all of our differences indefinitely, but our identity as women transcends our physical bodies. Instead, I focus on our commonalities. We all live within a common discursive community.[9] In other words, the shared meanings that emerge through our shared discourses are what bind us together. As women living in the United States, we have a shared history of cultural discourse. We live amongst a common saturation of media discourse. We use the same basic language. This commonality of discourse systems is where I focus my discussion.

Understanding discourse

In order to understand these various discourse systems and the power they exert, I divide our discourse into three distinct though interrelated categories—personal, interpersonal, and cultural.[10] The first category, personal discourse, includes the ways that we think of and communicate with ourselves. Even if we don't carry on an actual conversation with ourselves, we are in constant discourse with ourselves, and our understanding of ourselves occurs within the context of our interactions with other social beings. We understand our existence as we define our being in the world and our sense of self in terms of both ourselves and these others. We constantly filter what we think of ourselves through the lens of what we think others will think of us. Therefore, we maintain a running internal dialogue with ourselves. We monitor what we say and do, modifying it as we think necessary.

The second category of discourses, interpersonal, include all those ways that we personally communicate with others—both face to face and through some intermediary format such as telephone or e-mail. The key is that the communication is *person to person,* not necessarily *in person.* Interpersonal discourse is the primary method by which we learn the meaning of the world and how to communicate with others. As children, we are introduced to the world and all that is in it through our interpersonal communication experiences with our parents and other relatives.[11] As we mature, our circle of interpersonal connections grows to include friends, teachers, employers, and many others. The specific individuals we choose to confide in and turn to for advice also change.

Since interpersonal communication occurs on an intimate level, it holds great weight for us. Because we care about these special people in our lives, we want to look good in their eyes. More than wanting to be liked, we want their respect. Therefore, these interpersonal discourses from parents, relatives, friends, and guys have a strong effect on us. Unfortunately, the female body is often a topic for comment in our culture. Therefore, if these people whose respect we want openly comment on our appearance and our bodies, their statements are significant in the realm of how we experience our bodies. We are more likely to believe them, because we assume that they have our best interests at heart and are only looking out for us. It is more difficult to ignore a statement from someone we know and care about than some generic mandate from some unseen other. These interpersonal discourses reinforce and further strengthen the norms and expectations created at the third, the cultural level.

The final category of discourse is that which occurs at the cultural level and which creates those overriding influences on our day-to-day existence. Cultural discourses create and communicate the norms and expectations for everyone living in the community. We structure our lives in light of these discourses even though we are not always conscious of them. For example, we learn early on that little boys are to be little men and that little girls are supposed to be little ladies. For boys, this means that they should adopt a veneer of strength and machismo at all times. We see this idea embodied in the maxim "boys don't cry," which creates expectations for an entire host of behaviors. For little girls, being a lady means being quiet, demure, and chaste, taking up as little space as possible. Essentially a little lady must exist like a china doll—lovely to look at but kept on a shelf. She can be in the world as a decoration, but she cannot be in the world as a fully functioning child.

Included within these cultural discourses are the myriad media messages that inundate our daily lives and surround us from childhood. It is difficult, if not impossible, to go through a day without being exposed to some type of media message. Over 95% of all households have at least one television.[12] When we log onto our computers to check email, we are bombarded with things to entertain us, inform us, or entice us. When we go to the gym to work out, we can watch television as well as listen to our favorite CD or to a mix of favorite songs on our MP3 player. We also have films and video games. All of these combine to constitute media discourse.

Through these media discourses we see the ideals of larger cultural discourses come to life. "Real" people live out the expectations created through cultural discourse and are rewarded or punished accordingly. Because media discourses are so prevalent, what we see and hear through them has such a powerful impact on us that we are no longer consciously aware of all the underlying messages. We have internalized the narratives depicted through media systems so thoroughly that we tend to use them as guides to our everyday experiences.

All of these discourses—personal, interpersonal, and cultural—operate both independently and interdependently, feeding off the others, swirling together, creating a mass of power that is realized in the complex network of implied rules dictating the procedures or expectations of society that we are expected to follow. This mass of discourses and the power it exerts on us creates a situation where we feel as if we are continually being monitored. We function as if we are always under the surveillance of a social gaze.[13] The discourses that structure our lives also serve as a metaphorical gaze under which we monitor ourselves and discipline ourselves accordingly. Life in twenty-first century America is marked not only by our interactions with each other but also, and perhaps more importantly, by our engagement with and exposure to these various cultural and social discourses. We realize who we are through our dialogue with other individuals as well as with the discourses around us. Angela McRobbie explains that our sense of self is an "amalgam of fragmented identities formed in discourse."[14] The discourse that we turn to comes from books, education, mass media, friends, politics, community, relatives, and other sources.

For women, many of these discourses revolve around the way that our bodies should look. What we hear and see around us in discourse presents images or ideals of what we should or could be. These discourses exert power not by presenting direct mandates that must be followed in order to avoid punishment. Instead, discursive power is realized in the ability to gain access to our minds and, through our minds, to our bodies. Under its influence, we change our behavior accordingly, imprisoned in a metaphorical prison from which we cannot escape. Our everyday existence is one of continual, self-imposed surveillance through discursive regimes. Throughout this book, the stories of body dissatisfaction do more than demonstrate how these various discourses act. They bring life to the situation, and in bringing it to life, they demonstrate how little we truly know about the lived experience of body dissatisfaction.

Dissecting dissatisfaction in this book

This book is divided into three main sections based on each of the three discourses presented above. Chapters One through Three address the personal discourses of body dissatisfaction. Chapters Four through Six discuss interpersonal discourses. Chapters Seven and Eight highlight cultural discourses, including media. A final chapter addresses the future of body dissatisfaction as a discourse. Included as part of this final chapter are suggestions for positive behaviors that women can adopt to change their lived experiences of body dissatisfaction. A set of appendixes includes further information on resources and organizations related to body dissatisfaction, as well as a series of questions and exercises for working through the topics in this book.

Personal dissatisfaction discourses

Chapter One opens with a discussion of the physical changes young women experience when they are maturing emotionally, intellectually, and physically. Rather than view these changes as part of the natural process of growing up, many young women think they're just getting fat. In talking about their bodies, they say things like, "I'm the biggest I've ever been" or "I just want to look like I did when I was sixteen." The problem, of course, is that their bodies are easing into what they will look like in their adult childbearing years. Short of surgery, there is no safe way to change this genetic predisposition. To deal with their dissatisfaction, young women adopt many different strategies, including living in constant competition with each other in attempting to achieve a perfect body.

Chapter Two addresses one of the most frustrating pressures and choices faced daily by young women—what to eat and how to do it without getting fat. Many women enter college or the working world from homes filled with low-fat, fat-free, low-carb, and other "healthy" foods. Their new freedom is the first time that they are presented with a seemingly never-ending selection of foods when meal time comes round. To compensate for weight gains caused by changes in lifestyles, young women may start dieting, usually choosing the latest fad diet, and working out for hours on end. While none of the women that I spoke with admitted to currently suffering from an eating disorder, a surprising number of them spoke of the eating disorders they had had in the past or confided that their friend or roommate was currently suffering from an eating disorder.

Chapter Three explores the role of clothing in body dissatisfaction. More than just a way to cover up and retain body heat, clothing acts as a barometer of emotional well-being. If a woman looks attractive or cute in her clothes, then she feels good. If she looks less than cute, then she feels crappy. Looking cute is more than simply combining pieces of clothing which look good together; it is also finding clothes that look good as well as fit right and taking part in the social competition of being known to wear as small a size as possible. Yet there is no uniformity in what the numbers of sizes mean in terms of real body size and shape.

Interpersonal dissatisfaction discourses

Chapter Four examines the ways other people help enforce ideal standards of body size on young women. The female body is not private: It is a social body on which anyone can comment. Looking right in the currently acceptable way is a badge of honor. Looking wrong, then, is the adult equivalent of the dunce cap—something to be ashamed of. Parents and other relatives still play a significant role in the lives of young women who have left home. One statement from a parent or relative can be enough to send a woman running to adopt the latest diet or workout craze.

Chapter Five discusses the interpersonal pressures felt by young women by introducing the role that comments from other women play. Constant comparison to other women results in young women's participation in a particular form of discourse structured around their bodies, what I call *Body Shape Discourse*. In addition to explaining the various forms that Body Shape Discourse takes, Chapter Five also discusses some of its ramifications, such as Body Battles. Characterized by judging and snide comments about other women, body battles create an environment of hostility surrounding all female relationships. Even more disturbing, though, are the various methods of control that emanate from these battles.

Chapter Six concludes the examination of other people's comments by looking at the roles that guys play in female body dissatisfaction. For many women, college is about more than simply getting an education for the future, and working in the real world is about more than establishing a career: These are also the years to find a husband. Even for those women who don't plan on marrying right away, having a boyfriend seems like a mandatory accessory. Consequently, the opinions of guys are extremely important. As

Foxy observed, "A guy will get a girl's attention by compliment-
ing her on her looks." However, guys tend to say one thing and do
another. As noted over and over, guys say they want a girl with a
"little meat on her bones" but then date and praise girls that look
more like the anorexic ideal, as described by Claire, "the skinniest
girls in the class, the tiny size one cheerleaders." These duplicitous
messages leave young women in a quandary, trying to determine
just how they should look to get the guy. With no solid feedback,
most err on the side of skinny.

Cultural dissatisfaction discourses

The final aspect of body dissatisfaction that I highlight is the role
of cultural discourses, including media. It may seem interesting
that I end here, considering that most scholars begin with these
discourses. While I would agree that much of the lived experience
of body dissatisfaction is precipitated by larger cultural issues, I
believe that these issues are secondary to how we experience our
bodies. When I listen to women talk about their bodies, they don't
focus on cultural discourses about what it means to be a woman.
They focus on how it feels to be a woman. Therefore, I have chosen
to privilege these components of body dissatisfaction discourse
throughout this book. That said, as a scholar I believe that the role
of cultural discourse in helping create those feelings of dissatisfaction should not be denied or ignored and discuss this aspect in the
final section of the book.

Chapter Seven delves into the ways media add to body dissatisfaction amongst college women. Media venues present images of
an ideal woman. In a media-saturated society, this ideal woman is
everywhere young women turn. Women are intimately familiar
with what this ideal looks like as shown by Jasmine and Mandi's
description of the key aspects of her beauty: long hair, tanned, perfect body with a tiny waist, big boobs and not a big butt, "unless
she's Jennifer Lopez." Jasmine summed her up as "airbrushed and
perfect," the ideal that some women believe they should emulate.
The problem, though, is that as Jasmine's summary indicates, this
ideal is actually unreal: She is airbrushed or computer enhanced.
If she is on film or television, she has a team of beauticians, cosme-
tologists, and stylists available to create her look. In addition to images, the media also provide methods by which women can achieve
this ideal. Advertisements for diets, exercise regimens, and plastic

surgery options abound. The unfortunate reality of the situation, though, is that the divide between ideal and real is nearly impossible to traverse for most women.

Chapter Eight summarizes some of the larger ramifications of all this pressure and commentary. Knowing that their bodies are always open for possible critique, many women make pre-emptive strikes and comment first. Saying "I look like a heifer" puts the speaker in a position of power—or so it seems at the time. She is acknowledging her flaws before they can be pointed out by anyone else. Of course, this position of power is actually one of disempowerment, no different from the social stigmas hurled at those who don't conform to ideal standards. Punishment comes in various forms. She doesn't get the guy. She doesn't get the job she wants. She is the target of gossip. Interestingly, though, this constant stigma also creates a sense of longing for the golden era when "real women's bodies were appreciated." Each woman I interviewed dreamily mentioned this era without really knowing when (or if) it ever existed. More problematically, this intense focus on body and appearance keeps women running in a circle after some mythical impossibility. And they miss the other real problems that still exist—differential pay, ever increasing restrictions on reproductive rights, increasing violence against women: the list could go on indefinitely.

Future (dis)satisfaction discourses
Chapter Nine opens with a discussion of the problems of body dissatisfaction affecting older women who are also pressured to look young and thin. Even more troubling, we see ever younger girls trying to emulate the ideal. This creates the potential for a lifetime of cycling through dissatisfaction. The chapter then asks the question: What do we do about this problem? When I ask this question, I am inevitably first met with blank stares and silence, followed by an injunction to change the media. At times, it seems like changing media representations of women would be the easy answer—too easy. How do we change a billion dollar industry? Do we want to sacrifice freedom of speech principles? It seems as if a more workable solution is to start small. As my interviews demonstrate, simply asking the question, "What do you think of body image?" opens a door that most women have never walked through. For global change, we can't stop here. We have to talk to others. We have to break the power of silence with the power of speech.

Chapter One

Just look at my stomach

Just look at my stomach

Even though women have made tremendous advances toward equality, there still exists a societal obsession with ensuring that ideal female bodies are skinny, creating a Culture of Discontent that all women must live within. Attempting to achieve this ideal body, a mythological body that is always just a bit further out of reach, many women find themselves in a self-perpetuating Cycle of Dissatisfaction that is exacerbated by their internal comparisons to other women. Recognizing the complexity of this situation is the first step in moving toward changing the cycle of dissatisfaction.

Defining body dissatisfaction

I met Grace a few days before classes started in the fall semester, right after she moved to campus. She was eighteen years old, weighed 110 pounds, and comfortably wore a juniors size three, although she owned clothes ranging from size zero to size seven. As we spoke, Grace shared her concern that she would gain the dreaded "freshman fifteen" during her first semester of coursework. She told me how over the summer her mom had reminded her daily that she must "exercise and eat right." Her mom also said that if she wasn't careful, Grace would get fat since "fat thighs and big butts run in our family."

During the summer, Grace and her high school boyfriend had broken up. He was attending a competing university in a neighboring state and neither wanted to put in the effort to maintain a long-distance relationship or be tied down. She explained that the last time they were together, he told her that her stomach was "getting pouchy." Later that evening they broke up, and six weeks after the fact Grace still wondered if the real reason for the split was her "pouch."

As a result of this, Grace vowed that she would take advantage of the free fitness center membership available to all students on her campus by working out for at least one hour after class each day, doing 150 stomach crunches. She had also planned to eat only three fresh and healthy meals a day under her meal plan in order to keep her eating under control. Grace expressed an air of confidence that no matter what happened, she would not get fat. In fact, she shared with me her plan to wear the same dress to her college graduation that she had worn to her high school graduation.

Just after mid-term, Grace stopped by my office to chat. She looked tired and drained, the way many students do after mid-term exams. I asked how everything was going. She slumped into the wooden chair next to my desk and sighed, "Life sucks. College is hard. And I'm fat." Grace grabbed her stomach to demonstrate how her plan of being healthy and fit had only lasted for two weeks before the social pressures of new friends and the academic pressures of classes had taken over. Grace said that so far she had gained twelve pounds. She jumped up to show me the tag on her jeans and practically shouted how she now had to buy "damned size seven jeans. I'm fat!" Other than looking completely exhausted, she didn't appear much different from when I first met her a few months before. Grace, however, was convinced that she was a "big fat cow who won't ever get married or be successful now."

Grace's story is typical of the stories women share with me. They are faced with the intense pressures of being on their own for perhaps the first time, adapting to the college environment, and meeting the demands of a full-time course load. Nevertheless, the pressure that they feel and fear the most is getting fat. For Grace and other young women like her, being fat seems like the ultimate failure. They fear that if they get fat, they will fail college, be unsuccessful at work, and be doomed to a life of misery. They are convinced that their ultimate success and happiness is dependent fully on the size and appearance of their bodies. They believe the societal assumptions mapped onto the lives of fat women: that a fat woman is an undisciplined mess who lacks self-control and gives in to every whim and desire; that she is more concerned with where the next Big Mac is coming from than with how her personal appearance affects what others think of her; and that even when dressed in the most expensive designer clothes available in her size, she is slovenly and unkempt. Young women like Grace believe in this formula: if svelte, success; if fat, failure. It is tempting to dismiss these concerns as merely narcissistic and immature. However, the fact is that in the United States today, fat discrimination is rampant. Fat people are openly laughed at and scorned. Despite the work of fat activist groups like the National Association to Advance Fat Acceptance, it is not illegal to treat a person differently because of her weight.

Young women's concerns about getting fat are exacerbated by the fact that they are still physically maturing. Before puberty, young girls tend to be angular and bony, and many young girls look as wiry as their male counterparts do. As young women enter adolescence, their angular bodies soften and develop into the more curvaceous bodies of adult women and they physically mature into what they will probably look like during their adult childbearing years. Eating a well-balanced diet and getting regular exercise will help these young women maintain a healthy, regular weight, as Grace had planned. However, young women are unlikely to change the genetically predisposed size and shape of the body safely short of extreme diets, excessive exercise, or extravagant surgery. Nevertheless, young women repeatedly ignore their natural body development and say to me, "I'm at the biggest I've ever been," or "I just want to look like I did when I was sixteen."

Does any woman really like her body?
Women live with the various discursive representations of the female body and the disjunctures these images engender in many different ways. While some women may appear unaffected, many women like Grace participate in an ongoing personal battle, trying to accept the body they have and striving to move closer to the ideal body they believe they see around them. Even though these young women are aware of society's obsession with the size, shape, and appearance of their bodies and are also aware that genetics pre-determines body size and shape, many of them live with some form of negative body image, an extreme dissatisfaction with one's body. A woman suffering from negative body image will focus on what she perceives as inadequacies with her body. She will obsess over these perceived inadequacies and examine them as if they are under a microscope. Part of this micro-focus on perceived inadequacies—the negatives—involves a disregard for the positive parts of their bodies.

Defining *negative body image* as an extreme dissatisfaction with one's body may provide a basic understanding of the phenomenon, yet it doesn't allow for a holistic understanding of it. *Negative body image* as a phrase and concept doesn't fully encompass the lived experiences that women share. At some point in my interviews, I usually ask a question along the lines of, "What do you think about women and body image today?" The question typically evokes eye-rolling and exasperated sighs, or as Mandi, a twenty-year-old tourism and hospitality major, said, "I'm just sick of hearing about it. Everyone talks about it but do they do anything about it? No!" I was surprised at the vehemence with which she expressed herself; however, many of her insights were right on target. For example, Mandi discussed at length the mixed messages of the media. On the one hand, the media speculates on whether a given female Hollywood star is suffering from an eating disorder if she appears in public looking thinner than before. Gossip magazines will then run articles detailing her alarmingly fast weight loss and her possibly being anorexic or bulimic; they go on to discuss how Hollywood's unrealistic expectations cause more and more female stars to feel inadequate if they are any larger than a size two. On the other hand, these same magazines will simultaneously feature this newly thin star on their covers, in clothing spreads, or as a representative example of the ideal female body.[1] Surrounded by such hyperbole and double-talk, it is no wonder that Mandi and many other young women are frustrated with and tired of the phrase "negative body image."

Not only does this phrase, "negative body image," evoke dismissive behaviors and attitudes by young women themselves, but it is also unjust, placing the burden exclusively on them. However, this is not an individual problem or even a woman's problem. In fact, as noted by Angela Trethewey,[2] women's approaches to their bodies should be seen as responses to the social construction of the feminine body. Roberta Seid observed that the ideal feminine body seen in media images of models and actresses represents the thinnest 5% of all women.[3] But if only 5% of American women are represented in media images, then 95% are not. Therefore, the represented ideal is more *unreal* than *real*, and most female bodies are considered bad by media ideal standards. These media images of the ideal über female are not the only source of the intense feelings that women experience about their body image; another comes from the culturally approved custom that everyone, from relatives to friends to strangers, can comment on the appearance and changes—real or perceived—that occur in young women's bodies.

As will become clear in the following chapters, all these pressures influence what young women think and feel about their bodies. It is more than their just being unhappy with how they look; they feel frustrated, discouraged, and inadequate, leading to a feeling of low self-esteem. Everywhere they turn, they are reminded of how they don't measure up to the cultural ideal of female beauty. Limiting these experiences to their own concept of negative body image seems to imply that the phenomenon is just an ailment that a woman herself suffers from, like a biological or psychological disease. This further implies that, like other diseases, negative body image can be cured with simple professional and perhaps pharmacological intervention. In reality, though, the lived experience of negative body image is much deeper and more intricately complex, a societal and not just a personal problem. It is a state of being that often encompasses women's sense of self. To more accurately reflect the complexity of these experiences, I use the phrase *body dissatisfaction*.

Discussing the cycle of dissatisfaction
Did this mirror come from a carnival?
The complex emotions and experiences of body dissatisfaction create an environment in which a woman feels as if she is always looking at herself in a fun-house mirror. The reflected image looks slightly familiar but drastically distorted. Inadequacies that in reality are minor become disproportionately obvious in the reflection. Adequacies that are significant become disproportionately invisible in the reflection. The mirror acts as the main site for a female version of hide and seek. At the same time that women strive to hide from the distorted images reflected, they also seek out those images. The mirror becomes an object to consult in order to examine isolated body parts instead of the entire body. When I ask them how they feel about their bodies, most women sigh and respond with a discussion of the specific part or parts of their bodies that they are most dissatisfied with: "See how my stomach sticks out;" "I hate my thighs. If only they didn't have these fat pockets on the inside." The mirror is then used as a tool to help focus this dissatisfaction, resulting in a further distortion of the actual reflected images.

Women who are dissatisfied with their bodies are persistently aware of their appearance and overall size. They feel as if each time they go anywhere, their bodies—and by extension their entire being—is under a spotlight. They feel as if they are constantly being judged and found lacking in some significant manner. At the same time, each woman thinks that she is the only one who feels these things. Therefore, they either silence themselves from discussing their feelings for fear that they will be perceived as some sort of loser, or they apologize for their perceived flaws in order to acknowledge their awareness of the social norm. In either case, they create a situation where they are constantly frustrated with their bodies and themselves.

> Daisy: "I think every girl thinks she could lose like five or ten pounds. I don't know. Even though people tell me I'm skinny, I still feel like I could lose some."

Daisy was twenty-two years old and majoring in public relations with an emphasis on event planning when we spoke. Like so many other young women I've met, Daisy appears to be succeeding in all aspects of her life. Throughout her college career, she had received good grades and had several job prospects waiting for her after graduation. While in college, she had found her soul mate, married him six months before our conversation, and was adjusting to the changes married life brings. She had no significant health problems and acted genuinely happy. Despite these appearances, though, she struggled with an overwhelming conviction that something was wrong with her or missing from her life. Her statement above summarizes the basic experience of body dissatisfaction for many women: a persistent tension or feeling of disjuncture between their reality and their perception of that reality. The reality of Daisy's body size varies from what she thinks it is: She is skinny but is convinced she's fat and needs to lose weight.[4] In order to survive and thrive, women like Daisy must find a way to manage this tension and navigate through the various predicaments engendered by it. The specific life details may vary, but the tensions experienced with body dissatisfaction are the same.

Returning to Daisy's statement, I find it interesting that she begins by talking about others: "I think that every girl thinks she could lose like five or ten pounds." When I first considered this portion of her comments, I dismissed it as Daisy's attempt to rationalize her own thoughts—everyone else thinks this way, so it's ok that I do too. However, after talking to so many other women who feel the same way and express similar thoughts, I realized Daisy was on to something. Every woman that I've talked with is unhappy with some aspect of her body size and shape. The overwhelming majority of them think that their bodies are too big and need to be smaller[5] and that it is their responsibility and duty to ensure that this change happens. Think about the impact of this fact—out of hundreds of women who participated in this project, *every one* of them feels that she needs to change her body in some way. Even more troubling than this is the fact that when I ask them if they know of any women who are happy with their bodies, they resoundingly answer no. It seems that body dissatisfaction is widespread and endemic to young women's experiences—a type of postmodern plague.

Like Daisy, Dragonfly is relatively thin. When we met, she was also twenty-two years old, a senior communication studies major, and a popular cheerleader on campus. To many, she would seem to be the ideal representative of today's college woman: smart, pretty, popular, and thin. Of all the women I've met, she was one of the few who regularly acted as if she was comfortable with her body. In fact, one of the reasons I wanted to interview her was because she did present herself as not feeling any body dissatisfaction. Despite these appearances, though, Dragonfly expressed dissatisfaction with her body: "There's no way I could ever fit into a size four and have washboard abs. I just don't think I will ever be like that." I found Dragonfly's comments to be quite surprising, especially her comments about her "abs," for she always dressed in stylish clothes and often wore things that revealed her stomach. As Dragonfly's case demonstrates, body dissatisfaction can't be discerned by simply looking at a woman. Even after studying the phenomenon and speaking with women of all ages, sizes, and shapes, I still find myself surprised that there are no demonstrable symptoms or signs of body dissatisfaction and no way of telling who feels it.

Do I have any choice?
Daisy's and Dragonfly's comments exemplify the level of dissatisfaction felt by many young women, demonstrating the depth of awareness each has of her body. Ladybug hates her "big boobs" that she feels are out of proportion with the rest of her body. Her friend Roxy feels that she doesn't "have any boobs to speak of." Jasmine hates her short legs that are "really fat." Often, a young woman will blame genetics for what she considers her body's flaws. Chazy is convinced she will never be skinny because she comes from a "bigger

family." Madeleine is reconciled to the fact that because she has "always been overweight ever since I was little," she "probably always will be." Eva and Annette are stocky and "built like our dad." Lola thinks she will always have body issues because her "whole family is short and stout and muscular." Each woman I've spoken with detailed the genetic predisposition of her body and the flaws caused by these genetics. It may seem that a measure of comfort would be provided in knowing these "flaws" either need the drastic measure of surgery to be changed or are simply unchangeable (after all, if you can't do anything about a situation, then you have to make the best of it, right?). However, what actually happens in the realm of body dissatisfaction is that a woman's genetic predisposition creates a sense of lacking that manifests itself in increasing levels of self-hatred, disgust, or low self-esteem. Genetic predisposition and its resulting emotions coupled with the mirror version of hide and seek create a self-perpetuating Cycle of Dissatisfaction.

The cycle begins when a woman looks in the mirror and sees "grandma's thighs," "mom's jiggly arms," or some other perceived genetic malformation. Through the mirror version of hide and seek, these areas become magnified in their grotesqueness. Thighs that are perfectly in proportion with the rest of the body appear as colossal "cottage cheese" ridden behemoths. A soft rounded belly resembles the jiggling bowl of Jell-O stomach of Santa Claus. The more the woman looks at these body parts of "titanic proportions," the more disgusted she gets. The more disgusted she gets, the worse she feels about herself and her value as a woman. Turning away from the mirror, she worries to the point of obsession about her supposed flaws. She feels a persistent sense of dissatisfaction, discontent, and disgust. These feelings simmer just below the level of consciousness until the next time she looks into a mirror or is otherwise made aware of her body. When this happens, the feelings bubble to the surface and the cycle starts again, plunging her deeper into the pit of self-hatred that epitomizes body dissatisfaction and enmeshing her more deeply in this cycle until it seems impossible to escape.

Did you order the discontent?

The cycle of dissatisfaction comprises women's complex feelings about their bodies, their relationships to food, the size and appearance of their clothes—all the personal dimensions of body dissatisfaction. As women live with this cycle, they also move about in the larger social world, living in the midst of various discourses.[6] In this larger environment, a Culture of Discontent is created through actions and discourse. This culture of discontent surrounds women's being in the world and influences their personal cycles of dissatisfaction. The culture of discontent is defined by an ever-present awareness of one's body size and is created in part through women's discussions with each other about their bodies. An inherent aspect of this culture is maintaining an intimate familiarity with the body's perceived problem areas. Consider the following exchange between Caitlyn and Isabelle, held after Caitlyn joined a gym:

Caitlyn: Like I said, I need to firm my...firm my arms.
Isabelle: Yeah.
Caitlyn: And my thighs and legs and then...
Isabelle: Yeah, but thighs are legs.
Caitlyn: My thighs mainly, my calves are ok. My inner thighs!!
Isabelle: I guess I don't really see your inner thighs that much.
Caitlyn: Yeah, it's a problem area.
Isabelle: Right.
Caitlyn: And it runs in the family.
Isabelle: Oh, really?
Caitlyn: Yeah.
Isabelle: Big stomachs run in my family.
Caitlyn: Really?
Isabelle: It's not good. That's why I don't want children.
Caitlyn: Oh, no...
Isabelle: It's so selfish, I know, but it's never going to go away. I'll look like I'm four months along forever. I have some big stomach muscles. But I like the arms. I'm really into that. I want that.
Caitlyn: Yeah, I know. Sometimes when I wear sleeveless, I don't like them.
Isabelle: I don't like it either because I put my arm down, and it all gets spreading out.
Caitlyn: Yeah.
Isabelle: I don't think that's very fair.
Caitlyn: No.
Isabelle: I think my arms should work better for me.
Caitlyn: Exactly.
Isabelle: So I kind of...I find myself standing like this like a lot.
Caitlyn: Yeah.
Isabelle: Like you know, standing around and it's kind of the equivalent of sitting like this so that your legs don't touch.

Caitlyn: Yeah. I stand with my legs apart.
Isabelle: Yeah, yeah.
Caitlyn: So, for my arms and…and then lose weight to firm my tummy.
Isabelle: Yeah.
Caitlyn: But you know I just don't think I'll ever have a flat stomach.
Isabelle: No, I just think…
Caitlyn: It's not in me.
Isabelle: I think I've just resigned myself … cause I have very weak stomach
    muscles. And so I think I'm just very resigned to like not having a
    flat stomach.
Caitlyn: Yeah.

This conversation is a fascinating example of how the culture of discontent develops and is reinforced by the mirror version of hide and seek. Caitlyn lists the areas of her body that she wants to target in her fitness program—arms, thighs, legs, stomach—nearly her entire body. Isabelle expresses her own frustrations with these same body parts. She has a big stomach that looks like she's "four months along." Her arms look all "spreading out" when she puts them down. And, like Caitlyn, she stands so that her "legs [inner thighs] don't touch" so as not to accent the unacceptable body parts. All they see are fat stomachs, arms, and legs. Zeroing in on these body parts magnifies them; the more the women look, the larger the body parts seem to grow. Yet it should be clear from the account of Caitlyn and Isabelle's conversation in the Introduction, as they commiserate about being a size two, that to most observers, they would appear to be thin and have an ideal body size. Despite this fact, each expresses the desire to change essentially her whole body.

Their discussion presents yet another facet of how the cycle of dissatisfaction and the culture of discontent become intertwined and move way beyond perception, affecting the very lives of women like Caitlyn and Isabelle. Their obsession with what they see as inferior body parts also affects their behavior in society, in how they appear to others. They are ever vigilant in how they monitor and modify their stance so as not to appear fat. Standing with legs apart and arms slightly sticking out is not a natural stance and in fact is quite uncomfortable. I see this stance replicated on college campuses and elsewhere around the country. The woman in question usually stands with her legs slightly apart and her hands on her hips or one hand on her hip and one hand holding something. An alternate version has the legs crossed so that clear delineations between the legs cannot be discerned. On occasion I've asked women why they stand in such an uncomfortable position. Grace explained that she saw "everyone else" standing like that and "didn't want to look fat standing next to them."

In addition to being unnatural, such a stance limits a woman's ability to fully participate in society. To understand the limitations created by such positions, try recreating one. It takes a lot of concentration for a young woman to maintain the position and look "natural," while positioning herself so that legs don't touch and arms don't spread out. Conversation, while not impossible, is difficult. In effect, a woman turns herself into a form of living statue, carrying her pedestal with her wherever she goes. Like a statue, she is frozen in a manner that highlights her "beauty." However, unlike a statue, a young woman is a living and breathing being. By limiting herself to the stereotypical beauty of statues, she limits her very existence and all possibilities of a full future.

Do I ever get to stop thinking about my body?
While being conscious of appearance may cause some young women to behave like living statues, these feelings may also immobilize them emotionally so that they never experience satisfaction with themselves. When I met Claire and Alice, they were both twenty-two years old with plans to enter Christian ministry after graduation. Claire planned on "traveling the world and seeing everything" before even beginning to think about settling down. Alice, however, was in a long-term relationship. She hoped to become engaged in the near future and was just waiting for her boyfriend "to grow up and realize he wants to marry me." Claire and Alice spoke eloquently and in depth about their body dissatisfaction issues. They seemed to feed off each other's comments and regularly encouraged the other to address them:

> Claire: I've just always been conscious of my body.
> Alice: Yeah, me too.
> Claire: I just grew up always being aware of what I was supposed to look like and stuff like that. It's kind of just this ever-present thing.
> Alice: It's kind of sad, you know? I just learned growing up that your body's never right or you're never ok with your body. You're always just like there's gotta be something else you can do.

Even though Claire and Alice don't act as if they are living statues, they are emotionally immobilized, feeling that they need to change. Each says she is always aware that her "body is never right."

Can I achieve perfection?

When a young woman looks into a mirror, it is likely that she is considering where she falls on a continuum that has the mythical perfect body on one end and the all too real less than perfect body she sees in her mirror on the other end. When I ask what this mythic perfect body looks like, I get the same response: tall, skinny, and big boobs. In other words, the body that young women want is the one they see splashed across magazines, movies, and television everywhere they turn. As we will see in later chapters, these images are often unreal and unattainable by natural means, yet they are still longed for. Marya Hornbacher, a recovered anorexic and bulimic, explained this phenomenon in her book, *Wasted:*

> We speak as if there is one collective perfect body, a singular entity that we're all after. The trouble is, I think we are after that one body. We grew up with the impression that underneath all this normal flesh, buried deep in the excessive recesses of our healthy bodies, there was this perfect body just waiting to break out.[7]

The perfect body described by Hornbacher is like a unicorn. Everyone knows about it and has her own idea of what it looks like, but no one has actually seen it in person. Not seeing it, though, doesn't stop women from seeking it.

Seeking out and thinking about attaining this perfect body creates a constant yearning for something that is not available to most women. Even if a woman subjects herself to complete reconstruction through plastic surgery, there is only so much that she can change. A short woman will never be tall; a big-boned woman will never be tiny. This state of constant longing can have serious negative consequences such as the anorexia and bulimia Hornbacher struggled with for years.[8] In some ways, comparison to a mythical ideal is even more dangerous than comparison to real women. With real women, there exists a tangible goal—something that can be seen. However, when pursuing the mythic, the ideal can and does change. It will always be just a bit further out of reach or just a few pounds away. We see this concept played out in anorexics—no matter how much weight an anorexic loses or how skeletal she appears to others, all she sees is how fat she is and how far she is from her ideal skinny image.

By this point, it should be clear that the body dissatisfaction lived with and discussed by young women is a much more complex and serious experience than simply being unhappy. It is a feeling of perpetual discontent, frustration, and lack of fulfillment. It is living in a culture of discontent with a sense that something is always missing. It is an understanding that their futures are bleak unless they do something now. They often feel like they are the only ones saddled with such hideously large bodies. Sometimes they may silence themselves for fear of drawing more attention to their bodies; at other times they may make fun of or criticize their physical appearance so as to achieve a sense of belonging and give a nod to the ideal. Whatever their response, they create an inner turmoil that creates and recreates these feelings of dissatisfaction. It is as if they are trapped in a mental and emotional whirlpool that keeps pulling them further and further down.

Body battles

Living with these swirling feelings of dissatisfaction is difficult. Adding to the burden is the fact that women are also social beings who live amongst other women. One of the results of this swirling of dissatisfaction is that their inner turmoil gets turned outward—through comparison and competition with other women. For at the same time that a young woman is looking into a mirror with a disapproving gaze and comparing herself to the ideal, it is likely that she is also comparing herself to others. Instead of viewing the bodies of other women in a friendly and accepting or confirming manner, the bodies of others are often viewed in a critical and criticizing manner. The end result is that within the culture of discontent, the body of each woman becomes the focus of comparison, competition, and battles, often resulting in negative feelings toward others and low self-esteem.

Each time another woman enters the scene, she is viewed first as an enemy and second as a gauge. She is sized up to determine where she falls on the body continuum. *Is she skinnier than me? Are her boobs bigger than mine? Does she have a big butt or fat thighs? Is her stomach flabby? Do her arms jiggle when she waves?* These types of questions create an environment of unspoken, though constant, competition among women. A new acquaintance is often viewed as a competitor first and potential friend second. While friendship with other women is not automatically precluded, body battles do make the possibility of friendship more difficult. Instead of bonding together to move beyond dissatisfaction, women move away from each other. They participate in internal struggles as they compare their own bodies with the bodies of other women.

Does she look skinnier than me?

These internal struggles that can lead to serious competition and body battles (discussed in Chapter Five) usually begin with some sort of comparison. Madeleine, an eighteen-year-old political science major who hoped to go to law school and "make a difference" described the way she compares her body to others:

> I always compare myself to other women. Like, if I see some really put-together woman walking down the street or something, I'll think I'm not good like she is. Like I'm not skinny enough. I always do that. I know it's bad, but that's what I do—compare my body, myself.

The act of body comparison further entangles each woman's sense of her body and her Self. Note that Madeleine, an intelligent and caring person, wavers between thinking that she's "not good" and "not skinny." The good and skinny factors become equated: They're the same. Based on Madeleine's comments and similar ones from other women, it would seem that skinniness is a prerequisite to goodness. In the culture of discontent the quality of being "good" is thought to have less to do with a woman's actions than with the dimensions of her body.

Comparing one's body to that of other women also appears to generate a deeper yearning for personal skinniness. Satania, a twenty-one-year-old political science and French double major, clarifies:

> I want to be myself and I want to be, to appreciate my body for what it is. I still find myself looking at thinner girls and going, gosh, why can't I look like that? You know you never will, and you're like why?

Yearning for thinness like this is usually a silent practice. In our conversation up to this point, Satania had presented herself as aware of her body "flaws" but accepting of them. Her self-image and self-presentation revolved around this illusion of self-confidence. Essentially, however, she wasn't truly happy but resigned to living with what nature had given her. After we had spoken for some time, she began letting her guard down and her true feelings out.[9] In the past she had adopted a defensive veneer to protect herself from the verbal barbs she was sure would be thrown her way.[10] As her trust in me grew, she dropped this defense.

Does anyone survive this comparison unscathed?
The potential of a skinnier woman coming onto the scene gives rise to yet another layer of vigilance. In comparing their bodies with those of other women, young women must be tenacious in their awareness of their genetic predisposition, their monitoring of body size, and their ranking on the body continuum. Alice describes how this vigilance often turns into animosity and vitriol toward other women:

> Even in a lot of women's friendships and other relationships among women, there's a lot of undercurrents of competition and comparison and condemnation. It's self-condemnation or to the other person because it's like you can't be friends with a woman who wears a smaller size.

This comparison, then, involves a woman's negative feelings as she gazes critically at her own body while thinking another woman's body appears more attractive. It becomes more than just a friendly contest between competitors. In most competitions there is a victor and a loser, while all parties benefit from the thrill of the sport. Today's loser may be tomorrow's victor. Body competition, however, is more like a traditional military battle where the victor defeats the loser, who slinks away in shame. In reality, both women lose. They lose out on the possibility of friendship. When a young woman meets another, the threat of this competition seems to be lurking just below the surface, preventing them from taking the chance that maybe this woman can be more than another opponent.

Perhaps the most dangerous aspect of this comparison is that it adds another layer to the cycle of dissatisfaction—a level of destruction. When a woman feels this way about herself, her cycle of dissatisfaction moves from the mental beating up and berating discussed earlier to these types of comparisons and competition with others. At times, these feelings may lead to outright aggressive acts exercised on other women, such as this story I have heard numerous times:

> I've heard it a few times on campus as part of the hazing and pledging process [of sororities]. The current sorority members go down and have them [pledges] strip down into their underwear and they will circle places on their body that are fat and need to be worked on.

This version of the story was shared by Mandi, who repeatedly stressed that the circles were drawn in permanent marker so that they would stay on the body for several days. Despite my efforts to confirm the story's validity, I have not been able to determine if it is a fact or an urban legend. None of the women who shared this story with me actually knew anyone who had experienced fat circling.

In her book *Pledged*,[11] Alexandra Robbins explores the various dynamics of sorority life—including fat circling. Robbins relates that several sorority sisters told her stories of fat circling similar to that told by Mandi. However, Robbins did not provide any details of specific incidents, nor did she ever witness any acts of fat circling—as part of the pledge process or at any other time. True or not, many women believe it to be true. They choose not to join sororities based on this story, which acts as another barrier between women bonding with each other. Instead of taking advantage of an opportunity to live with a group of like-minded women, the story and the potential of their fat being exposed drives women away.

Body dissatisfaction is clearly a complex dynamic in the lives of young women. While it may mimic negative body image, the stories shared here begin to illustrate that what young women experience is more than feeling unhappy with their bodies. Daisy is convinced that every girl thinks she needs to lose weight. Isabelle and Caitlyn want to change every body part. Madeleine is convinced that because she is not skinny like other women, she is not good. The cycle of dissatisfaction, persistent vigilance, comparison and competition, and yearning for skinniness lead to more than the negative feelings resulting from the comparison with other women discussed above. Many women take extraordinary steps to move closer—or at least appear closer—to the skinny end of the body continuum.

Chapter Two

The food is awful here

The food is awful here

Food is a necessary aspect of human existence; however, for women experiencing body dissatisfaction food becomes a primary indicator of their moral goodness. Each time they eat, or think about eating, they engage in an internal dialogue of what they should (or should not) eat. While some women succumb to eating disorders as a way of addressing their food concerns, most women do not. They may, however, participate in disordered eating practices. Understanding women's relationships with food is a pivotal component in addressing the lived experiences of body dissatisfaction.

Eating habits and behaviors

Sarah was twenty-two years old and newly graduated when we sat down for her interview. Having recently earned a bachelor's degree in history with a minor in Spanish, she was planning to teach English as a second language in Mexico for the next year with no clear career plans after that. We met at a local sandwich shop where Sarah ordered coffee and a plain side salad. After I ordered a cheeseburger and fries, she apologized saying that she was on a "new diet that will help me lose those fifteen pounds I gained as a freshman, plus another ten pounds or so." Looking at Sarah I couldn't figure out where the offensive extra twenty-five pounds were. Even though Sarah didn't appear excessively thin, she by no means appeared overweight. By most standards, she looked to be a healthy weight. During our conversation, Sarah returned four different times to the "freshman fifteen," wavering between anger and embarrassment at having gained the weight. She still chastised herself now for being so "lazy and foolish." Even though she admitted that perhaps this weight gain was simply part of the process of maturing, she insisted that she "knew better than to let it happen" to her. She repeatedly said that her mother raised her to make healthy food choices and exercise daily, so she had no reason for gaining weight.

By the end of our interview, Sarah seemed even more committed to her weight loss goals. She admitted that our conversation was the first time she had talked about her plans with anyone. Apparently, talking about it made it more real for her. After she left, I glanced at her plate. It looked like Sarah had moved the salad around without actually eating any. Thinking back, I didn't recall Sarah ever actually taking a bite of her salad. I wondered if perhaps Sarah's "diet" was an eating disorder. She never responded to my follow-up e-mails so I wasn't able to confirm my suspicions.

Who is really suffering from an eating disorder?
Sarah's story of food and weight struggles is similar to the stories of many young women. They've gained weight. They're worried about their bodies. They're taking some sort of measure to lose weight, either through diet or exercise. They feel guilty for gaining the weight or not doing enough to lose the weight. According to one study, over 90% of women in college have tried some form of diet within the last year.[1] Based on my discussions with women of all ages, this statistic, as shocking as it is, is understated. I have yet to meet a woman who has not tried some type of diet. This constant worry or obsession with food occurs in conjunction with the persistent body awareness discussed in Chapter One and heightens the culture of discontent within which young women live, creating a self-sustaining spiral that grows in intensity, adding yet another dynamic to young women's cycle of dissatisfaction. The more young women focus on their body dissatisfaction, the more they monitor what they eat. The more they eat and "miseat," the more they worry about the problem areas of their bodies. The more they worry about these areas, the more they focus on them, exacerbating their body dissatisfaction and starting the cycle all over again.

Is this behavior evidence of an eating disorder? Not necessarily. Eating disorders occur on a continuum of severity, yet when we hear "eating disorder," we often think of the extremes—not eating anything, or bingeing and purging regularly. However, as will become clear in the following pages, there are numerous other ways that eating disorders can be manifest in young women's lives. None of the women I've spoken with admitted to currently suffering from an eating disorder, although I was surprised to learn that several admitted to having had past eating disorders ranging in severity. Many women described how they would "starve" themselves for a short period of time in order to quickly lose weight for a special event such as prom. Others admitted to bingeing and purging on and off for several years. All of them were adamant in saying that they no longer practiced such behaviors. Based on the stories they shared with me, though, I suspected that many of them were still in the midst of an eating or exercise disorder.

What I found even more disturbing was the fact that every one of the women I interviewed knew of a friend, roommate, sister, or other woman who currently had an eating disorder. I was shocked. Studies estimate that approximately twenty-four million people suffer from eating disorders,[2] with over 90% of these individuals being women under the age of twenty-five.[3] If such a significant number of women under the age of twenty-five are suffering from an eating disorder, then it is highly improbable that all of the women I've spoken with for this project would be immune to this condition. Most likely, several of them were dealing with an eating disorder and either in denial about it or consciously chose not to discuss it with me.

Another possible reason for the vast disparity between stats and stories rests in the fact that eating and exercising disorders are often not a topic for everyday conversation. Even though many women discuss their favorite foods or popular diets, very rarely do they detail their actual eating practices. When I ask for such specific examples, a standard answer runs along the lines of "I try to eat three healthy meals a day." No amount of pushing or probing on my part elicits more specifics. In reality, addictive eating and exercise practices occur in deep privacy, as we shall discuss in greater length later in this chapter. The bulimic woman doesn't usually binge and purge in public or talk about her practices. She may go to a number of different stores and restaurants to purchase the food that will later be the focus of her bingeing. She may binge late at night when everyone is sleeping. She may cover the noise of her purging by running water while vomiting. She may go to the further extreme of vomiting into containers or plastic bags that she disposes of someplace other than her home. Likewise, the exercise addict tends not to limit her workouts to her local gym. She may do an hour of strength training at the gym and then supplement this with walking, running, biking, or other cardiovascular activities done outside the gym. Jenny's room-mate, for example, will spend one to two hours of the afternoon in the gym. In the mornings, she will go for a seven to ten mile run before classes. In the evenings, she will go to a high impact aerobics class after dinner. Before bed she will do a few hundred sit-ups. A typical day of exercise for her includes approximately five to six hours of work—yet only half occurs in the gym where she can be easily observed and monitored.

Can we avoid information about diet, exercise, and weight control?
While acknowledged eating disorders appear to be a rarity amongst the women I've spoken with, food struggles are preva-lent. They are intimately intertwined with body dissatisfaction concerns. Even if a woman is not concerned with food, it is dif-ficult to maintain this nonchalant stance when every time she goes anywhere today she is bombarded with diet and exercise information. The newsstand is covered with headlines such as: "What Will You Weigh in a Year? How to Change Your Weight Fate Now,"[4] "Fast Abs in 14 Days (And: Detox Diet Tips)."[5] Even magazines aimed at teens are in on the game: "Is Your Family Making You Fat?".[6] A trip to the local bookstore highlights just how mainstream the diet industry is. *The New York Times* best-seller list regularly features at least one diet or exercise book. In 2004, three of the longest running bestseller hardback books were diet or diet related: *The South Beach Diet* (fifty-one weeks), *The South Beach Diet Cookbook* (twenty-two weeks), and *The Ultimate Weight Solution: The 7 Keys to Weight Loss Freedom* (twenty-one weeks).[7] Television shows such as *Celebrity Fit Club* and the *Biggest Loser* feature the rewards of dieting and the punishment for not sticking to the regimen. Advertisements for Jenny Craig, Nutri-System, e-diets, Leptoprin,[8] or some other weight loss miracle program appear on television or computer ads. Twenty-first century America is obsessed with dieting and losing weight, with part of this obsession stemming from the fact that Americans are some of the fattest people in the world. According to the Centers for Disease Control National Health Interview Survey, over 50% of Americans are overweight and 20% are obese.[9]

The rise in obesity is surprising because Americans have access to an increasing amount of nutritional information available to help the general public understand and adopt healthy eating practices. For example, the Department of Health and Human Services in conjunction with the Department of Agriculture released new, easier to follow food guidelines in 2005,[10] indicating that a healthy diet should include two cups of fruit and two and a half cups of vegetables daily. Unfortunately, many Americans make bad choices, and their vegetable of choice is the French fry and their favorite fruit is juice with added sugar—not the types of fruit and vegetables necessarily envisioned in the guidelines.

Is everything fried?
When young women go out on their own for the first time, they are confronted with a clash of conflicting information. Parents or caregivers aren't there to ensure that healthy meal choices are made, leaving young women to make their own choices about what they eat. Macaroni and cheese, chicken nuggets, French fries, hamburgers, ice cream, cake, cookies, sodas, and all those other things that were deemed unhealthy at home are suddenly available—often in unlimited quantities. The temptation is difficult to pass up. After all, why eat salad when you can have deep-fried mushrooms with ranch dipping sauce or broccoli swimming in cheese sauce—or both? For these young women, following healthy eating guidelines can be difficult. Whenever I conduct interviews on college campuses, the most popular comment I hear is that the food "sucks." It's fried. It sits in grease waiting to be served. Fresh fruit and vegetables can be hard to find. When a salad is available, the lettuce often is brown and wilted, or is plain, nutritionally vapid iceberg. Temptations are many. As Diva explained, "Who wants to eat a grilled chicken breast with plain white rice when you can have mac 'n' cheese with chicken nuggets?"

Would you like a salad with that?
I went on a few field trips to explore what food options are available on campuses today. While there are more choices of places to eat at larger universities, there are a number of striking similarities in food services at both larger and smaller schools. Today's typical college cafeteria presents a variety of food choices. In addition to

the plastic trays, bins of silverware, and hairnets worn by the "lunch ladies" of old, there are now chefs—both male and female—in full chef regalia, including sparkling white toques, presiding over artfully arranged gourmet-looking dishes. On most campuses, a standard array of lunch options include at least: a made to order sandwich or sub station, one or two cold entrees, two hot entrees, two hot veggies, and the standard college fare of pizza, burgers, and French fries. The larger schools may have commercial fast food restaurants along with the more traditional college fare.[11] Most colleges also offer some form of salad bar, combining fresh salad ingredients with pre-made salads like cole slaw. Desserts usually consist of soft-serve ice cream and various baked goods. The physical set-up varies from a traditional cafeteria line to individual kiosks, each carrying a certain type of food. For example, one campus cafeteria offered the following kiosks: a baked potato and soup bar; a made to order sandwich station; a grill station serving hamburgers, hot dogs, fries and similar items; a made to order omelet station; a salad bar; individual kiosks for Mexican, Indian, and Italian foods; a soft-serve ice cream machine; and a mini-bakery with numerous cookies, cakes, and pies. In addition to cafeterias serving three meals a day, campuses also usually offer some sort of "quick place," reminiscent of a diner or coffee shop, which stay open all day and into the evening and are designed for hanging out, studying, and eating. Food options at the quick places usually include sandwiches, salads, soups, and coffee—lots of coffee.

Based on my observations and campus visits, it seems that it is indeed possible to maintain a healthy and nutritional diet while at college. One of my lunches, for example, consisted of a turkey and cheddar wrap made to order with lettuce, tomato, and spicy mustard. With this I enjoyed a side salad of lettuce, carrots, green peppers, peas, and dressing, all from the salad bar. I went on to supplement with a slice of cheese pizza, a plate of macaroni and cheese, and peach ice cream. And here is the heart of the problem: What started as a healthy lunch quickly morphed into a calorie and fat laden feast. The problem is not that there aren't healthy food options but, as Diva said, the problem is the numerous temptations. It's difficult to make the right choices when there are so many wrong ones easily accessible, in unlimited portions, on a daily basis with no extra charge.

For young working women, fast food restaurants, donut shops, and cafeterias are probably the typical lunch places that provide cheap, high fat food, offering choices similar to those faced by college women. All young women have to deal with the budget appeal of fast food. As Mandi said, "I know I shouldn't be fat, but it's hard not to eat junk when you can get a double cheeseburger meal for three dollars.[12] When you're in college, every penny counts."

What should I have eaten?

With so many temptations, young women struggling with the cycle of dissatisfaction are persistently aware of their bodies at mealtime. Each time they eat they have to keep themselves in check. Jasmine, an eighteen-year-old theater major who hoped to "make it big in Hollywood" someday and twenty-year-old Mandi regularly think about being fat:

> Mandi: There's not a day that goes by that I'm not like, "Oh, I shouldn't be fat."
> Jasmine: Yeah, it's always at the front of my mind.

Listening to Jasmine, Mandi, and others, it quickly becomes apparent that constantly monitoring food intake is a drive, a mandate, something that can't be turned off. Annette details the way this mandate tends to operate and how young women constantly worry or obsess over food:

> I never leave a meal without thinking what have I just eaten, what should I have not eaten. Seriously, every time I eat. There is not a time goes by do I eat a meal and not afterwards contemplate what I've eaten, what I should have eaten less of, what I shouldn't have eaten. Every time. I mean it, every single time.

Annette explains the worry about eating and "miseating," eating what one "should not have eaten." Her concerns demonstrate what I call the "shoulds" of eating and are determined less by nutritional guidelines and more by calorie, fat, or carbohydrate content. For young women focused on body image, the shoulds of eating appear to represent a more pressing and perpetual mandate than health or nutrition. In some sense, food has shifted from being a need for survival to a moral mandate. Eating the right foods becomes a tangible representation of how good (or bad) we are.

At least some of this food obsession grows from fear of the dreaded freshman fifteen—the extra weight that seems to appear by magic during the first year of college. Satania recalled that "freshman year, I put on a lot of weight." Isabelle worried about how she had "gained sixteen pounds since high school—the freshman fifteen, plus one." Happy observed that "I got the freshman fifteen, and I just want to go back to where I was before college." Psyche had recently realized that she had "started gaining the freshman fifteen." Liscious shared that her sister was worried because "she gained the freshman fifteen." During my interviews, the phrase "freshman fifteen" was used so many times that I thought it might be written on my forehead and the women were simply reading it.

She can eat how much without gaining weight?

Worrying about getting fat is worsened when women know one of those lucky few who have fast metabolisms. From the outside, it appears that these fortunate women have been blessed with the ability to "eat anything in the world and not gain a pound." Happy, a nineteen-year-old communication and media studies major who hoped to "get a job" and start a family after graduation, observed three times during our ninety-minute interview that it was hard to live with her fast metabolism roommate. Witnessing the roommate's apparent no-penalty-eating, Happy constantly feels she herself "should look that way" and be able to eat that way as well, eating "junk" and five or six meals a day. The assumption is that women with fast metabolisms eat anything and everything with no thoughts of the "shoulds" of eating. They become defined by their ability to eat at will and remain thin. They seem to be above the focus and concerns of the cycle of dissatisfaction. However, even though the fast metabolism women have been blessed with the ability to eat it all, this special dispensation is limited. Like the other young women I've met, the fast metabolism women still feel dissatisfied with their bodies and experience their own cycle of dissatisfaction. Despite the realities of their experience, in the culture of discontent, women with fast metabolisms are like rock stars. They seem larger than life and almost mythical, even though they are generally tiny. Where not eating a lot of food is considered a good thing, they are the bad girls who always eat. They eat everything and anything they want, and they never seem to be punished. In fact, they often are rewarded—with compliments.

Have you lost weight?
A common greeting amongst young women is what I like to call the Skinny Greeting: "Wow, have you lost weight?" or "You look great. How much weight have you lost?" In everyday conversation, one of the highest compliments that can be said of another woman is, "She's so skinny, and she eats like a horse." Comments like these—making them, desiring them—heighten young women's already existing persistent worry about being fat and highlight how examining and evaluating the body of another woman is a major focus of their lives. Most women participate in such practices though they may not be conscious of their behavior. When I ask women if they do this, they usually respond in the negative. As we continue to talk, though, their stories reveal otherwise. Desiring comments like these sets up the possibility of perpetual disappointment. If I think that I've lost weight and the woman greeting me fails to acknowledge this, then I am left to assume that I, in fact, do not look skinny. Or perhaps I do look thin but the woman greeting me is participating in a body battle with me or choosing not to play the game.

Participating on either side of skinny greetings focuses attention on weight loss as an essential activity of young women. If I am constantly mulling over and wondering about body size—mine and others'—eventually I will feel the urge or need to lose weight. Diva's comments demonstrate this situation. Diva was a nineteen-year-old communication and media studies major who hoped to "get a job and get married, not necessarily in that order" after graduation. A popular cheerleader on campus, Diva spent a lot of time in the spotlight and was constantly aware of her body because of cheering and the short skirts she wore. She explained her thought process: "I don't think I really need to lose weight. I just want to. It's the only thing. There's nothing else to do." Diva's justification "that there's nothing else to do" appears to be a rationalization of her desire to lose weight, as if she feels guilty about having and acknowledging this desire. Later in our conversation, Diva contradicted herself and revealed that she had much to do with classes, cheerleading, involvement in various student organizations, and spending time with her boyfriend and friends. She then explained that all of these things made finding time to work out difficult, and yet she did not recant her desire to lose weight. Perhaps she was trying to fit in with her peers who might also have been focusing on weight loss or passing the time in this way.

Disordered eating
Who ordered the disordered eating?

As a young woman continues to fixate over her body size, her desire to lose weight assumes greater importance. What begins as a wish often develops into an implicit mandate. Isabelle felt this mandate while living in a sorority surrounded by her skinny sorority sisters:

> I think it's crowd mentality. It's kind of like, well she's getting attention [for being skinny]. You just start picking up on people's cues. All of a sudden you're like, I should go run too or I guess I don't need that ice cream today. And it just kind of snowballs. I don't think we had anyone in that house who would be considered overweight.

Isabelle's snowball metaphor is apt. Like a snowball, the more the desire to be skinny rolls around in a woman's mind, the bigger it gets; and the bigger it gets, the more dangerous it becomes.

As this desire grows, young women start approaching the border between healthy and unhealthy behaviors. They move from being worried about what they eat to actively practicing various forms of disordered eating. The phrase *disordered eating* refers to dieting and related behaviors done solely for the sake of beauty and not for health reasons. A woman may need to diet for many health reasons—to control diabetes, to lower cholesterol, or to maintain acceptable sodium levels, for example; these practices are usually sound. Disordered eating is a more destructive practice that can run counter to more healthy dietary practices. The key difference between the two is in the underlying motivation: Is the diet precipitated by a recognized medical condition or for health maintenance, or is it a byproduct of body dissatisfaction? Merely going on a diet is not the same thing as disordered eating. Perhaps an easier way to understand the difference between normal diets and those that venture into disordered eating land is to think of the disordered eating diets as diets plus—plus the obsession and compulsion endemic to the cycle of dissatisfaction.

For young women, disordered eating takes many forms. At its most basic level, the disordered eater will engage in some limitation of food intake, such as skipping meals, taking smaller portions, not eating everything on her plate, or moving food around and pretending to eat as Sarah did during our lunch interview.

Twenty-one-year-old Annette and her nineteen-year-old sister Eva regularly practice this type of disordered eating together. When I met them, Annette and Eva both appeared confident and healthy. Annette, an elementary education major, spoke passionately about her plans to teach in an urban environment and of her interest in media and body image issues. As the younger of the two, Eva was still figuring out her life plans. At the time, she was majoring in professional writing and thinking of going into public relations or marketing. When our conversation turned to food and dieting, both sisters looked at each other and laughed. Annette then shared that, "We've cut out desserts altogether several times in our lives." These sessions of dessert deprivation had been prompted by a number of events such as eating "too much" on a weekend or just feeling fat. During these times, Annette and Eva otherwise ate as they normally would, but without the finishing touch of desserts.

At this basic level of practice, disordered eating doesn't appear all that much different from the dieting practices that many women regularly participate in. One could easily argue that skipping dessert is not a bad thing and could possibly be a good thing. But it may be just one facet of the larger, multi-dimensional practice of body dissatisfaction.

An intermediate level of disordered eating can occur when more severe and specific restrictions of food intake are adopted. For example, during the times I was conducting interviews, the South Beach and Atkins diets were popular, both of which advocate severely limiting carbohydrates and replacing them with a significant increase in proteins. Equally popular diets, variants of the Pritkin diet, advocate the exact opposite—consuming more carbohydrates and fewer proteins. While either of these approaches to dieting can work as part of a healthy lifestyle, one must be cautious: Dieting may lead to abuse or disordered eating. This abuse was demonstrated by Pamela, a twenty-one-year-old English major who planned to go to graduate school, "because what else can you do with an English degree?" Her version of the Atkins diet entailed the elimination of all forms of grain—breads, rice, pastas. At the time we spoke, her diet primarily consisted of meat and cheese with one fruit or vegetable per day. She reasoned that if a little change was good, a big change was better.

While all diets are meant to be short term solutions with the dieter's ultimate return to a healthy lifestyle, they have built in failure systems. The Renfrew Center estimates that 95-98% of people on diets gain the weight back within three years.[13] To understand this high rate of failure, let's assume that Jen goes on Atkins and loses twenty pounds because she has drastically limited her intake of all carbohydrates. Common sense dictates that this would result in a loss of some weight. After reaching her goal, Jen returns to "normal" eating and reintroduces carbs. She will most likely gain back at least some, if not all, of the lost weight—and possibly more. Therefore, she will need to go on yet another diet to lose the regained weight. The obvious result is a lifetime of yo-yo dieting.

A further complication on the continuum of disordered eating is modifying diets or even making up new diets. Annette and Eva, for example, told me about the more complex diets that they themselves created. One such diet required them to consume only 1500 calories per day with no more than 250 coming from "sweets or sugars." To stay motivated, they created a diet contract where they would "write down the rules and sign it and stuff." Eva observed that she "hated it" and was "hungry all the time"—no surprise, considering the recommended daily calorie allowance for adult women is two thousand per day. Eva finally said the diet was "stupid" and they agreed to break their contract. They did, however, try other extreme diets from time to time.

In its most advanced form, disordered eating involves even higher restrictions of food intake. Dragonfly and Ladybug discussed a friend who recently lost an extraordinary amount of weight, her "secret" weight loss trick being to eat nothing but lettuce every day. Even though such a diet is obviously dangerous and potentially life threatening, they focused solely on the "over one hundred pounds" she lost and the surgery she needed "where you get your skin all fixed up because it's just hanging there."

Are there dieting alternatives?
In their quest for thinner bodies, some young women will combine a higher level of food restriction with a meal replacement drink or energy bar, the premise being that you replace breakfast and/or lunch with this product and then eat a healthy balanced dinner. For example, nineteen-year-old Carol, a business major who hoped to work in upper level management in any industry "willing to hire me," explained how she and her friends incorporate these items in their "diet": "The last time I wanted to lose weight, I lived on Slimfast and Powerbars. I would drink a Slimfast for breakfast

and lunch, then eat a Powerbar for dinner. My roommates and I all did this for three weeks. It sucked after a few days but it worked." I asked Carol if she and her roommates worried about the potential of detrimental effects on their bodies from such a plan. She allowed that the thought had crossed her mind that she "might get hurt from not eating," but "any price" was worth it to be skinny.

Do you have a cigarette?

For many women, the promise of the immediate rewards of a skinny body often takes precedence over a concern for future health problems. This mindset can lead to the use of chemical assistance such as weight loss pills, laxatives, caffeine, and nicotine. Melissa, a nineteen-year-old dance major, hoped to turn professional after college. She survived on what she called the "Dancer's Diet"—diet Coke, cigarettes, and gum. Melissa was only one of several young women who said that cigarettes were the biggest component of their weight loss regimen. When we spoke, she joked about the long-term health effects of this diet. However, like Carol, Melissa felt that the price of future health problems was worth the promise of present thinness. For them, quitting smoking and possibly gaining weight is much more dangerous than the long-term prospect of lung, heart, and other problems.

In practice, the progression of levels of disordered eating is not quite as linear as I have presented it here. But too strong a focus on the use or avoidance of food can increase a woman's risk that her habit of disordered eating will develop into an eating disorder.

Have you eaten today?

Even though none of the women I interviewed admitted to having an eating disorder, several of them do seem to be bordering on eating disorders. To others, Melissa is clearly an anorexic; to herself, she is merely a dancer doing what it takes to succeed. By limiting her diet to caffeine, nicotine, and gum, she is severely limiting her daily caloric and nutrient intake—in effect, starving herself to be thin. Like Melissa, many anorexics appear thin but otherwise normal, keeping their serious eating disorders and related behaviors secret. They are ashamed of their behavior and, in some sense, of themselves, and they fear being found out and forced to discontinue the behavior. Remember that eating disorders usually begin with some sort of extreme dissatisfaction with the body. Therefore, the woman in the throes of an eating disorder struggles with a cycle of shame that cycles back and forth between dissatisfaction with her body and disgust with her behavior.

The two most common forms of eating disorders seen today are bulimia and anorexia. Bulimia is characterized by periods of bingeing on food followed by a purging of the food. The National Association of Anorexia Nervosa and Associated Disorders (ANAD) specifies the following behaviors as warning signs of bulimia:[14]

- Preoccupation with food
- Binge eating, often in secret
- Vomiting after bingeing
- Abuse of laxatives, diuretics, and/or diet pills
- Compulsive exercise

Usually the bulimic will engage in a number of these behaviors as part of her weight loss plan, with each woman creating her own regimen. For example, during the day she may take diet pills to control her appetite and help hide her compulsion to purge after eating. In the evening when she can be alone or when everyone else has gone to bed, she will participate in bingeing followed by purging. To help "cleanse" her system, she may regularly take laxatives and will probably also go through bouts of compulsive exercising. Unlike the skeletal appearance often associated with anorexia, most bulimics look normal, similar to many of the women around them. Physical indicators of bulimia are therefore limited but can include:[15]

- Swollen salivary glands
- Broken blood vessels in the eyes
- Teeth erosion and excessive cavities
- Calluses or other worn areas on the first and sometimes second finger

These effects result from the activity most commonly characterizing bulimia—vomiting. The bulimic may exercise any of a number of methods to induce vomiting—sticking one or two fingers down her throat; sticking a toothbrush, spoon, or other implement down her throat; ingesting a vomit inducing agent such as Ipecac; swallowing a piece of candy tied to a string and then pulling the candy back up her throat; and eating activated charcoal.[16] After time, many bulimics can vomit at will—without the aid of any form of outside assistance.

Bulimia tends to be a highly secretive form of eating disorder because the act of vomiting introduces an extra layer of shame into the process. None of the women I interviewed knew of a bulimic. However, everyone seems to know of the urban legend bulimic— the friend of a friend of a friend who always gets up and goes to the bathroom right after eating, presumably to vomit. And like other mythic legends that appear in the culture of discontent, the urban legend bulimic is sometimes revered and admired, not scorned or chastised.

To understand the cycle of bulimia, consider this description from Marya Hornbacher's *Wasted* in which she explains her experiences with bulimia while working at McDonald's:[17]

> At my lunch break, I would eat a quarter-pounder with cheese, large fries, and a cherry pie. Then I would throw up in the antiseptic-scented bathroom, wash my face, and go back on the floor, glassy-eyed and hyper. After work, I would buy a quarter-pounder with cheese, large fries, and a cherry pie, eat it on the way home from work, throw up at home with the bathtub running, eat dinner, throw up, go out with friends, eat, throw up, go home, pass out.

In this excerpt Hornbacher exhibits three of the five behavioral characteristics of bulimia—preoccupation with food, bingeing, and purging. Her preoccupation with food results in her buying the exact same meal—cheeseburger, fries, cherry pie. Her life is segmented into eating sessions followed by vomiting sessions with an intermittent period of what most of us consider real life—working, going to school, or spending time with family and friends.

Unlike the bulimic who eats large amounts of food, the anorexic eats little or nothing. Anorexics will often limit their intake to only a few hundred calories per day. According to ANAD,[18] behavioral warning signs for anorexia include:

- Deliberate self-starvation
- Intense and persistent fear of gaining weight
- Refusal to eat or highly restrictive eating
- Compulsive exercise
- Abnormal weight loss

When we think of the physical appearance of anorexics, we tend
to think of the advanced stages, extremely skinny, like the pictures
we've seen of skeletal women whose ribs we can count without effort. But the condition is not so noticeable in its earlier stages. Other
physical signs include:

- Excessive facial and/or body hair
- Sensitivity to cold
- Absent or irregular menstruation
- Hair loss

For the diligent anorexic, these physical signs can be and often are
hidden from friends and relatives. The anorexic will wear bulky
clothing to cover her extreme weight loss and growth of extra body
hair. She will adopt a new hairstyle such as a ponytail to camouflage
patches of lost hair. To mimic the monthly appearance of her period,
she will purchase and dispose of tampons and pads without ever
actually using them.

How can I be anorexic if I don't look like a skeleton?
Because anorexic behavior is so easily hidden, it is much more
common than we think. Every woman that I've spoken with knows
at least one anorexic woman; most of them know several. For example, Marie was a twenty-year-old communication studies major
thinking about going into marketing after graduation, although
she "really liked Starbucks" and thought she might be able to do
something within the company. Marie's roommate represents
a perfect example of a woman suffering from anorexia without
looking sick or skeletal. She described her roommate as "skinny,
wearing between a size one and a size three." Marie stressed that
her roommate's bones weren't noticeably apparent to the casual
observer. The year before Marie and I chatted, her roommate
had "gained a lot of weight." In response to this weight gain, the
roommate became convinced that she was fat and would continue
to gain weight if she didn't take steps to stop it. The roommate
started exercising at least two hours per day while simultaneously
decreasing the amount of food she ate. Most days she would have
a Lean Cuisine entrée as her sole meal, supplemented with a few
fresh vegetables or a piece of fresh fruit.[19] As part of her weight loss
"system," the roommate kept a daily food journal. Out of concern

for her roommate's health, Marie explained that she regularly read the food journal and calculated how many calories she was getting. According to Marie, the roommate averaged fewer than 1500 calories per day, and on most days took in fewer than 1000 calories. However, Marie calculated that with her workout and training schedule, the roommate would need to consume at least 2300 calories per day.

During our conversation, Marie also questioned if the roommate was even eating as much as she claimed. On more than one occasion, Marie had asked the roommate what she had eaten that day. In response, the roommate would get defensive and name some high calorie food that she claimed to have eaten while Marie was in class. After some quick sleuthing, Marie would usually find the same item still on the shelves or in the refrigerator—uneaten. Based on Marie's observations, her roommate was exhibiting all five of the behavioral signs of anorexia listed above.

Stories like that of Marie's roommate are found throughout my transcripts. Diva's roommate has followed a similar path. After gaining weight, the roommate became depressed and dedicated to the prospect of losing weight. A typical day for her is now one where "she sleeps, doesn't go to class, doesn't eat, wakes up at five o'clock in the evening and showers." Diva repeatedly stressed that the roommate "doesn't eat." The roommate's rationale was that she could lose the most weight in the least amount of time by not eating, and that sleeping as much as possible would help distract her from the hunger pains. Despite being confronted by Diva and other friends, the roommate persisted in her quest to lose the weight through starvation.

In Chapter Four, I present the story of another of Diva's roommates who over-exercises and participates in open competition with Diva and her friends to lose the most weight. I wonder how toxic the environment within their room was—Diva was dieting and exercising, one roommate was over-exercising and under-eating, and the other roommate was slowly starving herself to death. It seems that they have created their own subculture within the larger culture of discontent. Whereas most young women can use their rooms or apartments as a refuge, Diva and her roommates simply enter a more intense form of the culture when they go to their room. Their body battles are magnified—all they need to do is turn to one of their roommates to compare and compete.

It should be obvious at this point that the personal dimensions of body dissatisfaction are much more complex and time intensive than simply being unhappy. Young women who are stuck in the cycle of dissatisfaction spend inordinate amounts of time worrying about the size of their bodies. They routinely monitor and modify their stance so as to appear as thin as possible. They incessantly compare their body to the bodies of other women around them. Jasmine and Mandi constantly think about the fact that they shouldn't be fat. Annette tracks what she eats at every meal. Melissa survives on nicotine and caffeine with the occasional stick of gum. They methodically track the types of and amount of food that they eat. They waver between eating, disordered eating, and eating disorders. One would think that with all of these nonstop concerns, young women would be unable to worry about anything else. However, the personal dimensions of dissatisfaction also extend to the way they look in their clothes and the numerical size of that clothing.

Chapter Three

I look cute today

I look cute today

Also playing a primary role in women's experience of body dissatisfaction is the clothing that they choose. While clothes serve the necessary purpose of covering and protecting the body, for many women they also serve as a tangible demonstration of their sense of Self. Many women experience a direct connection between the size of their clothes and their emotional well-being, even though there is no general consensus on sizing systems. Examining the connections between clothing, food, and the body allows us to better comprehend the intrapersonal level of body dissatisfaction.

Clothes can make or break the day

Sue and I met in her campus apartment for her interview. She was twenty-one years old and preparing to graduate the next semester with a bachelor's degree in English. She had already secured an entry-level position in a New York publishing house. Sue's walls were covered with pictures of the New York skyline. The prospect of leaving the "flat corn fields" of Middle America and getting someplace with "people and concrete" excited her. Even though she had not yet found a place to live or figured out a way to afford New York rents, she seemed confident and put together.

My conversation with Sue was enjoyable as well as informative. Throughout most of our time together, it felt more like a lunch with one of my girlfriends than an interview. Not surprisingly, our conversation turned to the subject of clothing. Like body dissatisfaction and food concerns, clothing frustrations were a universal concern amongst the women I've spoken with. Sue's clothing concerns focused on what she would wear in New York so that she didn't end up looking like a "hick from the sticks." Her philosophy was that since "clothing makes the man" (or woman in this case), her clothing choice would be pivotal to her success or lack thereof. When I suggested that her ability to do a good job would probably be a better indicator of success, Sue was not convinced. We spent a lot of time discussing clothing—more so than during other interviews. She admitted to being a "clothes horse" and offered to show me her closets.

Sue had three closets in her apartment—a guest closet in the entry, a linen closet, and a large walk-in in her bedroom. All three were filled with clothes and shoes. The entry closet was devoted to coats and blazers. The linen closet was dedicated to shoes, purses, scarves, and other accessories. The bedroom walk-in was clearly her favorite, though. Sue had arranged the closet first by clothing type—bottoms or tops. Within each larger category, subdivisions were then devoted to specifics—t-shirts, button downs, tanks, etc.—which were further divided into dressy or casual and finally organized by color. I was impressed by Sue's organizational skills and her extensive collection of clothes. I was surprised when she started pulling out various items, telling me their size, and then throwing them on her bed, "Size three. Size nine. Size seven." By the time she finished, Sue had covered the bed with items ranging from juniors size three to size eleven and misses size four to size ten. She eventually threw up her hands in frustration and sighed, "I don't know what the hell size I really wear. It just makes me want to scream. It's absolutely ridiculous. How can I be a three one day and an eleven the next?" While Sue was the only woman who literally invited me into her closet to complain about the clothing problems she had, most of the women I interviewed shared with me the frustrations engendered by the contents of their closets.

Clothing is much more than a way to cover up; it is also a pivotal component of our search for self-expression and identity. The types of clothes we wear indicate our social status and the groups we belong to. It is an extension of Self. The clothing I choose to wear is one way to announce to the world my success and happiness. In society, our clothing serves a number of different functions. It provides a health benefit by acting as a barrier between the body and nature. Just imagine what winter in Chicago would be like without clothes to protect our bodies from ice, snow, and wind. Clothing helps us abide by the laws that prohibit nudity in most public venues. Its production and sales sustain the economy. In 2004, clothing sales in the United States totaled over 326 billion dollars, or more than one third of the total expenditures for personal consumption.[1]

For many young women, clothes are more than a decorative and protective covering—they also act as a barometer of emotional well being. Young women expect that a successful woman will always look great. Therefore, the way clothes fit often directly influences the way a young woman feels about her total Self on any given day, and the size she wears is a mysterious social indicator of her physical fitness, style, success, and attractiveness. Young women believe that if the number on the tags of their clothing is "too large"[2] they are fat and unattractive. Even though most of them know that sizes vary widely across manufacturers and that items of clothing which fit are in a range of sizes, they still allow their emotional ups and downs to be contingent upon this one number. The end result is a tumultuous up and down, back and forth shifting between happy and sad, cute and not cute, skinny and fat.

The clothing contingency

> Mandi: "I've recently come to the realization that I don't like to go shopping. I don't enjoy it. I don't have money to spend. I don't like trying on clothes. Like the other day, I was at the Gap looking at their clearance rack and most of the sizes left were extra smalls and stuff I can't wear. You try things on and they don't fit. I look in the mirror and they just make me look like a fat pig. That's depressing."

Shopping is one of the activities usually parodied as the ultimate domain of women, with the mall positioned as their supreme paradise. Shopping for clothes is projected as the Ultimate pleasure. Based on these assumptions, it would seem that Mandi's dislike of shopping is an anomaly. Surprisingly, though, she's not alone in this dislike.

Dilemmas like Mandi's are part of what I refer to as the Clothing Contingency, revolving around what a young woman sees as a direct connection between how she feels about herself and how her clothes look and fit. The mantra is, "If I look good, I feel good." A good day is one where she looks in the mirror and likes what she sees. Therefore, for at least one day she is free of the mirror version of hide and seek inherent in the body dissatisfaction struggle. Without any change in the actual size or shape of her body, the cloud of body dissatisfaction momentarily lifts.

Why don't I feel good?
Unfortunately these feelings of elation are usually temporary. Just as clothes looking good equates to one's feeling good, clothes looking bad—or thought to look bad—equals one's feeling bad. Marie describes how this aspect of the clothing contingency develops and can influence a young woman's attitude toward her Self and possibly her job:

> [The other day] I went to my internship and was walking around. It was like, oh my gosh I can barely breathe in these pants. It was just like the waist was really tight. Whenever I put on my clothes that I knew I felt confident in before, now I just don't feel good about it. It creates a lot of problems in my life.

Marie's story gets to the heart of the clothing contingency. She is physically uncomfortable, but the "problems" she focuses on are emotional, not physical. She no longer feels "confident." She doesn't "feel good." The situation "stresses" her out. She overlooks and ignores possible external causes for the tight waist—shrinkage, perhaps. Instead, she participates in a form of emotional flagellation. Within the implied dictates of the Culture of Discontent, gaining weight or appearing fat is anathema; therefore, for Marie, her pants not fitting the same way as before operates as evidence of personal failure.

Another form of the emotional flagellation and sense of failure dynamic of the clothing contingency is expressed by Diva, as she explains what happens to her when she goes to aerobics classes on campus:

> It's bad in there—the dance room with the mirrors. There's twenty other girls standing around. You look at the shorts on them and on some legs the shorts are glued to them and others they're just flimsy.[3] I look at mine and I'm like oh my god, my shorts are glued to me.

Like Marie, Diva's discomfort begins with the physical fit of her clothing. She perceives this difference in fit as a beacon broadcasting her failure and as a marker of the other girls' success. Like Marie, she never questions other causes for the difference. Maybe Diva's shorts have shrunk. Maybe the other girls purchased shorts in a size larger than needed. Instead, Diva immediately jumps to the conclusion that she is fat.

These two examples illustrate an interesting dynamic of the Clothing Contingency. In both cases, the feelings of unhappiness are self-generated. No one has said anything to Marie or Diva about the way her clothes look; however, both women are unhappy and uncomfortable, their feelings revolving around the ways in which they think they will be perceived. Secondly, while they blame themselves, they give to others—to the mythical ideal woman—the benefit of the doubt. Her clothes appear too large? Surely, she's lost weight. Her clothes are fitting a bit tight? They must have shrunk in the wash. Just like achieving the ideal body is always a bit out of reach in the real world (as opposed to the ideal world inhabited by the mythical ideal woman), achieving the ideal look of clothes is always a bit further down the road. Like skinniness, the fit of clothing has become another indicator of success.

Who needs plastic surgery when you have pliers?

Many young women believe that the perfection of the ideal body can be purchased without going to the extremes of plastic surgery. My conversation with Psyche, a nineteen-year-old art major who hoped to go into interior design, generated a fascinating example of this belief:

> I have this pair of size three jeans that I can never wear. But if I want a tummy tuck for the day, I lie down on the bed, grab a pair of pliers, and force those suckers on.

I was shocked and asked how she made it through the day in jeans that must be extraordinarily uncomfortable. She just shrugged. I also asked her how she went to the bathroom. She said that she just didn't eat or drink all day and "held it in" so that removing her jeans wasn't necessary. She was rather cavalier about her "tummy tuck for the day" as if it were just another thing women do in their quest for beauty. Psyche's actions here demonstrate another way in which women begin to imitate statues. While her excessively tight jeans may provide a slender body for the day, they also severely limit the things that slender body can do. Walking around would be difficult; the best and easiest thing to do is simply stand around and look skinny. Additionally troubling is her practicing—at least temporarily—a severe form of disordered eating. In order to wear the jeans, she must abstain from eating or drinking anything.

The clothing conflicts

Psyche's account leads to a discussion of a consequence of the clothing contingency, how the emotional barometer of clothing for women is complicated by an obsession with size, even when clothes fit properly, look right, and can be put on without the aid of tools. Many women invest emotionally in the actual number and cut displayed on the tags inside their clothes—even though these numbers are not visible to others. Clothing in junior sizes, for example, is usually a narrow straight cut, while misses usually has a somewhat curvy cut for women with more of an hourglass shaped figure. However, this difference is often overshadowed by the assumption that juniors are for skinnier girls and misses are for fatter girls. Satania explains:

> Misses [clothes] are cut for women with big hips and a butt—tiny waist, bigger hips. These are what fit me. If I buy juniors big enough to fit me through here [hips] I have a gap. I could have a party in the back of my pants. I've had to move into the misses section, which is like I'm getting older and fatter. You want to be the size that you are when you're sixteen. You want to stay like that forever.

Satania's unhappiness here revolves around the actual category of sizes—misses—which she associates with fatness. She clearly states that clothes in the juniors category are not cut for her body shape—if they fit her hips they leave room for a "party in the back of her pants." However, being aware of this fact does not diminish the connotation of fatness she feels is inherent in the misses label. As Satania's story illustrates, even if her clothes look right and fit right, she will never feel full elation because they are designated misses, not juniors. Clothing sizes—real and perceived—generate a related set of problems.

It seems that every woman I've met wants to wear a different size, in part because the size that a woman wears is thought to be an extension of Self. Women don't just *wear* a size, they *are* that size. To better understand this phenomenon, let's return to Isabelle's and Caitlyn's discussion from the Introduction:

> Caitlyn: We came back from somewhere and we were like I wear a size two now.
> Isabelle: Yeah, we were admitting to each other that we weren't a size zero anymore.

Caitlyn: Yeah.
Isabelle: And then we both talked each other into feeling that it's ok. I mean
a zero is what I always was. It's my base. But then all of a sudden
you're like a size two.
Caitlyn: I guess a size two is still small, but it's not what I am. It's not a...
Isabelle: Zero...
Caitlyn: Yeah...

During this discussion, Caitlyn begins by explaining that they were discussing how they "wear a size two now." Isabelle then responds that the problem is that they "weren't a size zero anymore." Caitlyn picks up on this linguistic change, later responding that a size two is "not what I am." This sight change in word choice shows how strongly these young women are defining themselves by the size on the tag in the back of their pants.[4] Self-confidence apparently decreases in direct proportion to the increase in this one number, as if it holds some sort of magical power over self-esteem and their very existence. Understanding this part of the contingency makes Diva's aerobics room story clearer. She is not upset just because her shorts are "glued to her legs," which indicate her alleged fatness, but also because she must buy a larger size to have her shorts fit well—supposed proof that she isn't skinny or is at least bigger than she used to be.

Fear of needing to wear a larger size and the resulting loss of esteem is illustrated in an anecdote by Foxy. When we spoke, Foxy was a twenty-one-year-old communication and media studies major. She was close to finishing her bachelor's degree and hoped to find a position in broadcasting—either as an on-air personality or behind the scenes in production. In this excerpt she discusses a close friend's shopping habits:

> We'll go shopping and she's like, "Yeah, I'm a size fourteen." Then she'll grab an eighteen and talk about how comfortable she is and how she loves herself. But if you were really comfortable, why do you have to lie? Why can't you be a proud eighteen? It's really annoying after awhile.

Notice that Foxy is frustrated with the friend's deception of claiming to be a smaller size and implying that it's ok to be a larger woman. Yet when it comes to the size/self connection, lying—even to your friends—is standard practice. Most of the women I've spoken with admitted that when asked about their size, they fudge a bit. The moral implications of lying are a lesser evil than that associated with being considered fat. After all, in the body battles the victor is she who wears the smallest size.

What do you mean I'm bigger than you?

The battle of the sizes is fought on many fronts. Sisters Annette and Eva, whose joint dieting practices I discussed in Chapter Two, told an interesting story of their size competition that was more than normal sibling rivalry. While in high school, Annette lost a significant amount of weight and started wearing a smaller size than younger Eva. In response, Eva began dieting and also started running five miles a day—without Annette. Eva said she "got a little jealous of her [Annette] losing all that weight." Eva's jealousy was multi-fold. She envied the new clothes that Annette's weight loss necessitated, feared that Annette would get more attention and be better liked, and worried that Annette's being a smaller size meant that she, Eva, was fat. In telling this story, Eva focused on her desire to wear the "same size as Annette or maybe one size smaller." She explained that she went to extremes, including borderline anorexia, trying to meet this goal. Eva eventually caught up with Annette's weight loss and was surprised to learn that "it didn't really make much difference in my life. All that suffering and worrying was for nothing."

Friends who normally support each other through all kinds of troubles also enter into competition when it comes to wearing a smaller size. Alice describes a typical situation:

> Just walking around, I don't look at Claire and think that she's going to blow away with the wind and I'm this big tank or something. You know, we're not that much different. But when we go shopping and Claire's looking at twos and fours and sixes and I'm looking at eights and tens and twelves, I'm just like ugh. I've never really had a friend before that was like, number-wise, a lot smaller.

Looking at Alice and Claire, it doesn't appear that they are that differently sized. While there may be a significant difference between Claire's two and Alice's twelve, there is not much difference between Claire's six and Alice's eight. However, that Claire *can* buy the smaller size and sometimes Alice *has* to buy the larger size is a trigger for competition. Alice's comments also illustrate a fascinating fact about women's clothes—there are no uniform standards for determining size.

The clothing conspiracy

As is clear from the foregoing interviews and from the experience of any woman who has shopped for clothing, there is no industry standard for sizing, no agreement on what numerical sizes correspond to what body measurements. Therefore, the body battle of sizes is one that can never be won completely. Until the early part of the twentieth century, much clothing was custom made by seamstresses and tailors and many women made their own clothes. In the 1920s, however, the clothing industry introduced standardized sizes,[5] boasting that women's lives would be easier. They could simply walk into a department store and pick the "right" size, and they could also expand their wardrobe by owning multiple items at a lower cost. Unfortunately, with the ease and freedom of standardized sizes came a heightened awareness of the body and its potential flaws. When clothing was customized, every article of clothing was individually measured, cut, and sewn for each woman's individual body. With standardized sizes, though, clothes are mass-produced to fit a proprietary generic female body of each manufacturer's choosing. Whereas clothing used to be made to fit the body, now the body must be made to fit the clothing. The situation begs the question: If standardization does not extend to the fit of clothes, then just what is standardized about standardized sizes?

What size am I again?

Currently, clothing manufacturers freely determine the body shape that comprises their proprietary fit—curvy, straight, etc. Sizing isn't standardized but the systems for categorizing sizes are. For most manufacturers, misses sizes are indicated by even numbers beginning at zero,[6] and junior sizes are designated by odd numbers beginning at size one. We have yet to see any uniformity in what those numbers mean. Complicating matters further, the cut on any given item of clothing can make two items of the same size from the same manufacturer fit differently; a "slim cut" will run smaller than a "regular cut," which runs smaller than a "relaxed cut." Every woman that I've talked to has a range of clothing sizes in her closet.[7] Sue's sizes varied from three to eleven. Chazy knows that if she buys jeans other than Levi's she'll have to "buy one or two sizes bigger." Psyche owns jeans ranging from size three to size nine and "all of them fit the same." Jasmine and Mandi explain this phenomenon:

Jasmine: Some days you'll go in one store and you'll be wearing whatever size. Then you jump like five sizes at the next store.

Mandi: And then you go to a store that runs big and so you're a smaller size. Then you're like, "Oh I like this store. This is good."

Jasmine: Those are the stores with the clothes that make me feel skinny.

Mandi: Yeah, those are the ones that make me feel good.

During my interview with Virginia and Jill, our discussion on the lack of uniformity in sizes took an interesting turn. Both of them were eighteen years old and planning to leave for college in a few weeks with undeclared majors. When asked about their career goals, they laughed and Virginia explained, "We have no idea what we want to do. We'll worry about that in four years." When our conversation turned to clothing sizes, Jill suggested we conduct a spur of the moment experiment to test just how bad the situation is.[8] Together we went to a department store in the mall where we were having lunch. Our goal was to see just how differently blue jeans within one store fit us. At the time, Virginia wore a size three, while Jill wore a size nine. Each of them grabbed five pairs of jeans in her size. When at all possible, they grabbed a "regular" cut to maintain consistency. Of this first batch, each girl had only one pair that fit well.

The next step in our experiment was to choose the manufacturers of those five pairs of blue jeans we had originally selected and find a pair that did fit right, regardless of size. The result: Virginia's good fits were one pair of size three, and two pairs each of size five and seven; Jill's were one pair of size nine and of size thirteen, and three pairs of size eleven. Each girl's five pairs were from different manufacturers.

We decided to add another phase to the experiment to see if sizes from any one manufacturer fit the same. Virginia and Jill picked a style of jeans that was available in different colors or washes. They tried on the same size from the same manufacturer in these different colors. None of the differently colored jeans fit the same as the initial jeans. At the end of our experiment, there were six different sizes between the two of them—all of which fit. We laughed about this as we left the store, but then Jill stopped laughing and said:

You know, only one size nine fit me. Maybe I'm just fooling myself by thinking I'm a nine. Maybe I've gained weight and am bigger than I think I am. Maybe I should go on a diet or start working out more.

Virginia and I both attempted to reassure her that she looked wonderful no matter what size she wore, but I'm not sure that she really believed us.

As Jill's comments illustrate, the problems generated by this lack of uniformity in sizing runs deeper than making any shopping trip a frustrating process. If a woman *is* a size and she doesn't know what this size really is, then by extension how can she know who she is? The situation sets women up for a life of intangibles and unknowns, while also adding yet another layer to the cycle of dissatisfaction. Recall that the cycle of dissatisfaction is triggered when a woman looks in the mirror and zeroes in on what she considers to be the problem areas of her body. The more she looks at these areas, the more grotesque they begin to appear, which in turn leads to feelings of inadequacy. Adding in the nebulous nature of clothing sizes adds another layer of frustration to the cycle. Because sizes vary so widely, women are thrust into the position of needing to try on clothes whenever they shop and look in the mirror. Therefore, each time a woman goes clothes shopping, she must re-confront the vision of her body reflected in the mirror. When she sees that an item of clothing doesn't fit—especially one in a size that she normally wears—she must determine what this means. Already feeling frustrated and often disgusted with the size of her body, it is quite easy for a woman to determine that this quirk of fit must be evidence of a fatal flaw, in this case being fat.

When is sexy really slutty and how can we tell the difference?

Part of the problem with fit is inevitably related to the fact that clothes are designed to look best on a thin, almost anorexic body. Even though there were skinny models such as Twiggy in the 1960s, the last twenty years has seen a rapid acceleration of this trend in the appearance of high fashion models. The curvy, healthy body popularized by Christie Brinkley in the 1980s has been replaced with the boyishly thin waif body of Kate Moss in the late 1990s.[9] Apparently, the goal of today's designs is to help achieve a sexually alluring appearance: another fashion mandate. A woman must not only look good, she must also look sexy … but not too sexy. How to manage this tension is not clear, and women are left to fend for themselves. If they make the wrong call, they run the risk of emotional turmoil. We see sexualized ideal women everywhere that we turn, and this ideal presents an interesting and unreasonable conundrum for women. They must possess the sexualized thin body of the ideal, but they must not be sexual. The social mandate of our culture is ambivalent about women who enjoy sex, or who are even thought to enjoy sex. These women risk being considered sluts, especially if they look slutty—despite *Sex and the Single Girl* in the 1960s and *Sex and the City* in the twenty-first century.

Such concerns were expressed in the following story by twenty-two-year-old Ladybug, a senior communication studies major hoping to land a position in a real estate firm:

> I have a hard time finding a bathing suit and dressy dresses, like for Senior Ball. Like the dress I have now, I love it but they're out there.[10] That makes me feel self-conscious because I'm afraid that people are going to be like, "She's just a big slut cause her boobs are out there."

Ladybug was very thin with larger breasts that were not out of proportion with the rest of her body. Even though her body looked exactly like a number of the Hollywood stars' bodies that are presented as the current ideal, she repeatedly expressed discomfort with her body—especially with her breasts.

Ladybug is reminded of this discomfort each time she goes shopping. Even though the current ideal body is thin with large breasts, the cut and design of women's clothing—especially bathing suits and "dressy dresses"—tend not to allow ample room for women with larger breasts and smaller bodies. Women like Ladybug, therefore, have to choose between clothes that fit on top but are too large on the bottom, or that fit the bottom and are too tight on top, leaving them to walk around with their breasts "out there." Neither option is acceptable, and either option will ultimately result in feelings of self-consciousness and fears of being considered a "big slut."

Angel, a close friend of Butterfly's, expressed a concern similar to Ladybug's. Angel was a twenty-one-year-old political science major planning to attend law school after graduation before helping her friend Butterfly who had political ambitions. Butterfly, having worked in politics for a few years, was now double majoring in communication and political science with a minor in English; her future plans included law school and graduate school, not necessarily in that order, and running for a national political office some day. Preparing for a Florida vacation, Butterfly and Angel went shopping for clothes, including new bathing suits. Angel was thin and, unlike Ladybug, did not have larger breasts. Butterfly described her as looking like a model in "Cosmo or Vogue." While the two were shopping, Angel found a bathing suit that fit her perfectly. Despite Butterfly's numerous compliments and repeated reassurances, Angel hesitated over actually purchasing the suit. She said:

> It was my first bathing suit like that and you can see my body.[11] A lot of my body. I think back to those magazines, and I don't look like those models so I shouldn't be wearing it. When they wear it, they're sexy. When I wear it, I'm slutty.

Angel's concerns about looking like a slut echo Ladybug's similar concerns and provide an extension of the connection: Size, Self, and Sex. Neither Ladybug nor Angel worry about *looking* like sluts. Instead, their concern is that they will *be* sluts if they choose the wrong clothing, echoing the size/Self connection where a woman doesn't *wear* a size, but *is* a size. Choosing the wrong size becomes a significant behavioral faux pas even though the connection between size and self is tenuous. Does appearance actually reveal anything about behavior? A slut is generally defined as a slovenly woman or a prostitute.[12] As illustrated by Ladybug and Angel's concerns, though, to be considered a slut a woman need not actually participate in sexual activity. She only needs to look like she has a lot of sexual experience to earn the title "Slut."[13] To avoid being considered slutty, then, a woman must choose the right size, with the clothing in question hugging the body but not appearing too tight.

What do you mean I'm plus-size?
While women struggle to figure out what size clothing to buy and worry about choosing clothes that look sexy but not slutty, they must also keep in mind one final clothing mandate: They should wear a small size. The smaller, the better. And they should take pains to avoid needing to wear a plus-size. Jasmine explains a typical response to being thought plus-size:

> I was looking at one of those big pictures in a store window with this girl wearing a real cute outfit from the store. Then I looked up and it's Lane Bryant.[14] And I was like oh no, no, no. I am not that size. And I looked at the model again and she's not even close to remotely being fat.

Young women tend to view the plus-size label as nothing more than a euphemism for fat. Since fat is seen as failure in the body battles, if plus-size equals fat, then needing to wear a plus-size equals failure. However, as with size and fit, there are multiple interpretations of what plus-size means. It appears designed to fit women larger than average. Today, the average size worn by women is a misses fourteen. Despite this fact, many manufacturers use fourteen as the starting point for plus-size clothes. This creates an interesting conundrum: If fourteen is the average, this means that perhaps as many women wear both larger and smaller sizes; therefore, how can it also be plus-size?

As part of my quest to find the standardized part of standardized clothing sizes, I decided to find out what exactly plus-size is by conducting an informal survey of popular plus-size clothing manufacturers. Using both the internet and catalogs published by the companies in question, I examined the most popular plus-size retailers. Not surprisingly, the numbers ranged all over the board.[15]

Manufacturer	Size Range
Ashro[16]	14–24
Avenue[17]	14–32
Eddie Bauer[18]	16–26
Elisabeth[19]	14–24
Lane Bryant[20]	14–28
L.L. Bean[21]	18–26
Roamans[22]	12–44
Silhouettes[23]	12–50
Sydney's Closet[24]	14–44
Ulla Popken[25]	12–38
Wal-Mart[26]	14–28

Based on these numbers, it seems that plus-size can include anything from size twelve to fifty. As if this weren't confusing enough, I found three companies that use a completely different set of designations:

Chico's[27]	0–3
Junonia[28]	0–6
Torrid[29]	0–4

These sizes have nothing to do with similar numbers used in misses and junior sizes or with each other. For example, Chico's zero equates to a misses size four, Junonia's zero to a misses fourteen, and Torrid's zero to a misses size ten or twelve. It would be ideal if an easier system could be devised. I'm not qualified to give a definitive answer, nor would I want to hazard a guess. A better question, though, is why does it matter? Is it really necessary to create linguistic demarcations between juniors, misses, and plus sizes? It is obvious that to create linguistic demarcations among sizes—juniors, misses, and plus sizes—seems illogical and is certain to engender negative connotations for those who pay attention to them.

The complex emotions and dimensions of the intrapersonal level of body dissatisfaction—concerns over body, food, and clothing— all feed into and off each other. When examining the clothing contingency in this chapter, what is especially interesting is that even without specific comments from other people, the stories shared illustrate how much time and energy young women devote to worrying about how their bodies look in clothes and what messages are sent as a result. Ladybug and Angel worry that people will think they are sluts. Diva, Satania, Caitlyn and Isabelle agonize over looking fat in their clothes. Marie thinks that she will be considered incompetent to complete her internship. Jasmine works to ensure she is not thought to need a plus-size. At the intrapersonal level of body dissatisfaction, concerns over body, food, and clothing all feed into and off of each other. What is especially interesting about this level of body dissatisfaction is the fact that even without specific comments from other people, the stories shared within these pages illustrate how much time and energy young women devote to worrying about how their body looks and what messages it implies about them. Are their concerns just simple paranoia mixed in with a smidgen of narcissism? As will become clear in the following chapters, it appears that young women have good reason to be concerned.

Chapter Four

You've gotten a little bigger

You've gotten a little bigger

In today's postmodern world, the female body is not just a private body; it is also a social body on which anyone can comment. In addition to women's personal experiences of their bodies, they must navigate the things that others say to them about their bodies. Presented as loving helpful hints, family members' words often serve to exacerbate women's body dissatisfaction concerns. Because family plays such a paramount role in women's lives, unraveling the myriad family comments is the first step in understanding the interpersonal influences of body dissatisfaction.

Socializing the female body

Jessica worked at a coffee shop where I do a lot of my writing (and spend way too much money on coffee). One day when the words just wouldn't come, she and I started talking about this project and, as happens so often, Jessica began sharing stories of her trials with body dissatisfaction and other related issues. Jessica said she had been a "big girl" her entire life with her dissatisfaction revolving around the fact that she's a "fat fourteen so I usually buy sixteens." Her situation was made worse because her mother constantly reminded her that she was fat. She remarked that if her mother told her one more time that she "has such a pretty face if you'd only lose some weight," she would probably kill her. After laughing at this, Jessica said that she felt as if her mother just didn't "get it because she's skinny and likes to spend five hours a day at the gym." Jessica shook her head in disgust and declared that her mother's obsession was a "big fucking waste of time." I kept to myself the observation that her mother appeared to have an exercise disorder and also that a woman need not even be really fat to receive such commentary; size fourteen is average.

Later in our conversation she confided that she was planning on entering her company's management training program in a few weeks so that she could "earn more money and move out of the house." When I asked how she would manage a full time work and training load with a full schedule of classes, she explained that she was temporarily dropping out of college because she had to move; she said, "I can't hear one more time how fat I am." Jessica admitted that her mother probably has "my best interests in mind and just wants to motivate me." Instead, the more her mom commented, the less likely Jessica was to do "anything healthy." Jessica also observed, "I don't really think I'm fat. I'm average, you know? But then my mom starts in and I feel like a big old cow or something." When I asked Jessica if she had ever tried to explain these feelings to her mom, she laughed and said, "Yeah, right. It's easier to just keep quiet and pretend like I care."

Whose body is it?
Up to this point I've discussed body dissatisfaction as primarily a personal and private struggle. The cycle of dissatisfaction begins when a young woman looks in the mirror and dislikes what she sees. Wanting to emulate the mythical ideal woman she sees in her mind, she often begins eating less and exercising more. To help create the illusion that she is close to the ideal, she will attempt to wear clothing that not only looks cute but also helps to make her look thin. However, when her appearance falls short of her expectations, she is immediately thrust back into the throes of the cycle of dissatisfaction. All of this worry about body size and attempts to control one's appearance through eating, exercise, and clothing is not just a practice in vanity. While we may live alone in our bodies, we also live within the larger social realm. This means that unless we are complete and utter hermits, we interact with a variety of others on a daily basis. In doing so, we often hear comments about our bodies. The female body is more than a private body; it is a social body— open for comment and available for viewing everywhere.

The maxim "Sex sells" is both well-known and well-practiced. Female bodies and body parts have become such an inherent aspect of advertising and marketing in twenty-first century America that we have grown somewhat numb to their presence. Pay attention to the way female bodies are used in television or magazine ads for every product imaginable.[1] The primary sexual body used to sell is a hyper-sexualized female body positioned to highlight the breasts and/or pubic area. Since most of these bodies are skinny models further enhanced through computers and/or airbrushing, their form comes to be viewed as the norm or standard for all female bodies. As women, we begin to think that we should look like them and that we could look like them if we only worked harder, ate less, bought different clothes, or took some other action to change our bodies.

Seeing the Self through others' eyes

Seeing female bodies everywhere also creates the perception that all female bodies are open for public scrutiny. We make comments about those women advertising Fanta soda, so why not talk about that woman drinking Fanta soda in the quad? Jessica's story about her mom's comments is a narrative common to young women's experiences of their bodies. Everyone—parents, other relatives, other women, and even strangers—feel that they have the right to make comments on the size, shape, and appearance of women's bodies.[2] Therefore, in addition to negotiating the body dissatisfaction women themselves experience, they must be constantly vigilant of the public perception of the size and comportment of their bodies. As I've already argued, getting fat is not just to be avoided; it is anathema, one of the worst things that can happen to a young woman. Because of this assumption about the evils of fat, other people try to "help" the "fat" young woman by commenting, critiquing, and cajoling her into realizing the error of her ways. All these remarks aggravate the burden of the body dissatisfaction that young women feel and seriously influence their self-image.

Through our interactions with others, we gain greater understandings of our individual Self. Not only do we determine and monitor the status of our relationships through our interpersonal discourses, but we also learn more about who we are. Charles Horton Cooley has defined this aspect of self-identification as the looking-glass self.[3] Cooley explains that when we look at ourselves, we not only see the reflected image but we also imagine how we will be viewed by others. Every action that we take is filtered through this lens. We struggle to define our Self in the manner that we desire; however, at the same time we struggle with defining ourselves the way others would have us do so. The closer that our relationship is with the individuals participating in the interpersonal discourse, the more influential the things they say become. We want to impress and be liked by those individuals we care about, such that the discursive mandates from a relative carry more weight than those from a random stranger. The multiplicity and variety of interpersonal discourses each of us engage in are varied; therefore, each of these relationships brings its own types of discourses and with them, its own discursive mandates.

As women, we use interpersonal discourse to help negotiate the struggle of determining who and what we are as women. Interpersonal discourse operates to introduce a specific, intense gaze into women's existence. As noted by Sandra Lee Bartky, "the gaze of the Other is internalized so that I myself become at once seer and seen, appraiser and the thing appraised."[4] That is, even as women observe others, they critically observe how they are being observed by others. Without the need or benefit of a mirror, women continually monitor themselves through the gaze of the Other. As women participate in interpersonal discourse with these Others, their bodies become the focus of this gaze, as well as of the discourse. One thing that remains fairly stable across relationships in our culture is the discourse that female bodies should be thin.

Mother knows best, right?

From the time we are born, our parents and caregivers influence us and teach us how to survive and cope. The child who hears, "No! Hot!" as she tries to touch the flame on the stove may cower and cry, but she quickly learns that stove = hot = bad. As we mature, the information we acquire increases in complexity. For example, the child learns that the stove is sometimes hot and sometimes not, and that hot can be good because it allows food to cook. One of the most important things that we learn from our parents or caregivers is how to communicate and relate to others. John Bowlby theorizes that the type of parenting we experience as young children continues to influence us as adults.[5] Bowlby identifies three attachment styles: secure or what we would consider "normal" parenting; avoidant or what we would consider abusive parenting; and ambivalent, which combines unconditional love with distancing measures. Parents may exhibit one or more styles throughout the lifetime of the child.

From the stories that young women share about their experiences of body dissatisfaction, we see an inordinate amount of the ambivalent style throughout the interpersonal discourse of mothers and other relatives. Mothers and these others clearly express their affection and love for the young women. However, when it comes to discussing the young woman's body, their discourse is more distancing and potentially damaging. Bowlby informs us that children who are raised with an ambivalent parenting style struggle with always trying to please others. Because the child never knows when affection will turn to disaffection, she strives to do everything possible to forestall the change. Therefore, when a young woman experiences ambivalent discourse revolving around her body, she internalizes it as yet another example of the gaze that controls her very existence. She internalizes the negative comments as proof positive that she is not worthy of their love until and unless she modifies the size of her body. Indeed, Jasmine and the other young women I've interviewed observed that at least a portion of its cause is "closer to home than anybody's willing to talk about," and that body dissatisfaction is initially learned by watching their mothers, grandmothers, aunts, and other female relatives worry about their own body size and participate in various behaviors to change. As they grow up, young women often adopt the routines they were surrounded with as children and consider this behavior the normal everyday experience of being a woman in the world.

If my mom thinks she's fat, then what am I?

The ways that parents and caregivers influence the development of body dissatisfaction are varied. One of the most common, though, is through behavioral modeling. When mothers enact specific behaviors related to body dissatisfaction and young women see this behavior repeated numerous times, the behavior eventually becomes normalized for young women. Throughout my interview with Psyche and Madeleine, maternal influence came up numerous times. The following exchange is representative of their concerns:

> Madeleine: My mom was always very body conscious. She'd be like "Oh, I look fat." So it's kind of hard because I do that too now. I think I'm going to be like that—always worried about being fat.
> Psyche: You think you're going to turn into your mom…
> Madeleine: I know. I think I will be like that. It's hard not to, though. It's learned behavior.

As Madeleine continued to talk, she began to realize just how much her own feelings of body dissatisfaction were a "learned behavior."

She observed that she always felt that her mother was skinnier than she was and therefore, if her mother considered herself fat, then Madeleine must be "enormous." Jasmine also grew up in a home where mom was constantly concerned about the size of her body. Jasmine's mother regularly said that she herself "needs to diet" and admonished Jasmine not to look at her "fat stomach." Even though it is unlikely that either Jasmine's or Madeleine's mother intended her comments to be interpreted as a standard of behavior, the impact of their words still stings and causes both women to modify their eating and exercise practices.

A more direct level of maternal involvement is described in the following story from Alice about how she learned a form of disordered eating: eating as an acceptable form of dealing with stress:

> I definitely learned from my mom because she was always on a diet too. I learned emotional eating from her. Like if something crappy happened to her at work, she would come home and grab that ice cream from the freezer. We would all sit together and eat ice cream. We were kids so we didn't have the right to go in the freezer without permission but if mom had a crappy day at work and she goes to the freezer and gets ice cream, then everybody gets to have ice cream, right?

Not only does Alice's mom teach by doing, but she also directly involves her children in her disordered eating. At the time, Alice thought the situation was just a party, but now Alice realizes that these ice cream parties still impact the way she handles her own stress. Like her mom, Alice frequently deals with difficult times by turning to food—usually ice cream. Alice continued to explain other body dissatisfaction lessons she learned from her mother:

> The majority of the time when I grew up I never saw [my mother] be successful at dieting. It was always this eternal condemnation kind of thing. Like, I screwed up again; let's try something else. It's like she never really thought of herself as being good enough and she was constantly dieting and re-dieting. And we'd go through and clean out all the chocolate and ice cream and potato chips and whatever from the house. Then my dad would get mad because he takes his lunch to school every day and takes chips and Little Debbies. So he would go buy some. And she'd be like, "Oh well," and we'd start all over again. That was just the cycle in my house.

From these stories, it appears that Alice's mom is involved in a dangerous and continuous cycle of disordered eating, turning to junk food when depressed or upset to soothe her emotions. Then she condemns herself for an unsuccessful diet and purges the house of all junk food, which is immediately replaced by Alice's father. Alice's mother is trapped in a cycle of extremes—overeating and undereating. And her children are right there with her. As Alice clearly infers, this influence lingers several years later.

Like Alice, Ladybug grew up in a home where her mother's body dissatisfaction affected the food options available to the rest of the family. After Ladybug's mother gained weight, her father started "teasing her." In response, Ladybug's mom "started dieting and not buying junk food and all." As in Alice's house, because mom feels fat the rest of the family is deprived—at least momentarily—of junk food. A fascinating aspect of these two stories is the role that dad plays. Instead of encouraging Alice's mom in her efforts to lose weight, dad rushes out and replaces all her trigger foods. Instead of reassuring Ladybug's mom that she still looks attractive after gaining weight, dad teases her. In both situations, dad's behavior serves to reinforce the assumption that women's bodies are social bodies open for comment from everyone. Therefore, Alice and Ladybug learn that to impress their daddy and stay in his good graces, they must not get fat and should not need to go on diets. As will be explored in Chapter Six, these early lessons continue to play out in young women's adult interactions with other men.

Can I ever become my model mom?

Even though young women are influenced by both parents while growing up, their mother or a female caregiver tends to exert a great impact on their sense of self and identity. The things that they do and say become an integral part of our discourses of dissatisfaction.[6] Christine Northrup explains that from the time young women are little girls the ways that their mothers discuss their bodies and eating habits directly influence the ways that they will continue to experience their bodies.[7] Even innocuous seeming comments or behaviors hold the potential for a lifetime of dissatisfaction discourse. Mothers, and other relatives for that matter, act as models which young girls emulate. What mommy does is the template for the way things should be done in later life, and their mothers' attitudes toward their own bodies provide a model to follow. Dr. Northrup explains that "our bodies and our beliefs about them will form in the soul of our mothers' emotions, beliefs, and behaviors."[8] While much of what we learn from our mothers about our bodies is direct, as in Alice's and Ladybug's situations, Dr. Northrup's point is that this influence may be more subtle.

Trying to and wanting to be like mom is a normal part of growing up. For those young women whose mothers have bodies close to the cultural ideal, the situation creates an especially tenuous proposition. As described by twenty-year-old Seville, her mother is the "most beautiful woman in the world" and a dancer who later became a "professional runway model." A communication and performance studies junior, Seville wasn't sure what she wanted to do with her life after college. She thought that she might like to "work with animals or something." A dancer herself, Seville was thin and seemingly beyond the personal struggles of body dissatisfaction, with a vibrant way of presenting herself. Nevertheless, as with so many of the stories shared in these pages, Seville's is filled with the contradictions engendered by living within a culture of discontent. As she discusses growing up in her mom's shadow, her own body dissatisfaction is evident:

> Her six-foot-tall, super-slim frame has always made me envious. She never comments on my weight or what I eat. She is also not at all concerned with her weight or what she puts in her mouth. Having a near perfect mother has created this exceptional world I feel like I have to live up to. I know my weight is much higher than my mom's and she's over a half foot taller than I am. My ex-boyfriend would consistently comment on her looks, and not being able to fit into your fifty-five-year-old mother's clothes is about the worst feeling ever. When you are at the mall, and guys are checking out your mom instead of you, it's a big ouchy. I know I will never be my stick skinny mother, but it doesn't seem to stop me from trying to be. I love her and she is as beautiful on the inside as the outside, but the pressure to be her is a killer.

Even though Seville's mother doesn't exert pressure or make comments, Seville still feels "pressure to be her." While Seville is aware of the mythical ideal body, she is also confronted daily with a living embodiment of that ideal, one who shares her genes. It seems as if she should be able to achieve at least this version of the ideal body. Each day that she fails to look like her mom, Seville's cycle of dissatisfaction increases in intensity.

It doesn't seem surprising at all when Seville says that she feels as if she must live up to this "exceptional world." Consider the various pressures that Seville raises:

- Her mother is a living embodiment of the ideal with her "six foot tall, super slim frame";
- Her mother never has to worry about her weight or what she eats;
- Her mother wears clothes in a small size and is "stick skinny";
- Guys who are Seville's age comment on her mother's looks;
- Men of all ages check out her mother;
- Seville weighs more than her mother, even though her mother is "over a half foot taller."

When we spoke, Seville wavered between wanting to accept the fact that she would never look just like her mother and the desire to still try. In addressing the phenomenon of body dissatisfaction, she noted that she wants it "to be gone" as much as she wants "to be a size zero." Whenever I think about Seville, I wonder if she will ever be able to find a solution to this conundrum. As troubling as the lived experiences of body dissatisfaction are for most young women, it seems that Seville's situation may be worse.

We often think that as they mature, girls tend to grow out of the phase of wanting to be just like mom. However, as these stories demonstrate, this may not be true. Alice still turns to ice cream in times of trouble. Ladybug continues to worry about being the butt of jokes if she gains weight. Seville struggles daily to live up to the exceptional world of her mother. Perhaps we want to believe that young girls will grow beyond this maternal influence, that just as parents and caregivers want their children's lives to be better than theirs, we all want the next generation of women to have grown beyond the frustrations of body dissatisfaction.[9] However, simply wanting it to happen is not enough to make it so.

I'm telling you this because I love you

Unconditional love is the sine qua non of parenthood. We know (or at least hope) that parents will love their children no matter what and want the best for their children—no matter what the children look like. However, because American society so often equates a woman's worth with the size of her body, parents will often encourage their daughters to lose weight as a way to try to help their daughters be accepted and loved by others. They do this because they love their daughters and want the best for them.

When is maternal love really child abuse?

The examples of negative parental influence presented up to this point have been indirect and most likely unintentional. Arguably, none of these mothers expected that her body dissatisfaction would cause harm to her children either in the moment or in the future. Annette, however, shared a more direct and disturbing story of maternal influence:

> I babysit for a couple of girls and right now the ten year old is on Weight Watchers. She is *ten*,[10] and she is not overweight. It's one of the craziest things I have ever seen. The girl has dropped several sizes. She and her mom both started the program, and I think it's almost like the mom is using her daughter to help motivate her or something. I think her mom is worried about her daughter becoming like her and having weight problems the rest of her life. She is *ten*.

> She eats very little. I pack her lunch and I have to measure out everything, count every pretzel. She has to add it up and tally the points. I see her in the mornings measuring out her milk and her cereal and then measuring out everything she has for lunch. She comes home after school and the first thing kids want, milk and cookies, she can't have. This girl has to flip through her Weight Watcher's points book to see what she can eat.

When I asked Annette if this girl was happy being on Weight Watchers, she responded:

> The first few weeks were horrible. I could have cried because the girl was not happy. She was grouchy because she was hungry. She's gained a lot of confidence now, because people are like, "Oh you look so nice." But I watch her. They have these huge mirrors in their house and I watch her walk past. She's doing what I do, what we do. You know? Like college students and high school students. Like looking at herself in the mirror. This never happened before. Now she's seeing how she looks—how good she looks and messing with her clothes. She was so carefree before and now she will be a dieter for the rest of her life.

This story is chilling for many reasons. What disturbed me the most, though, is that the girl is only ten years old. While most girls her age are playing or eating "milk and cookies," she is counting food points, obsessing about her total caloric intake and the size of her body, and already believing that her worth as a woman comes from being thin. This premise is being tacitly reinforced through compliments she now receives on her looks. While this young girl may be getting positive compliments, I have to wonder how much of her Self has been sacrificed and how this experience will continue to impact her as she grows up. As Annette observes, she is carefree no longer.

Anyone familiar with the Weight Watchers program knows that weight loss occurs after a serious restriction on the types of food consumed and the amount of calories ingested. It is a difficult regimen for the average adult and creates a feeling of deprivation coupled with moments of hunger even though the food amount allowed does provide enough energy to function. This begs the question of how subjecting a child to this type of diet unnecessarily is not considered child abuse or at least neglect. If the mother in question were denying her daughter food under other circumstances, she would probably be charged with criminal neglect or child endangerment. In this situation, though, she may think she is expressing unconditional love for her daughter and so the "neglect" is disguised as care and concern. I imagine that if I were to interview the daughter in the future, she would tell an even more disturbing story of body dissatisfaction than any I have heard to date.

While most parents do not go to the extremes of putting their very young daughters on diets, many of them do comment and criticize as a form of motivation. Sometimes these comments are downright mean. When Virginia was twelve, for example, she overheard her mother and a friend discussing Virginia's impending adolescence and her maturing body. Virginia's mom related how "Virginia is really starting to get a butt now" and how she "has her grandmother's legs." In telling me this story, Virginia practically screamed about how her grandmother had "big old grandma jiggly legs that were all dimpled and ugly." Virginia said that up to that point in her life she never really thought about her body. She said, "I was always a tomboy, too busy playing and climbing trees to worry about what I looked like." From that moment on, though, Virginia became "obsessed with having a tiny butt and thighs that don't touch. And never ever having jiggly grandma thighs!"

If my mom says I'm fat, then am I?

Many times mothers and others will say things such as, "You've gotten a little bigger" or "You've gained a little weight" to young women. While these comments usually are meant less to point out a fatal flaw than to motivate the recipient to take action, they usually discourage her. The following description from Marie exemplifies the situation:

> My mom will tell me you've gotten a little bigger. And then that makes me think well, if my mom's telling me this I must be getting bigger. I mean she's my mom so she loves me, right? She wouldn't say it if it wasn't true.

Because the comment comes from her mom, Marie grants it an unquestioned stamp of legitimacy. With no critical examination of the comment or of herself, Marie agrees that she "must be getting bigger" and her body dissatisfaction is exacerbated.

As with other aspects of body dissatisfaction, observations from mom are often not as straightforward as a simple comment. I met with Marie a week after her mom suggested Marie had "gotten bigger." To me, Marie appeared to be clearly on the thin side of the body continuum,[11] bordering on skinny. After hearing this anecdote, I began to wonder if Marie's mother's comments had anything to do with the mother's mapping her own body dissatisfaction onto Marie's body. Mothers and daughters often see themselves in the other. The daughter sees herself in the future, while the mother sees what she was, or could have been, in the past. At times, it is difficult to separate the present reflection of Self from the past reflection of Self. Moms will remember their own experiences and comment out of a sense of love and a desire to protect their daughters from making the same mistakes that they feel they've made.

What makes him think he has the right to say that to me?

Even though I've focused on mothers up to this point, they aren't the only family members expressing their opinions to young women. Every woman I've spoken with told a story of some other relative also making comments. For example, Shelly shared a story concerning her father and sister. Shelly was a twenty-two-year-old communication studies major preparing to graduate in a few months and attend graduate school. During her sister's sophomore year of college, the sister lost a significant amount of weight. Shelly's father, out of frustration, told the sister that her "knees are so skinny they look deformed." He then threatened that if she didn't gain weight, he was going to "drag [her] into the hospital." Like other parents, Shelly's father was expressing concern for his daughter. Unfortunately this concern ended up making the situation worse. Shelly told me that even though she had been concerned that her sister might be struggling with an eating disorder, she was worried after these comments that her sister would retaliate by eating even less.

While body dissatisfaction is primarily an issue affecting women's lives, men of all ages have a significant influence and are intertwined in the lived experience of body dissatisfaction.[12] Shelly's father is only one example of the many older male relatives who freely discuss young women's bodies with them. Not only are there a number of such stories, but their content and form is also surprisingly similar. Compare the following two stories from Marie and Happy respectively:

> Marie: My uncle is really bad. He's the worst. We went to Cancun last year at the end of the year and he was just saying, "Wow, you're getting bigger. You've gained a lot of weight." And I'm like, "Really? Where?" And he pointed out where—like here and here.[13] He made me feel fat. Then I saw him over break and he said it just looks like I'm becoming more of a woman, curvy. I don't know if that was a cover-up or not. He's pretty much the odd ball of the family. I get along with him. We laugh a lot and everything.

> Happy: I know he was just trying to make me feel better but he came over, my grandfather came over for dinner. He has told me several times that I look bigger or that I've gained weight. And I'm like, "Paw Paw shut up." I was like, you've got to be kidding me. And it was sort of a motivation to lose weight. At Easter, he was like, "You're getting fat." I never expected that from him. He's such a dumb redneck. I just never expected it. I mean I like him and all.

Both situations start with an innocuous family event—a family trip and a family dinner—shattered by the older male relative's comments. Neither Marie nor Happy expected these comments and, in recalling the event months later, both women made excuses for the relative. When I hear these and other similar stories, I repeatedly return to the questions I asked myself when I first heard them:

What prompted this relative to make such remarks in the first place? What made him feel like he had a right to comment on his niece or granddaughter's body size? Whether the woman had gained some weight or was simply maturing, the men in question act as if they have a proprietary interest in this particular female body, as if they are protecting an investment. Chances are, the men forgot the comments a few minutes after they were made. The women, however, remember the comments for months and often years later. I've spoken to women in their thirties, forties, and fifties who still remember and are affected by careless comments like these. When they tell me their stories, their emotions are clear. Many of them express intense anger, practically spitting the words out. Many more, however, display profound sadness and openly cry. Toward the end of their story, they inevitably turn to questioning themselves and wondering if maybe they really were—or still are—fat.

As the stories shared in this chapter demonstrate, one simple comment from a well-meaning relative—mother or other—can set off a chain reaction of emotions—anger, disbelief, belief, rationalization. More troubling and potentially damaging, though, is that such comments represent a form of power. By vocalizing their critical observations of the woman's body, these relatives exert control over not only the woman's body but also over her entire being. By simply accepting their relatives' comments as valid, each of these young women cedes control of her body to another. The women implicitly acknowledge that their bodies are social bodies, just like those sexualized bodies used to sell products. They are letting their relatives not only control their existence but also possibly lead them down a road to physical damage or destruction.

All of these linguistic attempts to control women's body size strengthen and reinforce each other. Even more troubling are the running dialogues that young women have with themselves about their bodies as a result. When they return to the mirror, they not only see their potential body flaws but also hear them through the voices of their loved ones. The intrapersonal and interpersonal discourses enter into dialogue with each other through each woman's experience of her body dissatisfaction. Individually, the discourses are strong; together they are super strong. They create a wall of control over the body that feels impenetrable. The lived experience of body dissatisfaction may begin as a personal struggle to accept and change the body; however, whenever a woman enters the public realm, she must confront the reality that her control over her body is only a small part of the story.

Young women are exposed to this discursive control from the time they are little girls. When they enter college, they face the added pressures of being surrounded by hundreds or thousands of other young women—all potential opponents in the body battles. As will become clear in the next chapter, all of these other women also freely add their voices to the critical commentary and control aimed at young women's bodies.

Chapter Five

You've got to impress the girl

You've got to impress the girl

Striving to achieve the mythical ideal body provides a common point of dialogue for women. As they talk about their bodies, women participate in body shape discourse, a particular form of discourse that helps women bond. However, body shape discourse can also result in body battles in which women openly compete with other women for the best body.

Good girls or battling broads?

I first met Katie when she took a class with me. Katie was an outgoing, friendly student who came by my office a few times to talk about class and to socialize. After we discussed body dissatisfaction issues in class, Katie's visits became more regular—two to three times per week. Katie explained that she was "really interested in body image and stuff." She continued, "As an actress, I know that there will always be a lot of focus on my body." By the end of the semester, Katie was asking if she could help with my research after she returned from her summer internship as an "actor"[1] with a major theme park chain over the summer. I told her that I would love to interview her when she returned and that we could discuss other ways she could help with the project. I wished her well with her internship and we said goodbye for the summer.

At the beginning of the fall semester, Katie and I agreed to meet for lunch at a bistro close to campus. As I was sitting down I tried to figure out what was different about her. We began talking, and I quickly realized the problem—her demeanor was flat. Before, whenever Katie spoke, she was bubbly and gregarious with an infectious sense of optimism. Something was clearly different now. Other than when she greeted me, Katie had not smiled. Her voice bordered on monotone. She was friendly, but that extra spark was gone. She seemed like a different woman. I finally asked, "Katie, are you feeling ok? You seem to be a bit off or something." She looked down at her food and shook her head.

After a few minutes Katie took a deep breath and began talking, "This past summer was hell." I didn't say anything and just nodded my head to show I was listening. Many students come back frustrated from their first internships after realizing that work is more often hard work than the glamour they had imagined. I expected to hear another story about a crazy, mercurial boss who wanted results, not excuses, or a rant about how she was expected to learn by simply having orders barked at her and then being severely criticized when she did her assigned job wrong—the usual student sagas in first internships. However, Katie's story was dramatically different.

Katie told me that after she went through her new employee orientation, she was assigned to be a no-name background character for the summer. "It was a dog or a weasel or some other crazy thing with four legs and a tail," she said. Her job consisted of performing in a show and spending the rest of her day walking around greeting visitors. Since her character was an unknown background figure, the only visitors interested in her were toddlers too young to know the difference between Katie's character and the other better known and popular ones; older children would cry and scream when their parents tried to force them to take a picture with Katie.

Katie said that she spent the summer feeling hot and neglected. She asserted that even though walking around Florida in July while wearing several pounds of fake fur felt like living inside a bonfire, the heat of her costume was ten times easier to deal with than the "crap" her co-workers forced on her. She described how her co-workers labeled her the "fat chick." I was somewhat shocked when Katie shared this story, for she was approximately five feet seven inches tall, wore a size seven, weighed probably between 130 and 140 pounds—and was definitely not fat. But Katie pointed out that most of her female co-workers were not like her. They weighed less than 110 pounds, several weighing less than one hundred. Every day in the locker room, they would jump on the scale and sing out,

"Ninety-eight pounds," or "102! I shouldn't have drunk all that beer last night." Many of these women were dancers or other featured performers who wore "normal" (for a theme park) clothes rather than full body fake animal costumes.

Katie continued by describing what the women did to torment her. After the roles were assigned, Katie expressed her frustration with her assignment to the woman whose locker was nearby. The woman looked at her, ran her eyes up and down Katie's body, and asked, "What did you expect? At your size you'll never be more than a background character." The woman then turned to the other women in the room and raised her voice, "You know, maybe she should consider a job as background scenery. Her ass is definitely wide enough to reach from stage left to stage right." As Katie told this story, I looked over at her to gauge her response. She appeared to be struggling not to cry. I remained quiet and kept my snide assessment of the woman's behavior to myself so as not to further upset Katie. After a few minutes of silent crying, Katie composed herself enough to continue with the story of her summer saga:

> I didn't want to look like I wasn't a team player, so I laughed with the rest of them. Maybe that was a mistake. After that woman's remarks about my ass, whenever I would pass one of the women in the park, they would make oinking noises. Every few days I would find magazine articles about diets or exercise programs taped to my locker along with an unsigned note telling me that I should try them.

Katie said that she tried to complain to her supervisor, but he just looked at her and noted that it wouldn't hurt her to lose a few pounds. He suggested she make more of an effort to get along with the other women and maybe they could teach her about "fitness and health stuff." She speculated that because she laughed at the first remark, all of the remaining actions were her fault since she "never let them know how much it hurt."

Katie's story sounded like a scene from the movie *Mean Girls.*[2] Yet these "girls" were adult women, some from well-known colleges. Katie ended her story by saying that the experience was "enlightening and educational." She said that she didn't plan on starting any "stupid diets" but she was reconsidering her career goals. She explained that she was going to focus on a career behind the camera now, instead of trying to be an actress or on-air personality.

Katie's story is upsetting but not that unusual. At some point, every woman seems to have experienced ruthless and scarring teasing similar to Katie's. The details vary but the damage remains the same. One of the goals of this project has been to discover why these things happen and to determine why it appears to be acceptable in our society for women to act in such mean and negative ways toward each other without fear of public scorn or ridicule. Undoubtedly, such behavior is related, at least in part, to treating the female body like a social body, which opens it up for commentary and criticism from others. In Chapter One, I asserted that women today live within a culture of discontent that requires an ever-present awareness of one's body. Teasing—remembered from the past and possibly anticipated in the future—is one of the causes of this culture, leaving women in a perpetual defensive state.

How do I look?

Women grow up in an environment where others are constantly commenting on and criticizing their body size. In Chapter Four, I focused on how the critical comments of mothers and other relatives get internalized by young women and incorporated into their personal body dissatisfaction dialogues. To these voices are added the voices of other young women (as well as the voices of guys, a topic to be discussed in the next chapter).

As young women mature and their bodies change, the critical comments often increase in frequency and intensity, eventually becoming accepted as a regular part of their lives and implicitly teaching young women that they must constantly monitor the way they look and act in public. As Susan Douglas noted in her book *Where the Girls Are,* "Women learn to watch themselves being watched."[3] They live as if they are constantly on stage, performing and waiting for the critics' reviews even though they are afraid of the criticism. One way that this commentary is avoided is through the living statue phenomenon discussed in Chapter One. A more troubling way occurs when a woman makes a pre-emptive strike and publicly criticizes her own body.

Do I look fat in this?

Women often try to protect themselves and head off criticism by engaging in the practice of criticizing themselves. When a woman makes a comment such as "I feel like a cow" or asks, "Does this make me look fat?" she is engaging in what I call Body Shape Discourse,[4] female friendship talk focused on the perceived adequacies and inadequacies of their own bodies. Such phrases can be heard regularly as part of pop culture humor. In pop humor, for example, body shape discourse is often used to poke fun at women's weight concerns in sit-coms, films, greeting cards, and just about any venue that combines pictures and words. Take, for example, a popular commercial for car insurance; a woman asks a man (her husband?), "Does this make me look fat?" Preoccupied with his newspaper, he responds, "You betcha." While the audience may laugh in response, the scene shows us that women's weight concerns are easy targets for ridicule, and that this concern is assumed to be a joke with such wide appeal that it can attract an audience and sell almost anything. It also raises another question. How should one respond? Agreement? Disagreement? No answer is exactly the right one.

Reducing these concerns about women's bodies to the stuff of humor may diminish their validity, which in turn can serve to reinforce the self-hatred felt by women expressing similar sentiments. However, body shape discourse is an important bonding ritual for women that not only occurs in female friendships but also can bring diverse women together in an act of friendship talk. In a sense, then, the friendship becomes a discursive construction that is lived out by the friends. Within the friendship, body shape discourse acts as a tool not only to allow the friends to commiserate about their personal body dissatisfaction, but also as a way to recreate and reify other body discourses.

Being stuck in less than perfect bodies provides a common point of dialogue that can instantly bind women to each other, allowing the relational space of friendship to be entered without the barriers or borders that usually limit such relationships. Even women who don't otherwise know each other and would not be likely to enter into conversation with each other will often find themselves sharing the most private details of their body dissatisfaction. For example, each time I enter a crowded fitting room, I am inundated with examples of body shape discourse. From the young girl frustrated over not fitting into the size three skinny jeans to the older woman disgusted with the lack of hip clothing in larger sizes, women come together in acts of body shape discourse.

Body shape discourse, therefore, can serve as a positive force in women's friendships. By verbally expressing our body dissatisfaction, we can befriend other women—even strangers. In this way, I have had numerous conversations with fascinating women I might otherwise have never met. In fact, to this day, a few of my closest friends are women I first met while commiserating over our bodies. In this sense, body shape discourse can be good.

When I first started thinking about and researching body shape discourse I asked a group of women to keep a journal for one month as a pilot project. In the journal I asked them to track all the instances of body shape discourse they participated in or overheard. At the end of one week, two of the women asked to drop out of the project. They found that they were simply spending too much time writing down examples in their journal. Before the end of the month, the remaining women had also dropped out for similar reasons. What I learned from this experience was that the way that women talk about their bodies represents a significant component of our interpersonal relations with each other.

Do I look like that?
Participating in body shape discourse introduces another, more intense, level of critical gaze. Therefore, it can introduce a more destructive and damaging discursive component into the relationship. In Chapter One, I showed how women often engage in personal, internal reflections as they compared themselves with other women, a type of competition that serves to heighten an individual woman's body dissatisfaction. In this chapter, I discuss the move from an internal dynamic and assessment of body comparison, mine and yours, to an external interpersonal expression. This can involve others in a dangerous, aggressive, and destructive conversation by means of linguistic games in order to gauge where each falls on the continuum of beautiful bodies. While a significant amount of this comparison involves the ideal images of media women, we also compare our bodies with those of other women. This interpersonal, in-person comparison has the potential to be even more powerful than comparison to media ideals. It is common knowledge that women presented in media images have the advantage of beauticians, make-up technicians, clothing stylists, and computer enhancements to make them look ideal. The woman sitting next to us does not have these advantages, though. Therefore, it becomes very easy to

say, "If she can do it, so can I." The effect of this dynamic of body shape discourse presents a doubly damaging proposition. First, each woman trains this gaze on her own body and disciplines herself accordingly. Additionally, though, this gaze is trained on other women, friends. Instead of viewing other women's bodies in a friendly and accepting or confirming manner, their bodies are viewed in a critical and criticizing manner. In other words, the anatomy of the gaze is inscribed into and onto the anatomy of women. The end result is that the body of each woman becomes the focus of friendship talk. Without even necessarily realizing it, the friends create surveillant gazes which feed off each other, strengthening not only the immediate surveillance but also the larger social and cultural gazes.[5]

As part of their personal body battles, many women will enter into actual competitions with other women to become the best or, in the case of one who possesses a near-ideal body, to maintain that supremacy. One form of this competition is realized when women enact a defensive mode of comparing and competing with other women as illustrated in this example from Diva. Diva and her friend Happy began a new diet and workout program in order to get into "bikini shape" for summer. Diva's roommate at the time was naturally skinny, "tiny," and one of those lucky few who "doesn't have to go to the gym." Within days of the start of Diva's and Happy's new program, the roommate challenged, "I can do it just as fast. Watch me." She then proceeded to under-eat and over-exercise in the hopes of losing more weight in less time. Even though neither Diva nor Happy reciprocated in competition, the roommate continued this regimen throughout the entire tenure of Diva and Happy's diet and exercise program. What is interesting about Diva's story is that the roommate turns a virtual competition of comparison into an actual competition of who can lose the most weight the fastest. By all outside appearances, the roommate is already a victor in the body battles. She is thin, close to the mythical ideal. However, the prospect of being left behind or being replaced by someone else as an ideal motivates her to take preventive steps and jump on the diet and workout bandwagon—a defensive move to protect her position on the body continuum.

Twenty-year-old Shirley provided a concise description of how these types of external body battles develop. A psychology major, Shirley planned to attend graduate school and then enter private counseling practice. She explains the general form of the battling process:

You pay attention to how tight her pants are compared to your pants. You say to your friends, "If my butt looks like that, tell me." You do it all the time. Some people let it go and some can't. It covers everything about how they [other women] look, how their hair is, and how my hair is. I'm bigger or I'm smaller.

Shirley describes another form of body shape discourse by including friends as allies in a public body comparison. If they laugh or agree to let Shirley know when her butt "looks like that," they implicitly agree with Shirley's assessment of the other woman's butt. If they say nothing, then the comment is left hanging and presumed to be valid. The only way to avoid being dragged into the battle is to contradict Shirley and run the risk of opening a rift in the relationship.

While discussing this particular facet of body battles, Isabelle observed that comparing ourselves to other women is "one of the most destructive things" that we do. Like Shirley, Isabelle will enlist the aid of her friends by asking, "Do I look better than her?" I doubt that either Shirley or Isabelle consciously seeks to involve her friends, but their seemingly innocent side comments and questions end up doing exactly this. Once the comment is thrown out there, the friends are left with an untenable choice—either become a battle ally or risk losing a friend. The end result exacerbates the already negative culture of discontent. In some sense, the culture comprises an environment where friends join with friends against other groups of friends creating battalions of battling broads roaming the earth.

Judging others

The scope of interpersonal body battles is much more complex than one's making snide comments to friends. The process moves from the quiet personal comparison described in Chapter One to off-hand remarks like those made by Shirley and Isabelle involving others, and finally to the cruel attacks directed at Katie. Sadly, the process doesn't end at this point. Often, even more blatantly devastating remarks will be made. The type of destruction resulting from this form of body shape discourse worms its way into all of the various friendships and relationships that women have with each other. The end result is that comments and potential comments from other women weigh extraordinarily high on the list of women's body concerns.

I wonder if she thinks I'm fat?

One result of constantly comparing oneself to other women is per-petually striving to impress them, for they could be the ones asking the next question or making the next comment. As with other facets of body dissatisfaction, seeking the approval of other women often results in rather ironic situations. During our interviews, Chazy described such a situation. At the time, Chazy was twenty years old with a double major in French and communication. She had no clear career plans and thought that she'd like to do something involving traveling and working with horses:

> One of my ex-boyfriend's best friends happened to be a girl. I'd say to him, "I have to put make-up on. I have to look good." And he's like why? I'd laugh and say, "You've got to impress the girl." I realized it was more important to impress the girl than it was to impress him. Like I was more worried about impressing his friend that I would be pretty or convincing her I was up to his standard or worthy of him and stuff. Looking back at that, I'm like why? I'm not dating her. I'm dating him. Why am I trying to impress her?

After Chazy shared this story with me, I asked if her concern with what the girl thought might be a form of jealousy. Even though the girl was "just" a friend, might she possibly be worried that the friend who is a girl could become a girlfriend? She admitted that she had thought about this possibility as well. However, she dismissed the concerns after her boyfriend explained that the girl was not only happily engaged but that he had never been interested in her in "that way."

When a woman is dating a man, she usually wants to be liked not only by him but also by the people closest to him. However, the feelings Chazy describe in this story go beyond merely wanting to be liked by the other girl. They entail a fear of judgment by the girl and the ensuing negative repercussions for being judged unworthy. The irony revolves around the fact that she is more concerned with what one of his best friends, another girl, will think of her than of what her boyfriend will think. The person that she knows and cares about be-comes less important than the unknown other woman who might just be a battle opponent or who might view her as a battle opponent.

Fears like those expressed by Chazy are common in women deal-ing with body dissatisfaction. In the culture of discontent, comments from other women are not only expected but can also carry more weight than comments from men.[6] Annette and Eva illustrate:

> Annette: Guys are just like, "Oh you look nice or whatever." Guys just don't notice things as much. But when girls comment, I know they mean it because competition is a big thing with girls.
> Eva: It's not just like something they're [women] just gonna throw out—"Hey you look nice today." You know when they mean it.
> Annette: Yeah, you know when they mean it.

As Annette and Eva's discussion demonstrates, women just don't throw compliments about other women around haphazardly; they compare and compete with each other. Therefore, when they do compliment you, it must mean something. It's thought to be more sincere, more real. The assumption is that if a woman takes the time to say it, then it must be true. Investing compliments from other women with more power than those from men is one of the reasons the skinny greeting has such impact. Women know that other women are competing with them in various internal and external body battles. Therefore, when another woman, a potential opponent, tells you sincerely that you look like you've lost weight, you truly must be thinner. The catch-22 is that the women's comments can tear you down as quickly as they build you up.

Do you believe she walks around looking like that?

The linguistic maneuvers of body battles appear as helpful hints when in reality they are mean-spirited jabs. Consider this example from Marie: "One girl said I look better with my clothes on than I do in a bathing suit." When Marie shared this story, I wrote *ouch* in the margin of my notes, remembering my own discomfort at being forced to don a bathing suit in front of my critical and criticizing peers. I can easily imagine the wound this direct critical observation opened in Marie. Marie explained that every time she wears a bathing suit now—four years later—she wonders if others think she would look better with some clothes on.

It seems that every woman has at least one story of being the recipient of similarly negative comments. Anabelle has a friend who will come up to her every time she is home and say, "Anabelle, you've gotten so much bigger." Jessica recalls a friend providing "constructive criticism" that her "butt is all jiggly like Jell-O." In high school, Ladybug was called "long breasts." Alice explained that she wasn't "super overweight but I also wasn't a willow, so I was considered a guy." The girls around her would reinforce this alleged guyness and say, "Well, you're not really a girl. You're not one of us." In retelling her individual story, each woman seemed to be reliving the anger and pain she felt when she first heard the remark. To some degree, these comments generate new concerns. For example, Alice had never considered the fact that by not being a "willow" she might somehow be less feminine. After being told that she was more a guy than a girl, though, she added this concern to her already existing list of body concerns and questioned her femininity. Each time she looks in the mirror, judging her level of "guyness" is now one of the things that she considers.

Attacking other women or making cutting comments to them is often considered as part of the status quo and therefore allows the underlying behavior to escape judgment or punishment. Alice explains:

> We all do this, right? I know who my buddies are and so we connect. And we're women and so we share our feelings, but if that person's outside that circle then we're just as guilty as by judging them and by saying, "Well I know exactly what she's like because she wears a size two." And we all, we all judge each other and evaluate each other. It breeds this inter-female competition thing.

The danger of considering such behavior normal is that engaging in it can then be done without fear of punishment. Catty comments will usually not be chastised by other women. Despite Alice's observations, there seems to be a general denial that such competition and its associated behaviors exist. When I ask women if they compete with other women, their first response is usually to balk. They respond with something along the lines of: "Why compete? I just let people be as they are." Many times they get defensive and proclaim that they like all people and don't judge anyone. As we continue to talk, though, the stories change. Just as their feelings of body dissatisfaction become apparent through their stories, so do their competitive actions.

The behaviors that comprise body battles occur nearly everywhere that women are—even within the confines of this project. I was surprised at how often within an interview I would find myself hearing snide remarks or revealing stories about other women. In talking about the women in their sorority, for example, Caitlyn and Isabelle participated in the following exchange:

Caitlyn: We had the "Ass Class," the class following our class.
Isabelle: There's a large portion of them that have asses—big, huge hips.
Caitlyn: Child bearing hips.
Isabelle: Oh god, they could pop a litter out.

The girls in the "Ass Class" weren't overweight or even disproportion-ately sized. They did, however, have the "asses" and "child bearing hips" that are common to many women. The sin of the Ass Class is that they dared to walk around with these things in the midst of girls who were skinny bordering on anorexic. In an environment where being a size two is a sin, curves like these apparently are a mortal sin; making jokes at their expense is not.

On one campus I kept hearing stories about the "Skirt Girls." A typical story is like this one told by Shirley and Liscious:

Shirley: The "Skirt Girls!" They wear mini-skirts through any weather. Like there's a thunderstorm but they have their skirts on with their rain boots.
Liscious: There's snow on the ground, but hey I'm in a mini-skirt.
Shirley: I have my snowshoes on, so I'm all right with my little mini-skirt.

In a different interview, Satania provided a more detailed descrip-tion of the Skirt Girls:

It's the dead of winter and they're wearing itty bitty skinny tank tops. And they're really, really thin girls. Like how could you dress like that in February? They were running around in basically nothing but galoshes.

The Skirt Girls stand out for being "really, really thin" and dressing in a manner considered inappropriate for the weather—wearing a mini-skirt. Each version of the Skirt Girls story emphasized the fact of their wearing boots with their skirts. At the time, one of the hot fashion trends was this exact style—fur-trimmed boots with mini-skirts worn in all sorts of weather. When I would point this fact out to the storyteller, her follow-up would be along the lines of, "But these girls are really skinny." It seems that the real complaint about the Skirt Girls is their skinniness, not their choice of clothing.

I ate a few meals in the main cafeteria of this campus, hoping to get a glimpse of the infamous Skirt Girls, but I never did. Interestingly it seems that the Skirt Girls are moving toward campus legend. Over a year later, I met with one of the women I interviewed. The day we met, the temperature was over ninety degrees with a heat index of 105. After lunch she returned to musing about why the "Skirt Girls" would dress like they did in the middle of winter. Even after a year, she continued to criticize them.

What's really going on here?

Making snide comments may initially occur as an innocuous way of dealing with the frustrations of body dissatisfaction. Unfortunately, their impact quickly spreads and generates more widespread damage, destroying women and their friendships with each other, often without their even realizing it. When one woman makes a battling comment, she makes herself feel better by tearing someone else apart. Momentarily, she is able to forget about her own body dissatisfaction and its accompanying frustrations. But the relief is brief. You realize that just as you are questioning and commenting on others, they might be doing the exact thing about you.

These comments become yet another layer in women's culture of discontent. These behaviors could be merely another form of gossip; we even have a nickname for such gossiping—"dishing." In reality, however, dishing is about control. When women dish, they reinforce the culture of discontent's implicit ideal beauty mandates—on themselves and on other women. When dishing, a woman simultaneously exerts three types of control:

- *Control over the woman who is the subject of dishing*—she is scorned for her failure to follow the "rules" and expectations of cultural norms;
- *Control over the woman who hears the dishing*—as she actively or passively participates in dishing, she also internalizes the message of the norm—or faces the possibility of being the next one dished about;
- *Control over self*—as women dish, they internalize the expectations for appropriate female behavior. They learn that they need to stay in line or face similar scorn.

In effect, through dishing like this, women end up acting like the culture police, making sure that everyone is behaving as expected. While they can't arrest deviants, they can attempt to arrest the deviant's behavior by talking about her. Even more troubling is that they exercise this same control on themselves. Katie, for example, changes her future career plans after spending a summer being labeled as the "fat chick." Likewise, Diva's "tiny" roommate enters into a diet and exercise competition with Diva and Happy so as to maintain her status as the possessor of the near-ideal body. Chazy dresses up and changes her appearance in order to impress her boyfriend's friend who is a girl. Shirley and Isabelle enlist their friends' help in reassuring them that their bodies look good.

Each of these women, and others like them, take affirmative actions to wrestle control of the social aspect of their bodies. While they appear to be making positive strides in moving beyond the cyclical nature of body dissatisfaction, the actual control they achieve as a result of body battle dishing is illusory—much like the relief felt by making a snide comment about other women. Knowing that she can always be the next subject of dishing, a woman walks around the world both outside and inside herself—watching herself being watched. She monitors herself even as she is monitored. She keeps up a running internal dialogue checklist: Is my face shiny? Are my panty lines showing? Am I showing too much cleavage? Am I not showing enough cleavage? Was I too harsh in my response to that jerk? Women may be doing this not because they necessarily care about these things but because it is a form of insurance against being the next topic of a dishing session.

Additionally, young women are surrounded by young men who have grown up in the same culture and who feel entitled to make critical remarks about the size and shape of women's bodies to them. We will take a look at guys and their comments in the next chapter.

Chapter Six

I like a girl with a little meat on her

I like a girl with a little meat on her

Added to the critical commentary of family members and other women are the things that guys say to women. Even in an age where women have numerous career options, they still confront the traditional expectations that they get married and start a family, increasing the importance of guys' views of women's bodies. Because women of all sexual orientations are confronted with guys' remarks, it is critical to understand the role such comments play in body dissatisfaction.

Guys: Do they mean what they say or what they do?

My interview with Lisa almost didn't happen. We were finally scheduled to meet in a campus coffee shop on a Saturday morning when my phone rang an hour before our appointment. Seeing Lisa's name and cell phone number, I thought, oh no not again. Before answering I decided that if Lisa cancelled again I would just give up trying to interview her. To my surprise, Lisa was calling to say that she was already at the coffee shop if I wanted to come earlier. Not wanting to miss the opportunity to finally meet her in person, I said I'd be right over.

When I arrived at the coffee shop, Lisa was easy to spot on this quiet Saturday morning. After getting my usual soy latte, I made my way over to Lisa's table and introduced myself. I tried to hide my surprise when she looked up—her eyes were red and puffy. I sat down and Lisa immediately apologized for her appearance. She began by saying that she and her boyfriend had spent most of the previous night arguing. Tears started falling when she noted that finally around four o'clock a.m. he said he was done and "officially" broke up with her.

It was clear that Lisa was still reeling from the shock of the break up. She explained: "Even though I'm only nineteen, I thought he was my soul mate. I was sure we would get married after graduation." Lisa ended up spending the first fifteen minutes or so of our interview crying and filling me in on the previous night's events.

I hinted that possibly this wasn't the right time for us to talk, but this only triggered more tears. After a few minutes, she said that she'd rather continue. She was convinced that going home would be even worse. We turned to the topic of food, and Lisa sighed. I asked her what was wrong and she responded that now she would "have to go on a diet so I can attract another guy." She continued, "You know, guys are so full of shit. They say they want curves on girls but then who do they date? The skinny chicks! The ones who look like walking toothpicks with a head." As we continued to talk about the things guys want out of relationships, Lisa allowed that perhaps breaking up wasn't all bad. She said that whenever she and her boyfriend went out to eat he would monitor what she ordered and how much she ate. Lisa looked like she wore a size five, yet her boyfriend would say things such as, "Are you sure you want to eat cream cheese with that bagel?" Lisa said that every time she ate something, she heard his voice in her head criticizing her choice.

When Lisa wasn't reminiscing about her relationship, she worried about how she would tell her parents the relationship was over. She explained that "they expect me to get married after graduation." She expanded on this thought: "That's what you do, you know? You go to college to get an education and meet your soul mate. Then when you graduate, you get married and start a family." I heard from Lisa a few weeks after our meeting when she emailed me with her "good news." She and her boyfriend had gotten back together and were "pre-engaged" with plans to get married in the summer between Lisa's junior and senior years. (She was currently a freshman.) I asked if she had discussed with him his habit of criticizing her food choices. She laughed and said that she was sure they would work it out eventually. I never heard from Lisa again, but I did hear from one of her friends that the wedding was "beautiful and Lisa looked super skinny."

If I get my MRS. degree, do I need a BA?
Even though most young women don't go to college today for the sole purpose of getting their MRS. degree, the thought of marriage is an ever-present notion. The college culture is one where

heterosexuality tends to be presumed, and the traditional practices associated with heterosexual relationships are what everyone expects. For example, when I collect demographic information in my interviews, I usually ask a question along the lines of, "How do you identify your sexual orientation?" Beyond evoking giggles and the occasional flushed face, the question often draws blank looks. Several times, I have had to explain what the question means. Many of the women were shocked to be asked such a question. A few of them worried, "Do I look like a lesbian? Is that why you're asking me that?"[1] Based on their responses to this question, most of the women I interviewed identified as heterosexual.[2] Associated with the assumption of heterosexuality is a presumption of marriage. Over the course of my interviews, I was surprised at how many women expressed the sentiment that getting their MRS. degree was one of their short-term goals. Marriage was not their main goal in college, but it was an expected part of their college plans. Like Lisa, they assume that after graduation, marriage is the next obvious step. One of my students explained to me that the mindset on campus is that if a woman "doesn't leave here with a big rock on her finger, she's a loser."

This presumption of marriage was concisely explained by Madeleine when the topic of marriage came up during our conversations. When I asked what her future plans were, she immediately replied, "Marriage." At the time, Madeleine was not involved in a relationship and had no potential boyfriends in mind but still knew that she would be married before or right after graduation. Later in our conversation, she reminisced about the number of her friends who were already engaged or getting married.[3] She remarked that "marriage is what college is supposed to be about, right?"

Even though Madeleine wasn't involved in a relationship, her sentiments sound like they were spoken around 1952, reminiscent of a scene from the 2003 film *Mona Lisa Smile*[4] set at Wellesley in the early fifties. The film depicts getting married and being a wife as the natural and expected "roles" the female students were "born to fill." In the film, the students are taught that in the future, their "sole responsibility will be taking care of [their] husband and children." It shocked me to hear these same types of thoughts repeated and believed over fifty years later.

Alice expressed similar feelings about the presumption of marriage. Unlike Madeleine, Alice was involved in a long term relationship of just over two years. When we spoke she was anxiously waiting and hoping for the relationship to move to the next level, or more accurately, for her boyfriend to decide that it was time to move to the next level. She and Claire discussed these dreams:

> Claire: I want him to propose to you now.
> Alice: All of a sudden propose to me in Florida.[5] I would love for him to propose to me tomorrow, I don't care. I love him. I want to marry him. No big deal.
> Claire: Go for it.
> Alice: Everyone knows this. I think he knows this.
> Claire: You'll get married.
> Alice: If he doesn't know this, then he's retarded, but ... he does know this. I appreciate the fact that he is taking it really seriously, though, reading about it and thinking about it a lot.
> Claire: Yeah.
> Alice: And it's not really like ... it's not really a question of if, it's just a question of when. He wants to ... he wants it to be good.
> Claire: Like here's the great thing is that when he does propose to you, you're going to know that he knows, he KNOWS he wants to marry you.
> Alice: Yes.
> Claire: And there's no question in his mind ... and there's not anything else and it's just like a go. Get married.
> Alice: And I'm willing to wait until that happens.
> Claire: It becomes better if you do.
> Alice: Yeah exactly. I don't want any other factor to affect his proposing other than the fact that if he doesn't propose right at this very second, he's going to explode. That's what I want ... that's what I want. And I don't...I don't want him to [propose] until that's what ... that's what it is.
> Claire: Oh.
> Alice: Yeah, cause I know already right now that he wants to marry me.
> Claire: True ...
> Alice: But he's not to that point yet where he's like, I'm just dying to marry you. And I guess until he gets there, then I'll just be his girlfriend and be happy. Cause I'm happy being his girlfriend.
> Claire: I'm sure it's fun.
> Alice: It is fun. But I really want to be his fiancée, because I really want to be his wife.

This passage is fascinating. Both Claire and Alice were seniors with job prospects already in line. For Alice, much like Madeleine, a significant amount of her time is spent thinking about marriage, yet her passivity toward the relationship is surprising. Even though she says "I really want to be his wife," she's "willing to wait." In feminist terms, she is acting in the traditional manner expected of women—suppressing her desires in order to privilege the man's. Instead of turning a feminist critical lens on these sentiments, I ask: What else is going on here? It seems that Alice, as well as many other young women, are attempting to balance the competing tensions of being a progressive woman with the rather traditional culture in which they live. That is, even though they are taking advantage of the opportunity to gain a higher education with an eye toward a potential career, they are also struggling with traditional societal demands that they find a man who is willing to marry them. The decision to marry is his, not hers.[6]

Young women attending college learn in the classroom and from their mentors that they can move beyond the traditional expectations for women. They witness many alternatives to these traditional expectations; the female professors they see fulfilled in many ways are but one example. Yet outside of the campus climate, these young women are immersed in a traditional culture. They hear politicians assert that family values require mothers to be home with their families. They are told that even in the twenty-first century, their ultimate worth as women is found in the cleanliness and decor of their homes. They realize that for doing the same work on the job as a man, they will only make seventy-seven cents for every dollar that their male colleagues make.[7] They see strong women like Hillary Clinton being publicly excoriated for being too masculine or too ambitious and upstaging her husband. Everywhere they turn, they see tangible proof that their worth is contingent upon what men think of them. All of this results in an inordinate value being placed on the things guys say and do or don't say and don't do.

The important point here is that because of this strong marriage presumption, getting and impressing guys is an important aspect of many women's young adult experience. Therefore, it is no surprise that the things guys say are important to women's sense of Self, including body dissatisfaction. Even women who do not identify as heterosexual are subject to the controlling gaze and discourse of men. An interesting example of this is presented by Gloria Gadsen in her study of how the male voice dominates in certain women's magazines.[8] After conducting a ten year textual analysis of *New Woman* and *Essence* magazines, Gadsen found that both magazines allocated nearly one fifth of the articles to male voices, which in turn operate to define women and their sexuality throughout the pages of the magazine. Even though the male voice did not represent a majority of the editorial commentary found, the male construction of ideal femininity and sexuality carried over into these other areas. In commenting on this fact, Gadsen observed that "if men can define women's gender roles and sexuality in a woman's magazine, women have not been successful in claiming a social space free from male dominance."[9]

The male influence over what "counts" as ideal femininity and sexuality is not limited to the voices of male authors in women's magazines. We see this influence in a variety of forms throughout society. Over thirty years ago, Laura Mulvey identified and explained the Male Gaze.[10] Focusing on classic Hollywood cinema and using Freud's concept of scopophila,[11] Mulvey discussed the pleasure we all gain from looking at the characters we see on screen. She observed that in films "women are simultaneously looked at and displayed, with their appearance coded for strong visual and erotic impact so that they can be said to connote *to-be-looked-at-ness*."[12] In other words, women on screen represent the prototypical sex object—they are there for our erotic viewing pleasure. That is, they are the desired sex object of not only their co-stars, but also of us, the audience. Of all the women in any given film, we know who these sex objects are based on the coding practices employed. For example, we know that the young skinny woman wearing revealing, tight clothing is the sexy one. Likewise, we know that the young woman wearing glasses and bulky, drab clothing is probably also sexy—the proverbial swan disguised as an ugly duckling. Underneath her boring unsexy costume, she's a sexpot in hiding. Different codes are used for different degrees of sexiness, or lack thereof. These practices also dictate how we respond to the woman on screen. We cheer for the ugly duckling, anxiously waiting for the transformation that will help her win the heart of the handsome leading man.

Despite its name, the male gaze is not gender specific and slips back and forth between men and women. Women also view the female characters on screen through a male gaze. While many women may not necessarily desire the female characters sexually, they desire to be like them. They want to be the girl that everyone wants—the sexy one. This virtual gaze also operates to reinforce gendered norms of behavior in which men look and women are looked at. Even when women look, it is presumed that they are incapable of looking of their own volition, so instead they must adopt a male stance. As observed by Naomi Wolf in the *Beauty Myth*, "What little girls learn is not the desire for the other but the desire to be desired. Girls learn to watch their sex along with the boys."[13] From the time they are young girls, women learn not just that they must act as the object of the male gaze of boys, but that they also must enact a male gaze on themselves. They must strive to appear sexy without being sexual.

Mulvey's observations are not limited to filmic depictions of women. They also apply generally to America's obsession with and passion for sexualizing all representations of the female form. It seems that everywhere we look, we see the female body being talked about, photographed, and displayed. A quick glance at the magazine covers at your local newsstand makes this point clear; a large percentage of the magazines have at least one woman on the cover. We all know that sex sells, so on one level it makes sense to feature a sexy woman on the cover of your magazine. If sex sells and you want to sell your magazine, then featuring sex is a no-brainer.

The problem, though, is that the impact of this saturation of sexualized female bodies extends beyond the sale of magazines. The ideal of these sexualized images is projected onto *all* women's bodies. This projection turns the metaphorical male gaze into an actual gaze that controls not only the bodies of women, but also by extension, their very being and existence. Adopting this male gaze and turning it onto themselves, many young women compare themselves to the computer enhanced, sexualized women they see presented in media images and turn to them as role models for their own bodies.[14] The end result is that the "ideal" bodies featured on magazine covers[15]—airbrushed, computer enhanced, and stylized by teams of experts—become prized over the "real" bodies of most women. Women whose bodies do not look like these ideal bodies are subject to potential scorn, rebuke, and ostracization.

For the young women who speak in this book, one of the most pressing male discourses they experience is that which they hear from the young guys around them. In fact, many of the examples included throughout this chapter come not from boyfriends, but from other guys who are friends. Both personal and in-person, the interpersonal discourse of young guys presents a living representation of the male gaze. As the guys in their lives comment on the body sizes and shapes of other women, young women face a constant reminder of how they think they must look. In the heterosexual environment that defines most of the college and young adult experience, these reminders can take their toll on women—heterosexual, lesbian, and bisexual. In order to be considered attractive and slip through the gaze without becoming the victim of specifically controlling interpersonal discourse, women strive to look like the women receiving the positive comments from guys, creating yet another controlling gaze that is internalized.

I can't stress enough that not all young women think college is about getting married. Some of them want to spend time establishing a career, traveling, and having fun before they think about settling down. For them, the mere thought of marriage in the near future is taboo. When marriage came up in my interview with Chazy, she cringed in horror and said, "I'm nowhere close to getting married or wanting to get married. I don't even want to think about marriage." However, even if we remove the prospect of marriage, having a boyfriend around is a required accessory, much like the right pair of shoes, and many young women want the companionship and comfort that come with a boyfriend relationship. As Virginia asserts, "a lot of women just want a man in their life. They want that approval from men." They may want tangible confirmations from guys of their beauty and desirability. Eva explains:

> I'm primarily trying to get a response from guys. That's horrible to say, but the idea of being noticed is important. I hate it. I absolutely hate it. I wish I could totally remove that from my life and not feel like I had to please the opposite sex.

Pleasing the opposite sex and the thought that such behavior is somehow mandatory is another example of being raised in a traditional environment.

Gotta get a guy
Most young women have moved far beyond their adolescent experiences. Adolescence is marked by a host of physical changes, including hormones raging throughout adolescent bodies. With these physical

changes come changes in the interpersonal status between boys and girls. Then, seemingly overnight, boys and girls who had previously thought each other infested with cooties suddenly found themselves drawn to each other. Whereas a simple brushing up against each other used to require intense spraying with "Cootie Bug Spray," boys and girls in adolescence found reasons to "accidentally" touch each other. Now that the young women are older and are primarily past their adolescent years, they may believe that they have matured and moved on. However, the emotional and psychological effects of raging hormones are still aflutter and are usually intensified, especially for those women who believe they should be attracting a man and seeking his approval.

Most young women living in a culture of discontent and struggling with a cycle of dissatisfaction are confident that there is a direct connection between their appearance and their ability to get a husband—the right husband. Therefore, getting the right body is thought to be the first required step to getting a dream life. Think about Lisa's remark that in light of the breakup she would "have to go on a diet" so as to "attract another guy." Even if this direct connection is only a figment of their imagination or of cultural norms, young women think that it is real and act accordingly. It seems that the prize for winning the body battles discussed in Chapter Five is more than just an ideal body. To the victor goes the perfect husband and the ideal life he is thought to bring with him.

We can add vying for men's attention to the competitions we've already discussed: competing for an ideal body, battling to see who can lose the most weight in the least time, and struggling to find out what size they really wear. Very often, women assume that every other woman is vying for the attention of the same guys they are. Claire provides an interesting take on this phenomenon:

> Like when you go to a club, do the men parade around? No. They sit and watch. And the women parade around and dress themselves up. They are battling for men's attention. It's like women are conditioned to compete with one another for the attention of men. You size up every other woman in the room, and you can't help it. It's just something that you do automatically and you're conditioned to do that. And when a man walks into a room, then even if it's a pajama party and you're all cool, you know … you know the minute that a man crashes your pajama party every single person automatically thinks about what they look like and what every other girl looks like in the room.

Body battles are about getting the attention and companionship of men, about getting the right body and getting the guy. The body is merely the spark that triggers the attention.

Can I be a lady if I don't have a man?

Even though most of the young women I've interviewed indicated some awareness similar to Claire's about how they were competing for guys' attention and how destructive these actions are, they had not fully internalized this fact. When I ask women if they compete with each other, the answer inevitably is no. "Competition is bad," they say. "I avoid conflict. What good does it do?" others say. However, like the competition of body battles, competing for guys is fairly commonplace and is so prevalent in some circles that the practice is often considered an inherent aspect of being a woman.

From the time they are young girls, women are told that little girls are made of sugar and spice and everything nice.[16] They are taught to be and act like ladies: nice, quiet, pretty to look at, submissive, and accepting a proper place in society that is secondary to men. They learn that ladies don't fight—especially with each other. A lady doesn't compete or assert her will about anything. Additionally, ladies should be beautiful in certain socially mandated ways. Sociologist Kristen Myers explains that a lady should strive to be sexually attractive, but not too sexual.[17] A lady's goal is to present a "well-groomed appearance" so that she is "seen as an ornament for her husband."[18] If a woman doesn't yet have a husband, it is even more important to present this well-groomed appearance or she may be doomed to perpetual spinsterhood. The ideal traits highlighted by Myers echo the concerns about looking slutty discussed in Chapter Three. Recall that Ladybug was worried that her senior ball dress would make her look like a slut because "her boobs are out there." In a similar vein Angel was worried that her bathing suit made her look like a slut because you could see her body. Even though neither expressed the desire to be a lady, they have both clearly internalized the mandates of ladyhood as something that is expected of them.

As we've discussed in Chapter Three, there is a problem in young women's looking too slutty. During the college or young adult years, young women are on their own for perhaps the first time, and they are unfortunately exposed to sexual behavior patterns that appear to be out of control. They must make choices. Therefore, they want to be in control of the message sent by their bodies and clothing. The stories I hear of the sex scene on many college campuses sound like porn scripts—mass orgies open to anyone who walks into the room, random "hook-ups," sex with multiple partners as a form of initiation to a student club or other campus organization, having sex out of boredom or because of inebriation, oral sex and anal sex to avoid pregnancy.[19] At times, it seems like "hooking up" is the main extra-curricular activity on many campuses. Even though most young women don't want to hook up with every guy they meet, they do seem to want to get a positive reaction from every guy. Not getting a reaction can be devastating, as Jasmine explains:

> I've noticed like the worse I feel about myself, the more I don't even want to see guys and their lack of response to me. Like you'll see a good looking guy and then you'll follow his gaze and see who he's looking at. And it's not anything that you can even come close to being, like some perfect woman. It makes me feel like crap.

For Jasmine and other young women, lack of response from a guy is equal to a negative comment—indirect, but with the same effect. I asked Jasmine what this "perfect woman" looks like. She laughed and said "blonde, tan, skinny, tall with long legs." Jasmine, on the other hand, looked a lot like Marisa Tomei—shorter, brunette, thin but not skinny. By most standards, Jasmine would be considered attractive, but in a different way than the "perfect woman" captured in the guy's gaze. Even though she is attractive, the guy's lack of response is internalized by Jasmine in the same manner as being told she is fat.

Why don't they just tell us what they want?
What do I have to look like to get a guy to notice me?
In young women's lived experiences with body dissatisfaction, it makes no difference if a guy does not compliment her and says nothing or if he says, "You're fat." Either way, the woman feels "like crap." Therefore, it becomes tempting for a woman to just avoid guys altogether rather than find out that she's less than what they want. Of course avoiding guys creates a conundrum for young women. If a woman needs to find a husband before she graduates, then she needs to be around guys. If she avoids them, then she won't be able to find the requisite husband. Even if she wanted to fully avoid guys,

I don't see how any young woman could manage such a feat short of cloistering herself.

It could be easily assumed that in Jasmine's story, the guy in question prefers a different "type" of woman than Jasmine is. Maybe he simply prefers blondes over brunettes or taller women over shorter women. His preference may have nothing whatsoever to do with body size or the fact that the "perfect woman" captured in his gaze is skinnier than Jasmine. However, Jasmine simply glosses over these possibilities and immediately jumps to the conclusion that no response is a negative response based on her less than ideal body size.

While the guy in Jasmine's story said nothing, I have heard numerous stories of women being the recipient of direct negativity from guys. The intensity of the offense varies. On the less intense end is a story shared by Marie. The incident occurred while Marie was talking on the phone with one of her "really good friends from home." According to Marie, they "hadn't talked all year," so she was expecting a lengthy conversation in which they would each catch the other up on the past year's events. However, her friend surprisingly cut the conversation short by saying he had to go because "Miss America[20] is on." Marie was shocked and hurt that her good friend would choose Miss America and "those women" over her. Even though the two of them weren't involved in a relationship with each other and neither of them wanted to be involved in such a relationship, Marie felt "insecure." She explained that she felt like she didn't somehow measure up to the Miss America contestants and that since her friend preferred them over her, she must be doing something wrong. Like Jasmine, Marie said she assumed that his choice was based primarily on her body size.

Stories of guys commenting on media women such as Miss America were mentioned many times. Many of them were more direct and intense than the one described by Marie. Ladybug's dad thinks "Salma Hayek is beautiful and perfect. Exotic looking." Roxy's boyfriend likes that girl "who's in *Victoria's Secret*—the girl who has dark hair and blue eyes and is Brazilian."[21] Angel is frustrated because the guys around her will "drool" at the girls in "those magazines"—fashion magazines such as *Cosmo* and *Vogue,* as well as men's magazines such as *Maxim* and *FHM.*[22] The magazine most often mentioned, though, is actually a catalogue, the *Victoria's Secret* catalogue. I have heard from many of my male students that they, their fathers, brothers, and every guy they know "subscribe to it" like any other magazine. Though purportedly a catalogue selling lingerie, the *Victoria's Secret* catalogue is often read like a catalogue selling women. The models present the ultimate male fantasy—leggy, big-breasted women sporting barely-there lingerie and posed as if eagerly awaiting to be consumed by the male gaze. Visually consuming these luscious lingerie dream women is common sport in many male residence halls and fraternities. And like most sports, this one is not relegated to the privacy of bedrooms. It is a public spectacle. I've heard of guys gazing and evaluating *Victoria's Secret* models in the student center, campus cafeterias, and at weekend parties. One of my students told me that he and his friends will bring out the catalogue at boring parties in order to "spice things up." Tapping into this public sport, the company turned the paper catalogue into a living catalogue with live runway shows televised two to three times a year. In a typical show, models strut up and down a runway wearing the same skimpy lingerie featured in the print catalogue, with the addition of stiletto heels that help them pointedly thrust their hips and breasts toward the camera.

Incidents such as these, where guys openly comment on beautiful models and actresses in public, heighten women's assumption that they should look like these ideal women of the media. While the impact of media ideal women on young women's body dissatisfaction will be fully explored in the next chapter, there are a few key components that relate to the interpersonal dynamics between guys and young women. Young women see media women like the *Victoria's Secret* models getting lots of male attention and compliments. They see men who are important to them—fathers, friends, and boyfriends—remarking on these women's beauty and perfection. Looking at themselves, they see something less than this ideal beauty. They, therefore, imagine that they are not beautiful and nowhere near perfect. They see the men around them distracted by these "perfect" media women so that these perfect women become living representatives of the mythical ideal end of the body continuum. When young women don't receive the same kinds or amount of attention as these ideal women, they feel confirmed in their thoughts that they are at the opposite, less than ideal end of the continuum. They feel justified in their assumption that to get positive male attention, they need to model themselves on these media women.

He said what about me?
Comments from guys are not restricted solely to women in the media. Liscious was a twenty-one-year-old communication studies major when we spoke. She planned on working for a year after graduation to "pay off loans and save up some money" and then go to graduate school. She describes a common scenario played out in cafeterias, bars, and other public venues:

> Over dinner you can hear comments that guys make about other girls. It's like, "Oh my gosh, look at her." Like if she's a big-busted girl and she's wearing a low cut or tight shirt, they'll be like, "Check her out."

Her story sounds similar to Jasmine's story with the addition of specific quotes. Whereas Jasmine thought guys are paying attention to other women, Liscious knows they are. Situations like those described by Liscious and Jasmine are even more frustrating than those where guys drool over magazines or catalogues. An actress or model can be dismissed as the stuff of fantasy[23] because these women have teams of experts to help maintain their beauty and perfection. On some level they can be momentarily pushed aside or forgotten. However, when the beautiful perfect girl is sitting at the next table over, it becomes more difficult to dismiss her or rationalize away her existence. The implicit mandates of looking the right way and being the right size begin to seem like explicit mandates.

Overhearing comments from guys like those described by Liscious help to create the perception of what guys want in women— or at least what women think guys want. Ladybug explains:

> Guys want someone with big boobs, skinny waist. They want somebody who's physically appealing to them and who is small enough that they can dominate over.

Ladybug's description echoes the ideal traits that ladies should exhibit—beautiful and submissive. In other words, for men the ideal woman combines the right beauty and demeanor. She is small, tiny, in both body and behavior. Her submissiveness combined with her skinniness makes her easily dominated in both body and spirit. Therefore, like the *Victoria's Secret* catalogue, she is pretty to look at but can be tossed aside when no longer needed. These perceptions of what guys expect in female beauty are often reinforced through direct comments to women. Angel and Butterfly, for example, are part of a co-ed honors fraternity. Guys in the fraternity regularly discuss the traits that they want in their "ideal woman." Butterfly explained this behavior:

> They analyze girls all the time. They have the qualititty instead of the quality. A qualititty is a perfect handful [of breast], not too hard, not too soft. The rest is negotiated.

After Butterfly told this story, she and Angel laughed and dismissed the comments as juvenile and typical of "boys." Later, however, they both indicated that they have each wondered where they fall in the spectrum of qualititties. These comments may be the stuff of juvenile male fantasies, yet Butterfly and Angel still internalize them as critical commentary. The guys' comments are added to the other swirling dictates, comments, and concerns of body dissatisfaction with the end result that Butterfly and Angel feel even more frustrated with their bodies and lack of qualititty.

The depth and extent of how guys' comments impact women's self-esteem is further illustrated in the following story from Eva:

> We were in Florida and this guy was like, "You look like a girl, exactly like a girl from my high school." And he's like, "She was your exact same height, exact same face." And then he was like, "Except she's really skinny."

Eva explained that hearing this guy's comments felt like he stabbed her in the heart. Up to this point in their conversation she liked the guy and thought he was nice. His comment shattered any possibility she may have held about him being the one for her. Of all of the things that can be said, telling a woman she doesn't look skinny is construed as the ultimate slam. Such a comment acts as solid proof to the woman that she is not measuring up to the ideal end of the body continuum, that she is closer to the grotesque end than the ideal end. Because the comment comes from a guy, it is even more troubling. To women like Eva, saying that they're not skinny is equivalent to a fortune teller predicting that they will be failures in later life. While they may successfully graduate from college, they are convinced they will not successfully fulfill the narrative of post-college marital bliss.

The most significant problem with the things guys say is that their words and their actions are often in conflict. The qualititty guys of Butterfly and Angel's fraternity present a perfect example of this conflict. Butterfly and Angel explained that the guys say that the supreme qualititty is a perfect handful, but then for fun they go to a local strip club to see the "girls with the biggest boobs." Since the ultimate qualititty is a "perfect handful," Butterfly and Angel questioned how the strippers with the biggest boobs factored into the equation. The discrepancy between words and actions results in even further feelings of inadequacy—if Butterfly and Angel thought that they didn't measure up before, they know it now.

Marie presented yet another example of guys' duplicity between words and actions:

> [Guys will say] I need a girl with a little bit of meat on her, like J. Lo. It just seems like they don't know. It just seems to me that a little bit of meat would be a lot bigger than J. Lo. And guys consider that a little bit of meat on her. In person, they look at skinny girls, though.

Satania makes a nearly identical observation:

> They say they like girls with meat on them and all that good stuff. I don't think they mean obese. I think they mean curvy. But then they date really thin girls. What I think is funny is guys want girls with big boobs but they want itty-bitty bodies. That just doesn't happen. It looks funny. You look like a top totty and you'll fall over.

Part of the problem here seems to revolve around interpretation of what a "little bit of meat" means. For the women, a girl with a little meat on her will be "curvy," "bigger than J. Lo," and not "really thin." In other words, a little meat is not skinny or really thin. For the guys in question, it appears that a little meat means not skin and bones but meat in certain places. Because guys say that they want meat but then go out with the skinny girls, another type of antagonism among women is generated. Women like Marie and Satania who have a little meat on them resent those skinny girls who don't and who therefore get the guys.

An additionally fascinating aspect of Marie and Satania's stories is their use of the word "meat" and the implied rhetoric it brings with it. Historically, "meat" has been one of the words used to objectify women, to reduce them to choice cuts, to consider them not as whole persons but as the sum of their parts. When a new woman enters the scene she is called "fresh meat." Singles' bars are euphemistically referred to as "Meat Markets." In fact the reference extends to nearly all places where men and women interact—school, the office, the Laundromat. I've even heard the meat market label used in reference to a church's singles-only Bible study. Despite the unsavory connotation attached to the word, neither Marie nor Satania questions its use. They merely repeat the story and focus their vitriol on the guys' unclear and contradictory messages. Apparently women have become so accustomed to being priced for their choice cuts that the word doesn't seem strange. Being considered meat is just another inherent part of women's existence. It is so common that I didn't even pick up on this impact of the word until I started analyzing the transcripts. Like Marie, Satania, and the rest of these women, I've grown immune to the fact that, as women, we're often considered to be nothing more than meat waiting to be picked up.

Contradictory and demeaning comments like these from guys leave young women to speculate about what is really expected of them. There is a constant tension between what young women think and what they are told, a constant negotiation between perception and reality. They think that they can have successful careers, yet are told that they should get married or else be considered losers. They think that beauty is in the eye of the beholder, but are told that the beholder only finds beauty in the skinny. They have relatives and other people chastising them when they gain weight as well as other women openly competing with them for the skinnier body and chiding them for being fat. They hear the guys around them comment on the beauty of the skinny women, yet listen to their fraternity brothers' discussion of the perfect qualititty, as Butterfly and Angel did. And they confront the open "parading around for men" that Claire noted that she and other women participate in. Faced with all this uncertainty, it's easy to assume that their best option is to emulate the skinny ideal. Reinforcing these assumptions are the myriad ideal women and miracle weight loss options saturating today's media.

Chapter Seven

She's got big boobs and she's tiny

She's got big boobs and she's tiny

Living in a media-saturated world, women are presented with numerous examples of the ideal female body. Even though most women know that this ideal is unrealistic, they still feel pressured to achieve it. In addition to presenting ideal images, media outlets provide a number of methods to help achieve this ideal. Deconstructing the rhetoric of ideal beauty generated through media establishes how the divide between ideal and real is nearly impossible to cross for most women.

Unreal media ideals

When I met Stacie she was living with seven other women in a four-bedroom house, two women per bedroom. Stacie was nineteen, while her housemates ranged in age from nineteen to twenty-two. Throughout our interview, Stacie punctuated her comments with stories from her life as well as her housemates' lives. We talked about many of the same issues that came up in my other interviews—food, clothing, guys, parents, classes, and of course, her own body dissatisfaction.

At the time, Stacie was taking a women's studies class where she had just read an excerpt from Naomi Wolf's *The Beauty Myth*. She kept returning to the topic of the way "those women in magazines" look. She and her housemates had recently started a strict diet and exercise regimen in preparation for spring break—two months down the road. Stacie described the steps they were taking to achieve their goals. After reading several diet options in various magazines, they had eliminated "all carbs, because they're evil." They banned carb-laden food from even being brought into the house.

They were "doing cardio every day and weight training stuff" three or four days a week. For motivation, they posted pictures of "those women" from the magazines around the apartment. Stacie took me into their kitchen to see the picture collages featuring numerous pictures of supermodels and Hollywood actresses posted on their refrigerator and cabinets. All of the women were achingly thin with their collarbones and ribs apparent in most pictures. The majority of the pictures featured the women posed to enhance their thinness and sexuality or walking down the red carpet. Stacie explained that she and her roommates thought that if they were surrounded by pictures of skinny girls like these, they would be more inspired and diligent about getting equally skinny and reaching their goal of having "killer beach bods" in time for spring break.

As a result of studying connections between beauty and media, Stacie was concerned that perhaps posting all these pictures wasn't such a wonderful idea. "You know," she said, "every time I see one of those anorexic looking models I feel like crap. No matter how much I starve and exercise, I'm never going to look like that." Stacie then revealed that she and her roommate Karen[1] stopped every morning for bagels. In the evenings, when their housemates thought Stacie and Karen were taking a power walk, the two were actually "carb-loading" at a friend's apartment. Stacie and Karen had decided that starving to wear a bikini for a couple of days of drunken fun and possible hook-ups just wasn't worth it.

Later in our interview, Stacie returned to the topic of "those magazine women." She mused over why looking at pictures of thin models and actresses bothered her. "I know they're all airbrushed and don't really look like that," she said, having seen a video in her women's studies class that showed in detail the process of computer "enhancement" of photographs. She was actually quite knowledgeable about the various "tricks" used in the industry—adding length to a model's legs, "shaving" her waist, adding shadows to make her breasts appear larger, "softening" facial wrinkles, and many other techniques. When I asked her if we as a society should do something to control or limit this type of stuff, she immediately responded, "Make it illegal. Outlaw it all. It's like false advertising. Nobody looks like those pictures—they [models and actresses] don't even look like those pictures." I asked her why she continued to look at fashion magazines and other such pictures if they bothered her so much. She just shrugged and said, "Everyone does it."

After spring break, Stacie stopped by my office to visit and share pictures from their trip. She looked tanned and tired, but no thinner than the last time we spoke. I told her how happy and relaxed she and her friends looked in the pictures. She laughed and said, "Yeah, tequila for breakfast will do that." She then pointed to the two skinniest housemates. "See them," she said, "Angela and Carrie. They won our dieting contest. They cheated, though. They used the see-it-twice method." I asked her what she meant and she explained that they "purged but never really binged. You know, they saw their food twice—before and after eating it." I was left speechless with Stacie's cavalier dismissal of her housemates' weight loss "method"—clearly an eating disorder. Before Stacie left she told me that the "house was on a new diet" getting ready for summer bikini season. She didn't share the specifics of the diet other than to say it was something they saw on *Celebrity Fit Club*.

Why is the skinny girl everywhere?

We are a media-obsessed society. In 2001, over 98% of all homes had a television and most of those had more than one.[2] Close to 70% of all homes have a personal computer with access to the internet and its advertising, with this number regularly increasing as the price of personal computers drops.[3] Drive down the road and you'll see billboards everywhere, from cornfields in the middle of rural America to the sides of buses in urban America. On the newsstand there are magazines covering topics ranging from news, celebrity gossip, fashion, and sports to more specialized topics such as diesel trains, tattoos for women, and goddess spiritualism. Walk into a store and in the background you'll hear music interspersed with "informational" sound bites—advertising. In fact, to see just how prevalent media saturation is, try to go twenty-four hours with no exposure to it.[4] You would have to avoid the packaging on many commercially produced food products and eschew the designer logos on clothing, shoes, and accessories. In my house, you would have to remove much of the artwork since it is pop culture themed. I wonder—is it possible in twenty-first century America to fully remove yourself from the presence of media?

Recognizing the constant presence of media in our lives is merely the first step in understanding the role that media play in our experiences. Working in conjunction with media saturation is the way we consume or use media. Susan Bordo has observed that the female body promulgated through media is a homogenized one.[5] Joan Jacobs Brumberg asserts that the homogenized ideal leaves "female socialization, in the hands of the modern media" and allows the emphasis to be on "external qualities (good looks) above all else."[6] Through this homogenization, "images function as models against which the self continually measures, judges, disciplines, and corrects itself."[7] Unfortunately, those images the media focus on are of super skinny models and actresses as symbols of success. According to Kim Chernin, by looking at media depictions of women, "we begin to read our culture's attitudes toward power in a woman."[8] We know the routes to success in this culture, and we learn that for women this success depends upon their ability to recreate the ideal women of media images.

The full impact of media images on young women's sense of self is often intensified by the lack of popular positive female role models. Despite the advances made in recent years by feminists, female activists, and professional women in numerous fields, there still exists a dearth of positive female role models popularized by the media who are prized for more than their sexual beauty. Even the images broadcast of Hillary Clinton, a professional woman and presidential candidate, have not influenced the stories and pictures of skinny celebrities. Since many women seek out role models from media images, the lack of strong females in media can result in the sexualized media version of women becoming normalized and turned into gauges against which all other women are judged as to body, self, and life.

The role that media plays in body dissatisfaction[9] has been researched by numerous individuals and from a variety of perspectives.[10] Despite the volume of work done in this area, we still don't have a solid grasp of the full extent of ways that media messages actually affect the way women feel about their bodies. Up to this point I have argued that body dissatisfaction is much too complex to be reduced to one simple cause like media. That said, I can't deny that based on the way young women talk about media's representation of ideal women and how this makes them feel, media do play at least some role in provoking and reinforcing their experiences with body dissatisfaction and their desire to achieve ideal beauty through thinness.[11]

Is the skinny girl really skinny?

Because the ideal media woman is so important to a young woman's idea of Self and understanding of her body, I wanted to see what young women think she looks like. Chazy says that she is "above five foot eight" and below 125 pounds." Claire identifies her as being "skinny with six pack abs." Madeleine points out that she's "real super skinny, blonde, blue eyes, and tan." Ladybug asserts that "she's got big boobs and she's tiny." Marie describes her as having "long legs and big boobs." Eva says she is "blonde, tall, thin with big boobs." Diva describes her as having "big boobs, tiny waist, big ol' bubbly butt, tan, shaved legs with thighs that don't touch, blonde hair and blue eyes." As these descriptions make clear, the ideal woman is more than just skinny. She has a range of ideal traits.

The uniformity of these descriptions is remarkably obvious. I expected to hear things like "thin," "big boobs," and "long legs." However, I was shocked that "blonde hair" and "blue eyes" were so often mentioned. Not all women provided details of hair and eye color, but when they did, blonde and blue were the only colors mentioned. As indicated by the mention of her suntan, she is presumed to be Caucasian. In other words, the ideal woman is her body, the sum of her choice parts.[12] Noticeably absent from these descriptions is any mention of personality, intelligence, or for that matter, facial features exclusive of her eyes. She sounds strikingly like a living Barbie doll and, like a Barbie doll, she is mostly the stuff of fantasy.

We see these ideal women in all forms of visual media including television, film, magazines, and the internet. The ideal beautiful woman has become an expected part of the visual aesthetics of entertainment found in these genres; however, we also see them in less expected places, such as newspapers. Alice brought up such an example from an ad in her campus newspaper. Alice explained that the ad was for some kind of business and showed a "dressing room or backstage or something similar." She continued:

> Every single girl in there couldn't have weighed more than one hundred pounds. There's a girl in the middle sitting in a chair and who is like the star of the show, but every girl helping her is really tiny, small.

An equally important aspect of the ad was that it was not for any product typically associated with femininity but for a "regular company," where many of these young women will work after graduation. The ad adds to the perception that thinness is an ideal everywhere, not just in places where women make their living based on their looks. Just as Lisa in Chapter Five remarked that she would have to lose weight to "attract another guy," most of the young women I've spoken with assume that they must be skinny to get a job and be successful.

Where is the line between fantasy and fact?
While everyone seems to know just what the ideal woman looks like, they also know what is done to improve her looks. As Stacie observed, even models and actresses don't "look like those pictures." Most women would follow their description with an observation that "she's airbrushed." Her idealness is amplified; she needs outside assistance to enhance her beauty, and often these enhancements look unnatural. Daisy described a picture of an unnatural woman on the cover of *Rolling Stone* magazine:[13]

> Her armpit wasn't hollow. Like you know how they airbrushed it. It looked like smooth skin on your face or something. You could tell that they had done it because it was so unnatural.

No part of the body is safe from digital manipulation or airbrushing—not even armpits. Additionally fascinating is how deeply Daisy inspected and analyzed the picture. Like Daisy, many young women consider pictures from all angles in order to discover the details and parameters of the ideal body. Part of this scrutiny involves a critical analysis of what makes the ideal body appear so ideal. This practice of analyzing pictures is similar to the male practice of looking at *Victoria's Secret* models. Like lingerie gazing, searching for signs of airbrushing and digital enhancing is a public sport. While young men are perusing lingerie catalogs in their dorms, young women are in their dorms examining magazines and catalogs that feature ideal media women, a practice which reminds me of a grown-up, distinctly feminine version of the childhood game of Where's Waldo. The grown up version is more aptly called Where's the Woman. In Where's Waldo, the goal is to examine a picture filled with myriad similar looking images and find the one true Waldo. In Where's the Woman, the goal is to examine a picture filled with myriad aspects of ideal beauty and find the true woman. Young women ask: What's real? What's enhanced? What looks good? What looks fake?

As part of this Where's the Woman game, one of the questions regularly raised is: If the picture on the cover of a magazine has been enhanced digitally, then at what point does the woman change from natural to artificial? In other words, when does the ideal move from being real to unreal? Perhaps more importantly, though, why are these unreal ideal beauties praised? Satania asks this exact question:

> You know that what you see on television or in a magazine is computer generated and you can't be that. I think that guys even know that, but these women are not real. It's not real. It just blows my mind that they want you to be something that's not even real.

Satania is right in that it does seem at times that "they" (whoever they are) want women to be something "that's not even real." It's easy to understand Satania's allusion to some kind of conspiracy aimed at young women. Looking at media images, young women see the creation of unreachable standards of beauty at the same time that they understand the implicit mandate that this is what they should and could look like if they worked hard enough. Trying to achieve these contradictory standards, they feel as if they are constantly scrambling after something that is just a bit further out of reach, similar to how the ideal end of the beauty continuum always seems to be changing, to be moving further away.

When thinking about Satania's comments, I ask: Is this a conspiracy or just part of good business practices? The goal of any form of media—film, television show, magazine, etc.—is to gain and keep an audience. To do this, the media product must constantly change so that people keep coming back. Who wants to see the same episode of a sitcom over and over? Likewise, ideal feminine beauty is a media product. And like films and sitcoms, the product must keep the audience interested by maintaining a position of constant flux and flexibility. Therefore, it seems reasonable to argue that changing the face of ideal beauty is no more a conspiracy than changing the characters on a sitcom. It's all just good business aimed at giving the consuming audience what they want. Unfortunately, what may be good business for media owners often adds to the feelings of body dissatisfaction for young women.

When did science fiction become the stuff of everyday life?
Conspiracy or not, the standards of beauty being presented by media
today seem to be moving further beyond the reach of most women.
Consider these observations by Chazy:

> Now we're doing computer generated women—taking one woman's arms,
> someone else's legs, somebody else's face. They airbrush the skin so that it's
> perfect without any pores. They shave off inches here. They enhance here.
> They do all kinds of stuff. You can't become that. It's pure fiction living inside
> a computer. But this is the standard that we feel we need to achieve.

Although Chazy's comments are accurate, they seem like the stuff
of science fiction. In fact, such a computer-generated woman was
the theme of the movie *S1m0ne*.[14] In the film, a director faced with
the prospect that his film will flop determines that extraordinary
measures are needed to save it. Using technology that allows for
digital fabrication of humans, he designs a new leading lady who is
the ultimate beautiful woman: Simone, created from the best parts
of real women. Even though she only exists on a microchip within
a computer, Simone becomes an international success. Her completely fabricated beauty is rewarded across all segments of society,
and she is heralded as the next big Hollywood star. Simone, though
wholly a product of imagination, becomes more well-known and
popular than her creator simply because she is thought to embody
ideal beauty.

While we have yet to see a media woman created to the extent
of Simone, we do see vestiges of such complete fabrication in other
forms. Perhaps the most famous media fabrication and representation of female beauty is Mattel's Barbie doll—ideal feminine beauty
immortalized in plastic. Created by Ruth Handler, Barbie debuted
in 1959. Handler's goal was to design a doll that looked like an adult
woman and would allow her daughter to recreate the dressing up
and fantasy play of paper dolls. Handler modeled Barbie after Lilli,
a German sex doll marketed to men.[15] Barbie's idealness is more
unreal than real. If Barbie were a living woman, she would always
walk on her toes and stand five feet nine inches tall and weigh one
hundred pounds—dangerously underweight. Her measurements
would be 39–18–33—dimensions not normally seen in nature. It
is doubtful that Barbie would be able to function in daily life with
such unrealistic dimensions. Even though she is only a doll, Barbie

is known internationally, the object of adult collectors and fan clubs and the subject of an entire magazine, *Barbie Bazaar*. She is the guest of honor at annual Barbie conventions around the world. However, she also has been the target of much criticism for the unattainable standards of beauty she presents.[16]

The impact of Barbie's depiction of ideal feminine beauty extends beyond childhood. As children playing with Barbie, young girls begin to think that she is what women should look like. For example, when she was ten years old, Psyche recalls asking her mom, "why she [her mom] didn't look like Barbie." She explained that she just wanted her "mom to be as pretty as Barbie." While critiquing her own relationship with Barbie in "Barbie Doll Culture and the American Waistland," English professor Kamy Cunningham asked, "Doesn't every little, and big, American girl want to look like Barbie?"[17] As they mature, young women learn that Barbie's body is not realistic. Nevertheless, Barbie's impact is still felt. Chazy observed that "Barbie's body is just ridiculous, you know? But imagine what it would be like if you did look like that?" Likewise, Jill wished that she "could have Barbie's curves."

Acting on wishes such as those held by Jill, in the early 1980s Cindy Jackson embarked upon a journey to become a living doll— Barbie to be exact.[18] Her quest for living Barbieness has led Jackson to undergo numerous plastic and reconstructive surgeries including:

- Upper and lower eye lid surgery
- Lip collagen injections
- Liposuction
- Breast augmentation
- Cheek transplants
- Hair plugs
- Butt lift
- Nose job
- Face lift
- Acid face peels

In addition to these, she has had her teeth capped and makeup tattooed permanently on. She has spent the last twenty plus years undergoing surgeries and other procedures to reach her goal. Instead of being scorned or chastised for what some would consider textbook narcissistic behavior, Jackson is referred to as the "high priestess of cosmetic surgery."[19] She is said to have a "beauty queen's face,"[20] a "glamorous body,"[21] and a "perfect face."[22] In other words, Jackson is commended for doing whatever it takes to achieve her goal. Today, she is considered by many to be a living Barbie doll but, like Barbie, her beauty is man-made. Despite this fact, she is praised and rewarded for her "beauty."

Barbie, as a doll, and Simone, as a character in a film, can possibly be dismissed as merely the stuff of fiction. Though a "real" woman, Ms. Jackson can also be dismissed as the stuff of fantasy, her ideal Barbie beauty coming at the expense and pain of numerous surgeries. It's easy to say that these "ideal women" aren't real and, therefore, cannot actually have much influence on young women's body dissatisfaction. However, they should not be dismissed. Barbie and Simone are merely two pieces in the complex social puzzle of body dissatisfaction that exists within young women's culture of discontent. The problem is not that fictional media women exist, that living media women are enhanced through airbrushing, or even that someone like Cindy Jackson tries to modify her body to look like Barbie. The problem is that by revering such unreal images as ideal, some women begin to think that these types of behaviors are normal and that they should do the same, often convincing themselves that they really do want to look like these ideal media women. More troubling, though, is the possibility of their turning the implicit mandates of these images into explicit ones, of emulating this idealized standard and enforcing it on each other—even when it becomes potentially dangerous. They accept the fact that extraordinary methods to achieve such beauty are acceptable and expected. In the face of numerous cultural, social, media, and interpersonal pressures to look the "right" way, they create their own culture of discontent, adopting the metaphorical male gaze described by Laura Mulvey and turning it into a living gaze. When they look at themselves in the mirror, they see themselves as they think others see them. They compare themselves to the computer enhanced, sexualized women they see presented in media images and turn to them as role models for their own bodies.[23] The end result is that the "ideal" bodies featured on magazine covers[24]—airbrushed, computer enhanced, and stylized by teams of experts—become prized over the "real" bodies of most women. Women whose bodies do not look like these ideal bodies are subject to potential scorn, rebuke, and ostracization.

Skinny girls get skinnier

Images of ideal women are only part of the media equation. Joining these images is the running commentary on the ups and downs of the weight of Hollywood stars. This combination of verbal and visual creates a rhetoric of ideal beauty that further exacerbates the thought that women's bodies are social bodies designed to be gazed at. We turn to Hollywood not only to see ideal beauty but also to learn how to emulate it. Weight loss and procedures to enhance beauty are now a regular part of our entertainment options.

How do stars get thin quickly?

Weight loss for ideal beauty is a prominent form of entertainment found in gossip magazines. We regularly see headlines touting the extra pounds gained or lost by a Hollywood star. More troubling, though, are the special feature stories glorifying weight loss and exercise secrets. Over the last few years, these types of features have become increasingly popular. The following represent only a small fraction of the myriad examples. In 2001, *US Weekly* presented a cover headline of: "Losing Weight: How Hollywood Stays Fit, Diets, and Sometimes Goes Too Far …"[25] A 2002 *People* cover advertised: "Hollywood's Shape-up Secrets: Forget Freak Diets and Wacko Workouts, Here are the get-real ways that stars stay fit."[26] A similar headline appeared later in the year on *In Touch Weekly's* cover: "Wow! They Got Thin … Fast! Star Secrets Revealed Just in Time for the Holidays."[27] A few months later *In Touch* featured "Oprah's Weight Loss Miracle: After Years of Yo-Yo Dieting, She's Found Success at Last. What's her secret?"[28] In 2006 *Life & Style* covers blared: "25 New DIET Secrets! How A-listers slim down FAST!"[29] and "Summer's NEW DIET SECRETS! How Oprah, Mariah and others are getting their sexiest bodies ever!"[30] We still see these types of stories today as illustrated by the following examples: STARS BEATING CELLULITE! Celebs say goodbye to every woman's worst nightmare. How the anti-cellulite diet really works."[31] Continuing into 2008 *In Touch Weekly* touted: "Drop Pounds in Days: SLIM FOR THE NEW YEAR. Exclusive Tips from Jessica Simpson and Lauren Conrad."[32] The same week, *US Weekly* offered: "2008's DIETS THAT WORK! 23 PAGE BONUS! The stars reveal the best ways they get thin FAST."[33] Notice that the dominant trend in these articles is the "secret" or "trick" that Hollywood stars are privy to. The assumption here is that by reading the article(s) in question you too can learn the secret and get thin quickly. However, this is another way that the line between real and unreal is blurred. The life of a Hollywood star is an unreal ideal for most people. However, all these articles promise that while we may never be able to live in a forty thousand square foot mansion and walk the red carpet, we can at least get a red carpet body.

In addition to the cover stories featuring star weight loss secrets, we also see cover stories revealing the "shocking" trans-formations—good and bad—of stars. One of the leaders in this genre is *Star* magazine. In September, 2004, *Star's* cover screamed: "Who Got Fat! Who Got Thin! 10 More Shockers Inside."[34] Recent feature stories reveal the shocking story of weight loss gone bad. For example, in May, 2004, *Star* advertised: "Mary-Kate Olsen Skin and Bones!"[35] In November the focus was on Renee Zellweger with the headline: "From Bridget Jones to Skin and Bones!"[36] The cover also asked: "Is she addicted to deadly dieting? Is she los-ing her hair?" and promised "Plus! More skeletal stars inside." Though *Star* may be the leader in this genre of cover, they are not alone. In May, 2007, *US Weekly* featured a "Ricki Lake Exclusive: HALF MY SIZE! FROM SIZE 24 TO 4 WITHOUT SURGERY!" Also promised were "Her diet & workouts" with a comment from Ricki that "It's a time of self-acceptance now."[37] In early 2008, *In Touch Weekly's* cover promised an "EXCLUSIVE" on Tara Reid, advertising "TARA'S TOO THIN! SHE'S ONLY 95 LBS." The cover explained that "She blames her weight loss on no room service in her hotel, but doctors warn her health may be in danger."[38] Note that these stories aren't just shocking, they're SHOCKING! Capital letters and exclamation points are a prevalent part of the shocking cover story and add to the spectacle of star weight loss.

Positioning drastic weight changes as merely another part of the spectacle that is Hollywood is troubling. Even more troubling, though, is the ambivalent nature of many of these articles. Consider this November, 2005 *Life & Style* story on Jessica Simpson. The cover sported a Before and After picture of Simpson next to the headline: "Jess gains 30 lbs in 3 months! Facing divorce, a heartbro-ken Jess binges on junk food!"[39] Inside, the article shows a picture of Simpson from July 22 weighing 105 pounds next to a picture of her from October 24 weighing 135 pounds—the advertised thirty pound differential. The text asserts that Simpson has been "gorging herself with junk food" when "just three months ago she was in perfect shape for the *Dukes of Hazard*."[40] The rhetoric reinforces the view that this weight gain is bad. Simpson is reportedly "pigging out" and "wolfing down carb-heavy pasta and desserts." She is quoted as saying, "Eating is the only comfort I have in my life right now." It could be argued that the article is simply pointing out a potentially dangerous health issue—gaining a relatively significant amount of weight in a short period of time. However, as with nearly everything else media-related, we have to look below the surface and ask what else is going on. Looking further, we find a contradiction. While the article criticizes the weight gain as bad, it also features a picture from December, 2004 from the set of the *Dukes of Hazard* with Simpson purportedly in "perfect shape" although the tag line indicates that she is "scarily skinny" at 110 pounds. Are we to believe that "scarily skinny" and "perfect shape" are the same thing?

A more recent addition to these types of magazine stories are television programs featuring the steps taken by stars to achieve the ideal skinny look. For example, Marie discussed how certain shows will focus on what stars do to "make over their body." She explained that the shows typically detail the workouts, the food plans, and the amount of time involved. In a related vein, Jasmine observed that stars will spend "hours each day and thousands of dollars each year" in order to get and maintain this ideal body. The process of body modification—even extreme modifications—thus becomes just another form of entertainment. It is discussed, debated, and dissected like the latest sit-com or movie of the week. Jasmine is cognizant of the fact that most women don't have this kind of time or money to devote to attaining the ideal body. However, she is still "fascinated" by the process and production of ideal Hollywood beauty.

An example of this type of extreme body modification as entertainment was shared by Butterfly. Butterfly explained that the main character in the *Legally Blond* movies is "built around Barbie." She discussed the steps Reese Witherspoon took to get the "right look" for *Legally Blond:*

> I watched the filming of it *[Legally Blond]* on HBO, and they actually set out to make her character built around Barbie. After filming started, she was still dieting to get skinny enough. So like that scene where she's in a bikini was shot last. And she's thin, really thin.

In other words, Witherspoon's diet regimen is positioned as entertainment, merely another part of the behind the scenes business of
making the movie. Presenting Witherspoon's diet and alleged need
to lose weight as a necessary part of making the movie, the idea that
the female body is a sexualized body to be gazed at is reinforced yet
again. Steps to make the real body of an actress look like the extraordinarily unreal body of a doll are not out of the ordinary—just
another day at the movies.

An additional, though opposite, example of body modification
as part of the normal business of making movies is presented by
Lola. Lola described the steps Renee Zellweger took in preparing
to play the role of Bridget Jones: "She ate donuts and stuff to gain
twenty pounds." Lola then detailed the criticisms Zellweger faced
after such weight gain, being called "disgusting" and "gross." Lola,
however, felt that at the higher weight Zellweger didn't "look bad."
She also observed that "normally she's a really muscley person who
is so skinny that it's almost unnatural." As with *Legally Blond,* media
commentary on this aspect of the filming was a regular part of the
media hype surrounding the film.

When does sexy skinny become scary skinny?

While being skinny is good, being too skinny presents a problem that
is also discussed throughout media. Every few months it seems that
the rapid and extreme weight loss of yet another Hollywood star is
splashed across the covers of tabloids and discussed on Hollywood
"news" shows such as *E! News.* A recent example of this phenomenon
is the weight loss of Lindsay Lohan and Nicole Richie, featured on the
cover of both *Us Weekly* and *In Touch Weekly* in May 2005. *Us Weekly*
asked: "Extreme Diets: How Lindsay and Nicole got skinny—but have
they gone too far?" The cover subhead commented on Lindsay's twenty-
four-inch waist and Nicole's weight under ninety-seven pounds.[41] *In
Touch Weekly* ran the following headline: "Scary Thin! Is the pressure
too much? Special Report—Why won't they stop losing weight?"[42] The
article commented on how quickly both women had transformed into
barely there, "pin thin" girls and speculated as to whether they were
suffering from an eating disorder. The text was supplemented with
various Before and After pictures as well as with what appeared to be
a staged picture of the two eating, each denying any eating disorder
problems and claiming that her rapid weight loss was due to growing
up, losing baby fat, eating healthy, and working out.[43]

While it may seem from these two cover stories that the media have finally turned a critical eye on the obsession with skinniness, this is probably only an illusion. In the same issue that questioned Lohan's weight loss, *Us Weekly* showed her on the red carpet and called her a style setter. Likewise, *Life & Style Weekly* listed Richie as having one of the top six "Hollywood's Hottest Abs."[44] In both magazines, the women were featured as "star dazzlers" on the Cartier red carpet. Lohan was also featured as "Best Dressed–Down Style" for her casual clothing selections and her "Best Accessories." Even more troubling, though, is that just over two months later both women were selected by *In Touch Weekly* as part of their top ten style makeovers.[45] Richie was selected as the number three biggest makeover based in part on her "slimmer silhouette." Lohan was the top biggest makeover and touted as experiencing a "Dramatic change!" The magazine went on to point out that "with her super-skinny look and blond locks—replacing her once-buxom bod and spunky carrot top—Lohan has totally transformed in just a year. She's lost nearly 20 pounds."

Presenting rapid and drastic weight loss like this as the stuff of entertainment further desensitizes us to the reality of such bodies. It's hard to dismiss drastic transformations such as Lohan's and Richie's as merely Hollywood smoke and mirrors. Lohan and Richie are not the stuff of fiction—they're real women who walk and talk like the rest of us. When we see them completely reconstructed without the extreme, unnatural measures of Simone or Cindy Jackson, we see that we really could be skinny if we only tried harder. As an extra incentive, we are reminded of what we will gain for doing this hard work. We will be in style and perhaps even style setters, just like them.

The skinny girl can be you

Media commentary on the weight loss and diet secrets of Hollywood stars keeps the phenomenon of the ideal skinny female body in constant circulation. It is impossible to pass by the newsstand without seeing a cover blaring news of skinny bodies. As with other types of media representations of women, it is tempting to dismiss this as just more media hype; after all, these women are actresses whose living depends upon having the ideal or "right" look. They are not us. They are more like Barbie, Simone, or even Cindy Jackson—fantasy brought to life. But there are other forms of media messages young women see which can influence them. Also in the mix are television shows such as *The Biggest Loser* which presents a group of individuals desperate to lose weight,[46] coupled with tidbits of biographical information that typically detail how unhappy and unfulfilled the individuals are in their current physical state. The shows are presented as competitions between individuals or groups to see who experiences the biggest final transformation. The contestants' identities are presented as being fully encompassed and contingent upon the size of their bodies, focusing not on health issues but on quality of life issues. The standard narrative is that the individual feels ashamed, embarrassed, and generally unhappy being fat and that if he or she loses weight, a better life awaits. Each week viewers see the diet and exercise steps taken on the route to transformation, highlighted by the weekly weigh-in in front of a panel of "experts." During this portion of the show, a system of rewards and punishments is created. Contestants who have met the previous week's goal are praised; those who have not are chastised and their resolve to lose weight questioned. The implication is clear—you're fat by choice and too lazy to change.

Watching these shows is another facet of the Where's the Woman game. Chazy, for example, "never misses" the show *Extreme Makeover,* another television show featuring body modification as entertainment. She often will schedule "viewing parties" for her friends. During these parties Chazy and her friends watch the show and comment on the contestants' weight loss, effort, and overall appearance—yet another facet of the body battles that comprise the culture of discontent. While the commentary in this case is directed at a woman known only through her media presence, the discursive controls discussed in Chapter Four are still present and experienced by all those participating.

A newer addition to the makeover shows are those that focus on body transformations achieved with plastic surgery as a magical beauty panacea.[47] They are usually presented as a blend of real-life and documentary. A typical show will follow the surgical candidate from pre-op through surgery and recovery. As in the weight loss shows, biographical information about the individual is part of the program. We learn that the young woman who has already had one breast augmentation is having a second one so as to attract a rich husband. We are invited to feel the emotional pain of the woman who is having liposuction so that the "pretty girl inside her" can come out. Many of these patients present their quest for plastic surgery not as a wish or desire but as a need. For example, on a 2005 episode of *Dr. 90210,* a sixty-five-year-old interior designer explained how she needed to get a face lift so that she could stay competitive in her business; her doctor agreed that this was a "necessary" part of her business life, the message being that what was once the ultimate act of narcissistic vanity is now necessary. No longer a matter of wanting to look good, now you *must* look good. More troubling is the fact that we are slowly desensitized to recognizing these procedures as surgical procedures. Even when we see Dr. 90210 in surgery, we see little if any of the blood that is a natural occurrence of cutting into the human body. If we see the patient after surgery or during her recovery, we see only a minute portion of the pain and bruising that are present. We don't see the permanent scarring, disfiguration, or death that can occur. Just as in the shows about less invasive makeovers, the focus revolves around the final transformation that brings the individual one step closer to the ideal end of the beauty continuum.

Through these shows, the practice of plastic surgery becomes normalized as just another method for being beautiful and sexy— less like a medical procedure and more like a haircut. It is merely another tool in the beauty regimen. Of course, there is a price, and to help educate the consuming public, magazines provide us with even more detailed information about what these procedures cost. For example, in March 2006, *Life & Style* ran a story entitled "How much does a Hollywood body cost?"[48] The article highlighted the transformations of Demi Moore, Anna Nicole Smith, and Dolly Parton with a detailed breakdown of the procedures each has had and the cost. According to the article, Moore spent over forty-five thousand dollars on her most recent transformation, Smith spent over sixty-five thousand, and Parton spent over seventy-four thousand. These figures are in addition to the thousands of dollars each has spent in the past.

To help the rest of us, Sandow Media introduced *New Beauty* magazine in 2006, described as "your source for all things beauty."[49] Its primary focus is cosmetic surgery. The fact that you're subjecting yourself to bruising, scarring, intense pain, and possible death are downplayed in favor of the long term aesthetic benefits of the surgery. All of these media examples reinforce the presumption that nothing is too extreme in the quest for an ideal image.

How can I get skinny?

Young women seeking a less invasive at-home version of makeovers can turn to media for help in finding methods to achieve them. Shirley runs down some of the popular options:

> Every time you turn on television you see Weight Watcher's commercials and Slimfast or that Tony Little guy with the exercise thing[50] or diet pills like Trimspa.

The message here is clear: Getting thin is not merely a product of genetics, other biological factors, or hard work. Skinniness is just another consumer product that can be purchased for the right amount of money. One can be skinny if one wants to and is willing to spend the money. For those who can't afford hi-tech equipment, plastic surgery, or pills, there are cheap alternatives.

Women's magazines notoriously are filled with the latest get thin quick schemes. In response to critical commentary from feminists and health professionals, most mainstream magazines today are conscientious enough to provide weight loss information that is at least semi-healthy. As part of my research, I regularly read a variety of entertainment, fashion, and women's magazines, and I rarely see any articles advocating the unhealthy methods touted in the recent past such as fasting or taking laxatives. In fact, most magazines today actively discourage the use of drastic measures and encourage speaking to a doctor before starting any weight loss program. This does not mean, however, that all the things in such articles can be considered healthy. For example, the September, 2005 edition of *Elle* magazine featured: "10 days to a New Body: It Won't Be Easy—but it can be done!"[51] The miracle plan that will provide this new body in such a quick time is a "2-hours-a-day, 10 day, crack-of-dawn boot camp led by Jack Walston, a former Navy SEAL, in New York City's Central Park." The program combines running with old school calisthenics. As a sidebar, the article provides a detailed description of the workout. The plan includes running 4.7 miles interspersed with hundreds of push-ups, sit-ups, jump squats, squat thrusts, and step-ups. In order to test the efficiency and effectiveness of the plan, the article's author volunteered as a guinea pig; however, after seven days she was sidetracked with a stress fracture in her heel, caused by the excessive running in the program. The severity of the fracture prevented her from finishing the full ten days. Despite her injury, she brags about the "new bump" on her biceps and the increased energy she received from the workout. In other words, the pain and stress were worth it in the end.

Arguably, exercise is better than starvation, juice fasts, or living on laxatives. However, it's hard not to question just how healthy a plan like this can be. After only seven days, the author limps away with an injury that prevents further workouts. Other than making note of this point, though, the magazine presents the exercise regimen with no critical commentary. No additional mention is made of injuries, soreness, or other negative side effects. Consequently, the author's injury appears to be nothing more than an anomaly. Even more damaging is that by including the detailed workout as part of the article, the magazine editors suggest that anyone can replicate the workout anywhere. While the "official" Navy SEAL workout is available in New York City and Hudson, New York, now even someone living in the smallest town of rural America can get a new body in ten days with the directions included in the magazine—without needing to pay four to six hundred dollars and without having the safeguard of a trained instructor supervising.

The media emphasis on skinniness and the steps taken to achieve it creates an environment where it is easy to think that anyone can get skinny. It becomes commonplace to think that since the celebrities did it, so can I. If Renee Zellweger can lose the twenty pounds she gained for a movie, and rather quickly, then why can't every woman lose the extra ten or twenty pounds she's carrying? The problem, though, is that it's not as easy as simply deciding to lose weight. Stars like Zellweger have numerous resources available to assist in fast and effective weight loss programs. They can pay thousands of dollars for a private chef and a personal trainer to come to their house. And if necessary they can devote eight hours a day to a workout regimen. Even if these resources were made available to all women, some things just can't be changed. A woman who is short can't make herself tall. Short legs are short legs. Big bones are big bones. No amount of dieting, workouts, or even surgery will change these facts.

The constant media emphasis on skinny also reinforces and recreates the premise of the female body as a social body, a body seen in ever smaller sizes. One of the ramifications of being a social body is that the female body then becomes not just a spectacle of a social gaze, but also an object of social control. Annette describes one popular aspect of this control:

> I feel like with magazines, anywhere you go you see it. You see it at the mall. You go to a grocery store and everything is dieter's stuff and low-fat this, fat-free that. Everything is so focused on losing weight and being thin. Even here at college, there's such a pull for the college image and the Spring Break look. I feel like I'm bombarded with it. Like you cannot pick up a magazine without one of the cover headings being New Diet Tricks. I buy into that. I want to read it. You know, find out what it has to say.

This constant reminder on "losing weight and being thin" works in conjunction with the personal and interpersonal commenting and cajoling comprising women's experiences with body dissatisfaction. The media presence merely adds another layer of surveillance and pressure. Annette succinctly summarizes the crux of this media aspect of the problem—it's everywhere. However, more than simply being everywhere, it's believable. As Annette points out, she "buys into it." Annette, Stacie, and other women want to believe that this month's diet tricks will prove to be the mystical talisman or provide the magical formula that will make their body dissatisfaction dissipate by helping them achieve the skinniness they desire.

Yet another ramification of the way media represent skinny women is that thinness becomes a marker of success. In years past, being fat was an indicator of success. Carrying a few extra pounds meant that you had money to spend on extra food. Today we see the exact opposite. An entire meal can be obtained for three dollars at many fast food restaurants: low cost, but high fat. To be thin takes extra effort and extra bucks. Therefore, just like driving a Lexus, wearing a Rolex, or carrying a Louis Vuitton bag, being skinny is another commodity available for purchase and available to those with money.

The rewards and punishments seen in media present a dangerous proposition because they are everywhere. When we turn on a sitcom and see a skinny girl and a fat girl, we know that the skinny girl will likely get the guy while the fat girl gets the laughs. The norms of the thin ideal and the rewards due her are brought to life through these media examples. Women are presented with myriad examples of what can be theirs if they try hard enough or spend enough money to buy the right body. Even though young women know that the ideal beauty they see throughout media is just another form of created media hype, there still exists a longing to "look like those women." Because we cannot avoid a media presence in our lives, we are surrounded by these ideal women. As we watch them, we learn more about the expectations of the cultural norms and behaviors specifically required of us.

Chapter Eight

Am I really fat?

Am I really fat?

Amongst many women, the common thought is that having an ideal body is a necessary prerequisite to being seen as a success and to receiving the rewards that come with such success. Situating body dissatisfaction within these larger discourses presents a specific way we can change their impact.

Society and culture

Lori first crossed my radar when she took an introductory communication class with me. Upon first impression she struck me as a quiet student who was more tomboy than girly girl. As the semester progressed, these impressions continued to ring true. Lori rarely spoke in class, though when she did contribute, her comments were poignant and enlightening. Whereas my other female students usually sit in their chairs with legs and arms crossed, trying to take up as little space as possible, Lori would sit all spread out—legs open and arms flopped at her side. She usually came to class wearing jeans, tennis shoes, and a t-shirt. My other female students primarily wore jeans as well, but they dressed them up with stilettos, blouses, and fitted jackets. Lori spent most of her time hanging out with the other guys in class, seemingly unaware of her female peers.

During office hours a few weeks into the semester, Lori stopped by my office to talk about ideas for her upcoming informative speech. As she was speaking I tried to maintain the smile on my face and control my shock. Lori planned on giving her speech on her involvement in a local Renaissance Faire, or as she called it "Ren Faire." She spoke with an enthusiasm and vivacity I had not thought possible. Her face lit up. Her words tumbled over each other. She practically jumped out of her seat as she described a typical faire. Moving past my initial shock at Lori's involvement in an activity not generally associated with tomboys, I enjoyed listening to her stories and agreed that the topic would make a wonderful choice for the speech assignment. My shock returned when Lori pulled out pictures of herself in full Ren Faire costume. Lori explained that the Ren Faire culture consists of distinct social groups that mimic socioeconomic divisions of the Renaissance era. Costumes reflect these divisions and are an indication of the social status of the character the wearer is portraying. Each individual chooses the level that she wishes to be, and Lori participated at the highest level: the rulers and aristocrats. This level was reflected in the intricacy of her costume's design and materials, which took hours to design and sew. She also explained that one costume, including accessories, costs over five hundred dollars. Until this point, I thought that Ren Faires were merely another fun and inexpensive pastime. I had no clue as to the amount of thought, time, and money that went into participating in them.

Returning to how she could incorporate her love of Ren Faire into an acceptable informative speech, Lori said she thought that it might be interesting to give her speech in full Ren Faire costume. I enthusiastically endorsed this idea, having regularly challenged my students to think beyond the usual Power Point and poster board visual aids. Despite my enthusiasm, Lori still seemed hesitant so I asked her what concerns she had. She then said, "Well, you know how you always tell us to make sure that our visual aids add to our speech without distracting the audience's attention from us as a speaker?" I nodded in agreement, secretly smiling to know that at least one student had listened to me. Lori continued, "Well, I'm afraid that my costume might be too distracting. See, it kind of shows off my body and, um, well, you know I usually don't go around showing off my stuff." Lori turned red at this last statement and started digging in her backpack for something. I took the time to think about how best to respond to Lori's concerns. While it was true that Lori usually kept her "stuff" covered up more than my other students, I didn't see any reason why she should worry. Lori appeared to wear a size eight or ten and had the curves associated with classic beauty.

Before I developed an appropriate response, Lori thrust a picture at me and said, "Here, see what you think."

My first response to seeing Lori in full Ren Faire gear was, "Wow!" Lori's costume was a stunning full-length burgundy gown of velvet and lace with a fitted bodice and flowing skirt. With it Lori wore a complex necklace featuring a pendant that dangled just at the top of her cleavage. It was hard not to focus on the expanse of cleavage exposed by the design of the dress. Her hair was upswept and adorned with small flowers that appeared to be baby's breath. I couldn't see the shoes that Lori wore, but she told me they were small heels in a matching burgundy velvet. Once I recovered from the shock of seeing Lori with such a different appearance from what I saw in the classroom, I explained that while her costume might be distracting at first, I didn't see where it would be a significant problem for her speech.

I finally asked the burning question: "What made you decide to get involved in Ren Faire? On the surface it doesn't seem like the kind of thing that I would picture you involved in." Lori laughed and said that most people who she told about her hobby said the same thing. She proceeded to explain how Ren Faire lets her be the woman she can't be in the "real world." Because she wasn't a typical girly girl, Lori always felt like people looked at her as less than a woman. At one point she mused about how no matter what she did, she would never be a skinny girl. However, she felt that the size of her body was more in line with the expectations of the Renaissance. For a few hours or days, Lori described how she felt desirable and beautiful. Lori hoped to land a position with one of the permanent Ren Faires after graduation so that she could work in an environment that appreciated "women like her."

Throughout my research, I have heard a number of women's stories. While all of these stories have an impact on me, Lori's story is, without a doubt, one of the saddest I have heard: In order to be happy, Lori feels that she must transport herself several hundred years into the past. Lori's story is not just the frivolous musings of an unhappy girl, nor is she the only woman who dreams of living in a time when "women like her" and bodies like hers were appreciated. In fact, having such dreams seems like a harmless way to deal with living in a culture of discontent; however, as with all dreams, they can be harmful if they do not prepare the dreamer to deal with reality.

Trying to determine how society has developed into a culture of discontent became a popular point of discussion during most of my interviews. While Chazy and I discussed this issue, she posed an interesting and important set of questions:

> Just sitting here thinking about the things we do to get that ideal body, it's like why are we trying? I'm sitting here and wondering why? Lots of questions are running through my head about why have we set this up for ourselves? Is it historic? Why do we need to dress up for the men? Why can't the men dress up for us and we wear rollers in our hair all day if we wanted or shave our head if that's what is comfortable? Why do we feel like we have to dress up for them?

The questions Chazy asks are important on many levels. In addition to attempting to figure out why so many women feel the need to conform to social mandates, these questions also bring to light the multitude of discourses that create the pressures that feed the cycle of dissatisfaction. To understand just how we have arrived at the point at which female bodies are considered subjects for social commentary with the "best" bodies being thin bordering on anorexic, it helps to turn to a brief review of the historical changes in society that precipitated today's state of affairs and body discourses.

A very brief review:
From the Industrial Revolution to today

The Industrial Revolution in the United States accompanied changes in the day-to-day life of all Americans, with one of the most significant changes to society being the sharp divide between the public sphere and the private sphere. According to historians Barbara Ehrenreich and Deirdre English, American society had been "gynocentric" beforehand; the "skills and work of women were indispensable to survival"[1] and the home was the center of both work and leisure activities. Out of necessity, in both the home and the fields, men, women, and children had worked side by side without concern or thoughts that women might be too weak to perform some activities. As progressive changes came to the country, a sharper divide began to develop between work and leisure activities. The creation of a vigorous marketplace in the public sphere generated a new system of work activities based outside of the home environment and became the primary domain of moneymaking work activities, while the private sphere of the home became the primary domain of homemaking and leisure activities. An unfortunate consequence of this change was that work done in the marketplace gained a specific monetary value, while work done in the home did not. There was, of course, much work still done in the home to maintain it as a domestic and leisure refuge; however, unlike public work activities, this work was unpaid, inherently devalued, and trivialized as nothing more than women's work. In other words, men worked for pay; women worked for a sense of accomplishment. A discursive prejudice developed focusing on women's work arising from a sense of duty and responsibility for their family. Even though women "worked," what they did wasn't considered "real work," because they didn't earn money. The fact that the things they did allowed their husbands to do "real work" was ignored.

With the establishment of a separate public work environment, men were placed in a new role of workers who left the home to enter the cold marketplace of work. Women, meanwhile, were expected to stay at home and create a warm, inviting environment as a refuge to which men could return. Women were expected to be the angel of the house, where the house was the heaven to which they were chained. They were assumed to be too fragile to work in the marketplace or to engage in certain intellectual activities. Charlotte Perkins Gilman, for example, was advised: "Lie down one hour after each meal. Have but two hours intellectual life a day. And never touch pen, brush or pencil as long as you live."[2] This sharp divide between public and private domains effectively shifted the focus of society from gynocentric to phallocentric. Male attitudes, behaviors, and actions became prized over all things feminine. Women's work became constant and never-ending. Whereas the workday of the public market ranged from eight to ten hours, the workday of maintaining the home ran nonstop for twenty-four hours. For working class women who had to take in laundry or mending, as well as for those who were forced to work in factory or other jobs, the situation was even worse. Even though they worked in the marketplace just like men, they were still expected to be the angel in the house while at home.[3] They were presumed to still be in charge of maintaining the house as a leisure based refuge from the marketplace.[4]

As the changes engendered by the Industrial Revolution took hold, cultural discourses supporting them began circulating, many of which were housed in the formal institutions of law, medicine, and religion. Each institution put its own spin on its specific discourse; however, they all frequently revolved around defining and explaining ideal femininity with the discourse of each institution reinforcing the others and serving to maintain the limited, submissive roles which defined women's existence in the nineteenth century. For their part, women were becoming increasingly frustrated with the isolation inherent in being segregated to the home. Even before the Suffragists began agitating in the middle of the nineteenth century, groups of women were banding together in "benevolent associations, charitable institutions, and mutual support groups."[5] Through these organizations, women provided a range of assistance and services to less fortunate members of society. More importantly, though, participating in these organizations allowed women the opportunity to venture out of the home to meet and talk with other women. As they did so, they began to understand the lure of the market and the potential limitations of being chained to a house. Concurrently, American society saw the rise of the "Woman Question" or "Woman Problem,"[6] focused on what to do with women or how to keep them under control and in their place—the home. The goal was to find ways to encourage women to maintain the private sphere without question and to see this responsibility as part of their moral duty. The solution to the problem was provided by men hiding behind the guise of their professional expertise—physicians, philosophers, scientists, lawyers, and other experts who all agreed that women presented a problem of control. Women thus became "something to be investigated, analyzed, and solved."[7]

While twenty-first century women have more options, the impact of these earlier discourses and "traditions" can still be felt at times. The role of the woman was described in these traditions as primarily one of being pleasant, agreeable, and submissive. She was to care for the man's domestic, social, sexual, and emotional needs as well as his house and children. Through all these discourses, a woman's sexuality has come to be increasingly and intricately interwoven with the size of her body given the preferences of men today. To be sexually alluring, an ideal woman must maintain a small presence. That is, she should be small in demeanor—submissive—and small in size—skinny. Cultural discourses work together with media and interpersonal discourses to help foster a persistent feeling of dissatisfaction in those who do not achieve the ideal. As will be seen in the following pages, there are numerous reasons that women could—and arguably should—be dissatisfied with their existence today, but the size of their bodies should not be the central focus.

It's everywhere

This history of control through discursive rules, mandates, and laws has helped foster today's environment where the female body is considered a social body. Happy observed that public discussion about the female body is "in our face every single day," which in turn adds to the discontent that seems endemic to women's culture. Happy further describes the situation:

> Being thin is all I want to think about. I mean really, you pick up a magazine; you see it on TV. You even walk outside and it's there. Every day, you see someone, and you're like, Oooh, she needs to eat. It's in your face all the time.

Happy describes body dissatisfaction as being "in your face all the time." Her comments demonstrate the intertextual nature of body discourses—the personal moves to interpersonal, which moves to media. Together they create a rhetoric of ideal beauty, which creates the situation Happy describes.

Happy's comments indicate that for her and women like her, what they think about their bodies is contingent on what society thinks. Nevertheless, women are not empty vessels waiting to be filled with the thoughts of an outside entity. They don't need to be told what to think or what to do. The problem is that women are rarely afforded the opportunity to determine their own body destiny. Everywhere they turn they seem to be surrounded by reminders of how they should look. They face "gentle warnings" that they're getting bigger from parents and other relatives. They confront openly critical and mean remarks from other women. They receive contradictory messages from the guys in their lives. When they turn on the television or open a magazine, they see numerous ideal women who remind them that they themselves are somehow deficient. Each day they must find a way to navigate through all these social norms and discourses telling them they need to be other than they are.

In other words, the body dissatisfaction that is everywhere and that young women live with arises from a confluence of personal, interpersonal, and social factors. These forces swirl together, creating a tornado of pressures that assaults women's psyches, defining the culture of discontent that leads to the cycles of dissatisfaction that comprise women's lived experiences of and within their bodies. Laverne discusses an interesting perspective on this confluence of factors:

> Society plays a big role in how we see each other. People invest a lot in their body image, but that's only because society has let us invest in it. People have been allowed to invest time and psychological thought and perceptions. That's why we have Slimfast. That's why we have build 'em up Tony's[8] exercise program or other things. We worry about what people think about our bodies. We have all those things that let us always pay attention to our body image instead of other things. So we get caught up in it.

Laverne's observations here make clear that the relationship between a woman and her body is like a ménage a trois—the woman, her body, and society. It is intense and personal with a sexual aspect. Everything that she does with, to, or on her body is considered public fare, not just a result of her personal experiences.

Can't I forget about being fat when I'm in class?

Even in the classroom, young women find it difficult to escape the constant societal gaze. Isabelle noted that when "you walk into a classroom and people are just sitting down, I feel women as well as men check me out." Isabelle explained that each time she enters a classroom, she feels like she's running a gauntlet and that one false step will result in her social demise. The part of the gauntlet that bothered her the most was the women and their critical gaze, not the men. Isabelle's fears echo those voiced by Chazy, Annette, and Eva in Chapter Four. Because women know that other women are in competition with them, they fear their critical judgment more than the judgment of men. While young women may want to impress a guy, they feel a mandatory compulsion to impress other women.

A different version of pressures felt in the classroom is provided by Diva:

> In class, I'll be sitting there thinking about class stuff and all, trying to pay attention. Then a girl will sit down beside me and she's like fussing with her shirt and all, making sure that her fat rolls aren't into her shirt. I've even seen Dr. Smith[9] do it. She does it a lot. And then I'm sitting there and I'm like I should sit up straight. I should do my shirt like that. Now, that's all I think about. Now every time I go to my classes, I make sure my shirt is right and not stuck in my fat rolls.

With this story, Diva demonstrates what may be thought of as the male gaze in action when she exercises it on the girl "fussing with her shirt." That is, she doesn't just notice the girl; she critically evaluates her appearance. She notices the girl's "fat rolls" and the actions the girl takes to conceal them.

Simultaneously Diva internalizes the gaze and modifies her behavior—she sits up straight—and wonders if she should do her shirt "like that." Diva later clarified that before this incident happened, she hadn't thought much about how her body looked while she was sitting in class. She assumed that in the classroom, she was "safe" from any form of critical gaze. After this incident, however, Diva said that she now goes to class and always adjusts her shirt. She makes sure that she sits up straight and monitors these things continually throughout the class period. Diva and Isabelle's stories appear to confirm the presumption that as young women in American society, they are prized first for their bodies and only later for their education.

Why do we put pressure on ourselves?

It should be clear by now that for young women today, the influence of a critical gaze, or even the possibility of such a gaze, is always present. I've noticed, for example, that in my interviews there comes a point where the women begin to turn a critical eye on themselves. Chazy and Satania's thoughts are representative of the questions most women begin to ask:

> Chazy: Why do we put pressure on ourselves? Is it because we want to meet somebody? Or is it because we want to get married and have the perfect life? But everybody's perfect life is different. Why do we put these standards on ourselves?
>
> Satania: Why do I put pressure on myself? I'm engaged. I've got somebody who I've found who loves me for more than just what I look like. But I still find myself being unsure. I want to look a certain way. Why do we care? Not that I would let my body go and not care, but you know what I mean? Why do I feel like I need to impress anyone really? It's weird.

Notice that Chazy and Satania ask nearly identical questions, focusing on their self-inflicted "pressure" to be thin. They then connect this pressure to the need and desire to find a mate—"get married and have the perfect life." Both waver between questioning why they do this and knowing that they shouldn't or don't have to. Both identify that they pressure themselves to look a certain way out of motivation to "impress" others. They ask good questions, important questions. Not surprisingly, they aren't alone in asking these questions, and in seeking answers. While we were talking about the various societal pressures to maintain an appropriately skinny body, Ladybug commented that "we're just screwed." This pithy statement accurately summarizes the way many young women feel. When it comes to the female body, it does seem at times that women are living in a perpetual catch-22. Every move that they take gets them into another type of trouble.

Skinny rewards

Young women are well versed in the rewards that come with looking the "right way." They know that the road to success is best walked on skinny legs and seem to define these rewards in the amount of attention they receive. Liscious pointed out that a friend of hers had lost 50 pounds recently and was now treated differently "by guys because of the weight she's lost." Butterfly argued that "the only girls who really get attention on this campus look like they walked out of one of those magazines." Similar sentiments were expressed by most of the women I've interviewed—guys want the skinny girls. One could argue that this phenomenon is limited to college guys and their relative immature focus on physical appearance. That is, because they haven't had a lot of worldly experience, they are still heavily influenced by what they are told is sexy, and since ideal media women are depicted as sexy and super skinny, this is what they want. However, the approval from guys is only one form: Social rewards come in many forms from multiple sources.

During my interview with Laverne, the issue of image-based rewards came up repeatedly. As a twenty-two-year-old family and consumer science major, Laverne hoped to find a job in some sort of counseling position working with elementary school children. On the topic of rewards, she noted:

> The feeling that you need to be skinny, I think it's more than just girl/boy pressure. Your parents reinforce it. Your grandparents reinforce it. Your employer reinforces it. It comes up so many times. I would just say that people

have a bias when they're hiring people. Like it's not a joke. It plays into every aspect of how you're viewed as a person. It's like your physical appearance determines your potential.

Laverne highlights several sources: "your parents," "your grandparents," and "your employer." These individuals usually don't come right out and say, "You must be skinny to succeed." Instead, as discussed in Chapter Four, they tend to focus on less direct things. Jessica's mom, for example, told Jessica that she had such a pretty face and just needed to lose some weight. The clear implication is that Jessica is flawed until and unless she loses weight and may, therefore, not be happy or be a success. Laverne's observations come from a more-knowledgeable perspective than that held by many others. Like all these women, she has grown up in a society obsessed with skinniness. What sets her apart from many young women is that over the previous two years she had lost 110 pounds. In discussing this weight loss she was quick to clarify that "I did it for myself, not others." However, she also observed that "people treat you differently, on a daily basis" even though no one commented directly on her weight loss. She continued to note, "that's how people get caught up in the criticism of society and they adopt a thin mentality." She said that people spoke to her differently after her weight loss, as if suddenly she was a person worth talking to. People who before never fully acknowledged her began acting like friends. She was now a more socially acceptable size.

How do you get the dream job?
In the employment arena, it seems like common sense that for most professions body size should not be a determining factor in whether one is hired or not. An individual's education, experience, and qualifications should be the things that determine who is hired. However, in practice this is not always the case.[10] Unlike race, gender, religion and other traits covered by Title VII of the Civil Rights Act, in every state except Michigan it is not illegal to discriminate against someone for being fat.[11] Women are especially damaged in this way, for research has shown that "overweight females are penalized for their obesity in the wage sector."[12] While young women may not be familiar with the academic literature and studies that discuss the links between job success and body size, they have heard anecdotes of what can

happen to fat women in the corporate world. Consider Foxy's summary of the situation:

> If you have a woman who is insanely smart but she is bigger or not as attractive and then you have a woman who looks like a Barbie doll and isn't as smart and they're going for a position where they're going to be in touch with people, they'll be judged on their looks. The Barbie woman will probably get the job even though the other woman is better qualified for it.

I asked Foxy if her assumption was based on personal experience. She indicated that while she had never personally been discriminated against, she had heard about it in her business classes. Most of the women I've interviewed expressed a similar awareness and had plans to diet before entering the job market, much like Sarah whose story opened Chapter Two. A recent graduate, she was still trying to lose her "freshman fifteen" in anticipation of beginning her first job.

Getting the job isn't the end of the worry, though. Rewards and punishment on the job can also be appearance-based. After graduation, Isabelle planned to begin a full time position as a chemical engineer for a Fortune 500 company. In a field dominated by men, she regularly faces harassment and discrimination that is appearance based, which in turn impacts how she feels about her body. She describes a situation she experienced while participating in a summer internship at this company:

> It's not like my ideas are ever discounted or people ever say, "she's just a woman," because that's not PC. What they do is belittle and degrade you in different ways, in ways like lewd comments. I mean I was asked about my virginity at the lunch table. I was sitting at lunch with eight different guys and they were like, "Oh Isabelle, like you would still hate a guy if you weren't having sex with him after two months" or something like that. This conversation about my virginity is just completely inappropriate. I feel like that's now how the power play goes on between men and women. I just feel like it plays a very large part of my life, in my image of my body.

Isabelle explained that this conversation made her feel like she was reduced to nothing more than a sexual body. Because her body is close to the ideal, her male colleagues approached her as if she were nothing more than a body. They completely ignored the fact that she had earned the right to be there professionally, as they had.

How do you get the dream life?

Being thin is not just about getting the guy or getting the job; it's about getting the lifestyle that is thought to come with skinniness. Shirley explains:

> We want the It girl or the It physique that we see on TV. Like pink is the in color right now. Everyone loves pink. And why do we love pink? Because we see it in ads, in stores, and with other people wearing it. And then we're like, "Oh I've got to get me a pink shirt. It's the in color." Just like the color is in, that skinny body is in. People think that being skinny with perfect sized boobs or the perfect sized feet and the perfect jaw line and the perfect hair according to that look will get you to where you want to go. It will get you the perfect job making the best money, and then you'll get your husband and live happily ever after. You know, in a beautiful house and then you'll have a nanny and kids. So like that's the thing, the body ideal that's put out there comes along with a whole bunch of other stuff. So like if you are the perfect size or the size that people want to be, then you'll get all that other stuff that you see that other people have.

In other words, the "right body" is thought to be the determining factor for getting the trappings of a "good life." For women, the path to the American dream seems to be less about hard work than about a hard body. Bolstering this thought is the system of punishments that come with having the wrong body. Ladybug provides an example:

> "We get ostracized for gaining weight. Everybody used to say you've got to be like Britney Spears. Now they're saying she's fat cause she gained like three pounds. "[13]

Ladybug's example focuses on how varying slightly from the expected norm is considered a negative, even for a famous personality.

Thinness as a commodity and indicator of success reinforces it as a mandate—to be successful you must be thin. We see representative examples of this mandate enacted throughout media. For example, with actresses, there seems to be a direct relation between their popularity increasing and their size decreasing. Diva observed that when a female star first gains public notice, it will be "like she's changing the media perception. It's cool to have meat on your bones. Then two months later she's just as small as everyone else.

She's tiny." Mandi provided a specific example of the disappearing actress phenomenon:

> It seems like in Hollywood, when stars first come out, they're normal size. Then as they start to get bigger, bigger, bigger, their weight goes drastically down. Like the Friends cast, when they all started they were normal, and then they started fading away.

This phenomenon is one that is repeated over and over with each new batch of actresses. The examples of Lindsay Lohan and Nicole Richie discussed in Chapter Seven are just two of many. Even stars who are already thin become thinner as their fame increases. Take the case of Nicole Kidman, who is six feet tall and naturally thin. However, in recent years—most especially after landing a modeling contract with Chanel—her thinness has moved toward skeletal.

Whenever the issue of the disappearing actresses arose in my interviews, the discussion tended to focus on the fact that losing weight to be a "big" star just seemed to be assumed. As with other aspects of ideal beauty, young women tend to accept it normal. Skinniness is thought to be another job requirement just like good acting skills. The rewards of being a thin actress are further played out in the types of roles women get. As an example, Ladybug describes sex scenes:

> You look at sex scenes in the movies and it's only the pretty, hot, perfect girls who are doing them. I remember that movie with Jack Nicholson and Kathy Bates.[14] She had a nude scene and everybody was like, oh sick. Why is she getting naked? I was like, why not? She wants to.

Ladybug's observations here focus on the rewards that the "pretty, hot, perfect girls" get—the sex scenes, while imperfect women who do so are open to public scorn.

Doing a sex scene on film may not seem like a typical reward; for many women, it probably is not. However, the key here is that the woman chosen is deemed sexy. She is the one that men want, the one who earns the reward because she is skinny. Caitlyn presents another spin on the rewards that come to the skinny: "The models always get the hot guys. When a big woman comes along it's a big deal, like with Camryn Manheim on *The Practice*. It was a big to-do that a heavy woman was on TV." Because we see these situations so often, we become desensitized to them, losing sight of the fact that we are being bombarded with skinny perfect women being presented as the norm, the sex object under the male gaze brought to life, and the entire image internalized by the viewing woman in her personal cycle of dissatisfaction.

The myth of the magical golden era

All of these discursive mandates and narratives work together to maintain the status quo. As Dragonfly asserts, the entire situation is "something that suppresses us." She explained how she sees this suppression working in everyday life:

> It's just another way that women are lesser than men. Because they [men] can still control the way we think about our bodies, it's better for them.

This suppression works to create a micro-focus in which women become so involved in their body size that they miss the larger ways that women's existence is suppressed and their entire situation seems insurmountable. It creates a continual sense of longing for a mythical golden era where being skinny was out and being fat was cool, much like Lori's involvement in Ren Faire activities. Marie and her friends "talk about how we wish we grew up back in Medieval times when they had corsets." Satania "always jokes that I'd like to go back to the 1700's when the pale-skinned, kind of bigger woman is what was attractive. Now it's tan and thin. I'm waiting for us to come back in style." Similarly, Ladybug observed that "in the 1700s the plump lady was the ideal." Madeleine dreams of living in the "1800s when it was cool to be pale and overweight." Psyche wishes she lived "in the 1970s when size ten women were the norm." While the specific time period differs, the dream for a golden era stays the same. These women and others like them long to live in an era where "bigger women" "like us" are in style. They yearn for the time when "girls with bodies like Marilyn Monroe"[15] were considered the beauty norm.

I find it interesting that these women fantasize about a mythical era when they and their bodies were "in style." While a larger size female body may indeed have been the beauty ideal in medieval times, the 1700s, or even the 1800s, women in these eras faced many other obstacles.[16] For one thing, they were often treated as property to be bartered or sold away. They were unable to own property in their name. If a twenty-year-old woman and a ten-year-old boy, sister and brother, lost both their parents, the estate would go to the boy in its entirety. He would have sole authority to determine how much, if anything, went to his sister. Physical life was equally difficult during these times. Women could be beaten and raped at will with little or no recourse. Laws against rape and assault weren't implemented and applied until the late nineteenth century, and even then they were usually applied solely to middle class white women.[17] Modern medical facilities and treatments were not yet created, so disease was rampant. The average life expectancy was less than forty years old. Despite these negatives, for young women living within a cycle of dissatisfaction, the trade-off seems good: to live in a world free (or thought to be free) of body dissatisfaction.

Even in Psyche's dream era of the 1970s at the height of second wave feminism, women still confronted open and legal discrimination. Looking closely at Psyche's dream era, it looks more like a nightmare. For instance, in most states women could only obtain credit in their husband's name, so if they divorced they were left with none. Additionally, married women applying for credit were often asked to sign a baby letter in which they promised not to get pregnant over the term of the loan. A woman could be fired from teaching for getting pregnant, and in most states men weren't even allowed to teach at the elementary level. Flight attendants, still called stewardesses, were bound by strict beauty and weight requirements in order to keep their jobs.[18] Marital rape and sexual harassment didn't happen; while these behaviors were widespread, they were not labeled as such, nor were they considered crimes. A woman who complained about her boss's demanding sexual favors would likely be asked what she did to prompt such behavior or have her complaint dismissed with a laugh and a "Boys will be boys" comment. Curiously, at a time when feminism was making its mark and women were learning what their possibilities were, changes were occurring in terms of body ideals—changes that would culminate in the paralyzing body battles we see today. Some larger female bodies, like Elizabeth Taylor and Sophia Loren, were considered beautiful, but the trend toward thinner was already clearly in place. Twiggy became famous in the mid to late 60s and introduced a new standard to the concept of female attractiveness that evolved into the standard we see today.

Comments like these about the mythical golden era of larger bodies present an interesting illustration of one of the more dangerous aspects of body dissatisfaction. The cycle of dissatisfaction and its ensuing behaviors result in women's losing sight of what is really happening to and around them. Their micro-focus on body size and ideal beauty produces a situation where the body becomes the sole focus ... in other words, a textbook example of missing the forest for the trees—or in this case the tree trunks. These are smart women. Many of them consider themselves feminists and have studied feminist history. Most of them know how women were treated in the past and that even today women have not achieved full equality with men. When it comes to the body and beauty, though, they seem to forget all of these things. Instead of remembering how women were treated in the eighteenth and nineteenth centuries, they only remember that those bodies are fat by today's standards.

Even more problematic is that these dreams sadly attest to the fact that they're missing the larger issues faced by women today. Thirty years after feminists took over Atlantic City in protest of the sexist nature of the Miss America contest, pictures of nearly nude women are still splashed across newsstands, billboards, and the sides of buses. Thirty years after feminists stormed Wall Street, women still earn only seventy-seven cents for every dollar earned by men.[19] Thirty years after women broke into the ivy covered walls of colleges and universities in larger numbers, less than 25% of senior faculty positions are held by women.[20]

Instead of considering these problems or trying to change today's beauty standards, today's women dream of living in another era. They assume that skinniness is just a fact of life that we're all stuck with, just another story line in the overall narrative of femininity. Through these dreams of the mythical golden era, they demonstrate that for them, their destiny is determined by their bodies. If their bodies are right, then all will be right with the world.

Chapter Nine

Body image is the biggest issue women have

Body image is the biggest issue women have

Women and girls of all ages experience some form of body dissatisfaction. Instead of simply accepting this lifetime of cycling through dissatisfaction, it is time to ask: what can we do to stop it? While focusing on the larger cultural discourses and media discourses is one option, it is more feasible to start at the personal and interpersonal level. Talking to others about the various aspects of body dissatisfaction is the first step to realizing a change to a culture of satisfaction.

Where do we go from here?

At one of the parties I attended during graduate school and long before I ever dreamed of this project, I found myself sitting on a couch with two friends drinking beer and munching on snacks. We discussed a variety of issues—graduate school, our recent winter break activities, politics, music—the usual party fare. At some point in the evening one of my friends looked around to make sure no one was listening. She then leaned in and whispered, "Can I ask you guys a question about your bodies?" My other friend and I looked at each other and hesitantly assented. She then said, "What size clothes do each of you wear?" Neither of us spoke. I was in a mini state of panic. Weight and clothing size are things you don't usually share with others, and when you do, you tend to fudge the number down a bit. The first friend continued, "It's just that I've never been skinny but I've never been fat either. In the last few months, though, I've had to start buying clothing sizes in the double digits. I keep thinking that makes me fat." Relieved to know we wouldn't be judged harshly, my other friend and I divulged the magic numbers, and the conversation then turned to our bodies. One of us was currently participating in a commercial weight loss program and the other two were former fitness instructors still carrying around the mental baggage of the fitness industry—lose weight, be skinny, have hard muscles, and if you have time, be healthy. For the next hour we passionately discussed our individual struggles to obtain the "right" body and our collective frustration with the myriad cultural messages dictating what the "right" body should look like.

Returning home that evening, I reflected on my earlier conversation; it seemed familiar. Was it simply a matter of déjà vu? I eventually realized that within the previous twenty-four hours I had found myself in similar conversations at least three times, and I started to remember the multiple talks throughout my life on the same topic—with friends, with family, and with random women in dressing rooms, restaurants, bars, and other places. I struggled to think of one woman in my acquaintance who liked her body. I could think of no one—not one. All the women I knew were either openly dissatisfied with their bodies or struggling to maintain a public façade of body acceptance while privately counting calories and working to lose their flabby thighs or harden their sagging stomachs. Since that moment of clarity, I have been devoted to studying body dissatisfaction and talking to other women about the complex emotions and behaviors that develop around it.

Like the young women who speak in this book, I have moments when I feel profound dissatisfaction with my body. I've met women of all ages who feel this way. We seem to have those moments when we yearn for the sexualized ideal body we see everywhere, or at least wonder what it would be like to have it. Even though I study this subject, I occasionally find myself cringing at the vision reflected in the fitting room mirror. I pause before wearing a tank top and exposing my floppy upper arms. I change out of my low rider jeans on those days when my stomach feels exceptionally bloated. I think about passing on dessert when I haven't worked out in a few days. While the majority of individuals suffering from eating disorders are young women between the ages of eighteen and twenty-five, the larger problem of body dissatisfaction is not exclusive to this group of women. In my research I've spoken with girls as young as eight years old and women in their eighties who suffer from it. While the specifics of the pressures they feel differ, the bottom line remains the same—they are not happy with the size and shape of their bodies and feel that they must do something to change it.

From girls to women, we're all dissatisfied

I began this project because I wanted to see what young women thought about the issue. As our future leaders and perhaps the ones who will move beyond body dissatisfaction, they should do more than suffer silently. While the young women I spoke with were aware that the body dissatisfaction they feel is not limited to their age demographic, they also felt that it is something women must learn to live with. Claire's explanation of the situation is a typical response:

> Well, I really think that body image is the biggest issue that women have. I think that I've met one woman who claimed that she never had any body image issues, and I'm like how did you grow up in America and not? But, she didn't. Just the way that we're told that our bodies are supposed to look and the way we do look are usually like this totally different thing. There's so much about it in our society and culture and that determines where you're going and your future and stuff like that. It's something that I think every woman deals with.

While Claire's observations may seem like hyperbole, they may be more accurate than we'd like to admit. As we age, we may worry about the size of our bodies less frequently or we may resign ourselves to our "flaws," but our discontent seems to be often simmering just below the surface. However, young and mature women are not alone in these concerns. Girls of ever younger ages are also experiencing it.

At what age do we start worrying about our bodies?

In her pivotal book *The Beauty Myth*, Naomi Wolf observed that "sex is held hostage by beauty and its ransom terms are engraved in girls' minds early and deeply."[1] There is a presumption of heterosexuality in much of society, and young girls learn at an early age that one of their life goals, perhaps their primary life goal, should be to get married someday. While my niece was in pre-school, I was shocked to learn just how early this "life lesson" begins. Arriving early for her pickup one day, I stood in the corner and watched her play. She was dressed in an oversize formal dress like many little girls use to play dress up. As the game continued, I realized that she and a few of her classmates were acting out a wedding ceremony with my niece as the bride. One of the boys was the groom, with another boy as the minister, and several children as the audience. The ceremony was completed by one of my niece's teachers pretending to cry at "the beauty of young love." At the time, my niece was three years old.

Wedding play like that of my niece could be viewed as just an innocuous past time. For example, when I was growing up I regularly played Army with the neighbor boys but now consider myself a pacifist. However, some things that kids pretend to do during play are reinforced through myriad cultural, media, and interpersonal discourses; my niece's wedding play is one of these. Even though we may never do these things as adults in real life, the memory and the expectation that these things are normal and ideal in society remains. Young girls, therefore, navigate and live within the multiple messages and mandates arising from these discourses; the end result is a feeling that they must achieve the female ideal that society creates.

Some of the pressures influencing young girls are learned from their mothers and others around them. Recall Alice's story from Chapter Four of learning to connect eating to her emotions by participating in her mother's erratic dieting behaviors. In that same chapter, Annette discussed an even more direct example of parental influence in the story of the ten-year-old girl whose mother put her on Weight Watchers. In my daily activities, I continue to come across examples like these. Recently while waiting in line at my local coffee shop, I overheard a mother and her two young daughters discussing what they should have to eat and drink. Both girls wanted to have hot chocolates with extra chocolate. The mother quickly tried to dissuade them saying, "No, you don't want that. There're too many calories. It will make you fat." After a few seconds of arguing back and forth, they compromised with the mother, agreeing to get the hot chocolate but without extra chocolate. The three then ordered bagels to go with their drinks. When the barista asked if they wanted cream cheese with their bagels, the mother responded, "I was good last night and didn't eat much dessert so I do." The girls looked at each other and then the eldest said, "We had dessert last night, so I guess we better skip it." I estimated the youngest daughter to be between nine and ten years old, with her sister appearing to be thirteen to fourteen years old. I was fascinated by how quickly the girls changed their desires based on their mother's comments. After they sat down, their mother left for a few minutes. While she was gone the girls reminisced about how much they really wanted the extra chocolate and the cream cheese. The older daughter then said, "Mom's right, you know. We can't afford to get fat. It runs in our family, you know." Her sister shook her head in agreement. These girls have already internalized the social mandate that they must be skinny. Likewise, their mother has internalized the thought that it is part of her "job" to nudge their behavior accordingly. Not only does she speculate that the extra chocolate will "make you fat," she also models eating behaviors that the girls in turn mimic.

In addition to interpersonal pressures like these, young girls are influenced by many of the same social and cultural factors that affect young women in college.[2] For example, an interesting study from the field of psychology found that even brief exposure to Barbie dolls may influence how young girls feel about their bodies. Such exposure leads to "lower body esteem and a greater desire for a thinner body."[3] As a standard staple of girlhood, Barbie's influence may be even greater than gauged by this study, which focused solely on the role that Barbie the doll plays. Today, young girls have a plethora of choices on how they play with Barbie. Barbie is available in books, on video, as the star of video games, and singing on CDs.

One of the more interesting Barbie options available is the Barbie website.[4] Upon entering the site, girls are told that they can "B who U wanna B" by a thin, fashionably dressed animated Barbie. The site evokes visions of fun and play with its bright colors and multiple options of interactive things to do. Girls can choose how they decorate the page or they can read Barbie's diary and designate "who's a cutie and who's snooty" by attaching virtual stickers next to their names. Girls can also practice being Barbie by going to the mall with the site's virtual Barbie and helping pick out her clothes for upcoming events. Girls can heighten their Barbie experience by designing their own Barbie-themed clothing on a companion site that is merely one click away.[5] Visitors to this site style their own Barbie t-shirts by choosing their own Barbie, their chosen design elements, and personalized touches such as their name or "number."[6] For fourteen dollars and ninety-five cents they can then purchase their custom designed Barbie shirt. Like the wedding play of my niece, this type of play introduces a heightened level of reality into young girls' lives. I have to wonder how young girls who have had the opportunity to virtually play as Barbie will be influenced in the future. I speculate that such play may exacerbate the thoughts that they should emulate Barbie's body as young women.

Media discourse in general tends to heighten young girls' desire for the thin ideal through two distinct though interrelated components: "portrayals of thinness as a desirable trait ... and portrayals of fatness as an undesirable trait."[7] Communication scholar Kristen Harrison has found that exposure to these types of media discourses can predict the likelihood that an adolescent girl will fall prey to an eating disorder and does impact the way that such girls experience their bodies.[8] While research like this seems to show a connection between social discourses and young girls' feelings of body dissatisfaction, we need to continue to delve into the various other discourses impacting body dissatisfaction. Children may be more easily influenced than adults by outside factors, but only by talking to them will we begin to understand the things that they highlight as important to their lived experiences.

Just as young girls feel body pressures similar to those experienced by young women, so too are they adopting some of the same behaviors to achieve the ideal body. According to Dianne Newmark-Sztainer, over 50% of teenage girls participate in unhealthy weight control behaviors including skipping meals, fasting, smoking, vomiting, and using laxatives.[9] In 2005, the Associated Press reported that girls as young as nine are now using body building steroids to help them achieve the thin look of models and Hollywood stars.[10] Even though the dangers of steroids are well known and their side effects include stunted growth, increased facial hair, and a deepening of the voice, it seems that achieving the ideal thin body is worth the risk for some young girls.

Yet another example of behavior modification is found in Rachel Simmons's book *Odd Girl Out*. While conducting research on aggression in young girls, Simmons spent time studying how young girls act in their typical daily environments.[11] At one point Simmons was invited to a birthday sleepover hosted by one of the girls participating in the study. During the party, the girls participated in standard sleepover activities—giving each other pedicures, gossiping about Hollywood celebrities, and eating pizza, chips, and other party food. Simmons' description of the girls' spontaneous activities after dinner demonstrate the breadth of body dissatisfaction today:

Almost as soon as her toes are done, one girl, willowy as a reed, hops on the stationary bike and shouts, "I'm going to work off my dinner!" A few others jump up and begin clamoring for a turn. For the next hour, the girls climb on and off the bike, making sure to announce the number of calories they are burning with the regularity of train conductors .... They are nine years old.[12]

Simmons's observations are fascinating as well as fear inducing. These are nine-year-old girls participating in activities we tend to associate with older girls. I have to wonder just how many calories a nine-year-old who is "willowy as a reed" needs to work off and why she thinks she needs to worry. Even more troubling, though, is to ask how many other young girls feel and act this way.

At what age do we not have to worry about our bodies?
At the opposite end of the spectrum, older women also feel pressures to achieve the ideal feminine body. Women of all ages verbally express dissatisfaction with their bodies. My journals are filled with entries of body dissatisfaction conversations I've overheard while sitting in cafés and restaurants. While older women may no longer worry about the freshman fifteen, they appear to have adopted other concerns. Women in their thirties worry about getting back to their twenty-year-old bodies after pregnancy. Women in their forties worry about stopping or at least controlling the weight gain and middle age spread that often precedes menopause. Women in their fifties and older worry about not ending up like "those fat and dowdy grandmas we always see on TV and in movies."[13]

Again, media discourses feed into these body dissatisfaction concerns. For example, body size during and immediately following pregnancy has taken on an elevated importance in recent years. Whereas pregnancy used to be a time when a woman could let down her constant body vigilance and enjoy being "fat," it is now expected that she will continue her vigilance. This phenomenon is fed in part through the media's obsession with "Bump Watch" articles. The bump watch occurs in three phases. The first phase begins when a star appears in public with a stomach that "bumps out" instead of being completely flat. Such a telltale bump generates endless speculation that the star may be pregnant. The most obvious problem with the bump watch philosophy is that it operates under the misinformed perception that a perfectly flat stomach is normal for women, when in reality a "normal" stomach will be slightly convex. An inherent result of this presumption is that anything other than a flat stomach is presumed to indicate an unusual state—pregnancy, or if not pregnant, then fatness. During my interviews I see the internalized impact of this phenomenon when I ask women what specific parts of their body they're frustrated with. At some point most would respond like Jeanine who grabbed her stomach and screamed, "My stomach! Look at this flab." When I looked at what she was grabbing I couldn't see anything other than a little pinch of skin in her hands.

In phase two, the bump watch heightens after a pregnancy is confirmed. The media go on full time bump watch, charting how much and how quickly the bump grows. This is not necessarily new; the public has continually been obsessed with which Hollywood stars are pregnant. However, in the recent past this obsession revolved around whether the woman was married or not. Now that society is less concerned with marriage as a necessary precursor to pregnancy, the focus is on the woman's body: Is she gaining more weight? How big are her breasts? Is she not gaining enough weight?

Once the baby is delivered, phase three kicks in and the media clock starts ticking for how long it will take for the new mom to lose the baby weight. For example, the November 21, 2005 edition of *Star* magazine featured Britney Spears "post baby." The article observed how just five weeks after giving birth, Spears was already "flaunting a flat tummy."[14] A more in-depth discussion is found in the January 23, 2006 edition of *In Touch Weekly*. A five page article detailed the steps taken by Hollywood moms to achieve "amazing transformations" after delivery.[15] The article presented brief summaries of the techniques used to lose the weight, before and after pictures, and the amount of time the "amazing trans-formation" took. The examples of weight loss techniques range from Sarah Jessica Parker's "no chocolate diet" to Courtney Cox's "beach walks." Some of the more extreme examples include Kate Hudson's six hour daily workouts, Denise Richard's low carb 1300 calories per day diet, and Christine Taylor's non-exercise routine of running around after her three year old daughter. The amount of time taken to lose the bump included Michelle Williams's four weeks, Denise Richards's six weeks, and Heidi Klum's one week. Phase three media commentary creates the perception and ex-pectation that even after pregnancy, the most important thing a woman can do is lose weight—quickly.

Like pregnancy, entering middle age used to be a time when a woman could let loose, at least a little, and enjoy a little extra weight. As we have entered the twenty-first century, though, our definition of when one crosses over into middle age or old age is constantly changing. A recent survey shows that 60% of Americans believe that "the sixties are the new middle age."[16] While the full impact of this line of thinking remains to be seen, we already see an expectation of youthful appearance extending into women's forties and fifties. One of the most recent examples of this is the hit show *Desperate Housewives*.[17] The show revolves around the lives of six women, including one who is dead but provides narrative voice-over and commentary.[18] The show broke ground on many fronts, including the casting of five women over forty in leading roles. As the desperate housewives, these women received mountains of media coverage, both for the show itself and for representing the new face of middle age beauty. In itself, this type of media coverage is not surprising. However, what was surprising is that all of the women present an older version of the ideal media woman already revered and praised. The housewives appear thin like younger media ideals with relatively wrinkle free faces. Adding to the illusion that all middle age women could (should?) look like them, Bravo developed a spin-off reality show, *The Real Housewives of Orange County* featuring the real life adventures of five "real" housewives. Like their fictional counterparts, these housewives present thin and wrinkle-free examples of middle age female beauty.

Middle age and even older age women no longer have the safety net of age to look forward to as a solution to their body dissatisfaction. A recent study published in the *International Journal of Eating Disorders* focused on body image issues in women who were sixty to seventy years old.[19] The results indicated that over 80% of these women still took measures to control their weight and just over 60% of them struggled with eating disorders. These statistics nearly mirror those of young women, raising the question: Have body dissatisfaction and eating disorders now become part of the normal course of events in the life cycle of women? It would be interesting to examine if the same discourses that impact young women influence older women as well. Anecdotal evidence repeatedly demonstrates that body dissatisfaction doesn't magically disappear as one grows older. Based on my conversations, I would argue that as women age, they don't stop feeling the influence of the discourses that impact young women. If anything, more discourses are simply added into the mix. In order to fully understand the full scope of the phenomenon, further research is clearly warranted.

What can we do to stop feeling dissatisfied?

With body dissatisfaction so widespread, it often seems as if it's just part of the natural course of events—if you're born a girl, you will grow to dislike or hate your body and spend inordinate amounts of time thinking about your body and trying to change it. However, this course of events is not a given. Even though so many women live with body dissatisfaction, for example, most of them don't fall prey to eating disorders. Some girls and women find ways to move beyond a state of dissatisfaction and accept their bodies for what they are. While these women may be small in number, they present a glimmer of hope for the rest of us. Their ability to find a way to accept their bodies also begs the questions: Are we really stuck with this state of dissatisfaction? Is living within a cycle of dissatisfaction and the mirror version of hide and seek all that we can expect of our lives as women?

During my interviews, I always ask a question along these lines. I tend to get a variety of responses. Some women feel that we are in fact stuck with constant body dissatisfaction. Alice's response illustrates this perspective:

> You know, we're emotional and so we eat. Then we think that we're fat because we've eaten too much and so we go, and for emotional reasons we go and exercise. Things like that happen with women. I'm not saying that it doesn't happen with men, but because of the way that women in general are wired, we're more susceptible to that. We're definitely susceptible to the things that, not just the media but everything we see tells us to be skinny. Everything that we hear tells us to really look critically at the way that we look.

Alice's comment about the way women are "wired" alludes to a common thought about body dissatisfaction—it's just part of women's biology. The error in this way of thinking is obvious when one looks at non-Western cultures where a larger female body is prized as ideal. Despite this fact, many women like Alice still believe that women are nearly always going to feel some level of body dissatisfaction.

Alice's remarks also demonstrate the state of desperate resolution and constant longing generated through believing that women are stuck with body dissatisfaction. Angel more succinctly summarizes the feeling when she asks: "What can we do about it?" Psyche's response is even more pointed: "I don't think it's ever going to stop. It's just gonna be a vicious cycle." When we were discussing the future of the problem of body dissatisfaction, Mandi asked: "How much smaller can these people get?" As we now see more and more ideal women at the size zero mark, I have to ask the same question. Rhetorically, these women are already nothing, they are a zero. Where else can we go?

Can we really change the media machine?

Because we live within a culture of discontent and seem to be regularly struggling with our own cycles of dissatisfaction, feelings of desperation like those expressed by Psyche, Mandi, and Angel are not surprising. However, when I ask the question of what our future holds, an interesting thing occurs. The first response is usually along the lines of those in the previous section—negative and resolved to the status quo. After some discussion, though, the interview participant often begins to allow for the possibility that the future might be changeable. Isabelle, for example, initially said that "we're stuck with it for now." As we continued to talk, she suggested that perhaps we could see change and hypothesized that the key is to "find another way to portray women and another way to manipulate what a woman should be thinking, 'cause it went from the kitchen housewife stuff to into all of this." By "this" she explained that she meant super-thin sexually alluring ideal women. Isabelle explained that if we began to see more healthy versions of beauty labeled as ideal in media, then perhaps we needn't be stuck with body dissatisfaction.

Butterfly's response is similar to Isabelle's. When asked about the future, Butterfly asserted that the current state of affairs would stay this way "until someone actually makes the media wake up, which isn't going to happen." As our conversation continued, Butterfly expanded on her proposed solution:

> I daresay the moment you start to actively change the mindset in the media, it's going to take a generation, a complete generation to actually get through to the minds of, of the general population of women, to realize that being skinny is good, but it's not worth risking your health.

Notice, though, that even in discussing the need for change, Butterfly still advocates for a thin ideal when she says that "being skinny is good." Her response with its embedded ambivalence demonstrates why changing media is an easy answer but not the best answer. Real change has to come from another direction.

In recent years, we have seen some movement toward wider representation of female bodies in media discourse; however, the total number of these women who are pictured is still drastically fewer than the media ideal woman. When I ask for specific examples of models who women feel represent the ideal, I am barraged with names—Kate Moss, Giselle, Heidi Klum. When I ask for names of plus-size models, I am met with a blank stare and the occasional stumbling, "Uh, there's that one. What's her name? She's Steven Tyler's other daughter," in reference to Mia Tyler. Or I hear something such as, "There's that blond woman. She's real popular. What's her name," in reference to Emme. When I ask for examples of actresses representing the thin ideal, names come flowing out: Jennifer Aniston, Courtney Cox Arquette, Hillary Duff, Lindsay Lohan, Reese Witherspoon, Kirsten Dunst, Renee Zellweger, Nicole Kidman, Angelina Jolie, and many others. When I ask for examples of plus-size actresses, I hear the same type of stumbling responses as for the models.

Media ideals are only one small part of the complex body dissatisfaction equation. I would argue that media should be just one part of a multi-layered answer.

Toward a culture of satisfaction

I chose to open this chapter with my personal story for many reasons; one of the most important is that I want you to understand that even though I have dedicated approximately one fourth of my life to studying the phenomenon of body dissatisfaction, I still struggle with my own cycle of dissatisfaction. I am confronted daily with intimately personal reminders of what it means to be a female body in this society. Only yesterday I was smacked upside the head with the clothing conspiracy while trying, futilely, to buy a pair of jeans. For the past few years I've been wearing a low rider boot cut style of Levi's jeans. They always fit, and I don't have to deal with the horror that passes for a fitting room mirror. For whatever reason, that particular style no longer exists, so I am now left with the task of finding a new regular jean. Deciding to stick with Levi's (it's a nice easy way to make a public statement about the ridiculousness of the designer jean industry), I found a style that appeared to be similar to my old favorite. I grabbed my "size"[20] in short and medium lengths. I then grabbed an alternate style that looked cute. My dressing room results? The short length didn't button—not even close. The medium length buttoned but was so long that I could have cut off the extra material and made a matching pair of shorts. The alternate pair never made it past my upper thighs. I walked out of the store disgusted, thinking that perhaps I should have skipped the nachos appetizer with lunch.

I share this story not to depress you. I am now fully recovered from yesterday's fiasco, and after this writing session I plan to go out to purchase a pair of jeans that fit. The purpose of my story is to demonstrate how the culture of discontent and the cycle of dissatisfaction work hand in hand. Yes, we live within a culture that mandates we look and act a certain way. At the end of the day, though, there are no culture police who will arrest us for refusing to adopt these cultural standards. We ourselves are the police every time we choose to modify our actions so that we fall in line with the mandates established by the various body discourses I've discussed throughout the book. The key is to find a way to turn off this policing eye that enforces cultural mandates on ourselves and on other women.

Every woman's experience differs; there is no one solution to the problem. If you take nothing else from this book, I hope you take away the fact that body dissatisfaction as a lived phenomenon is complex and filled with various nuances of experience. With this in mind, I do not presume that I have the ultimate answer to the problem. What I offer in the following pages are suggested avenues of action that we can take to start to turn our body dissatisfaction into satisfaction. The basis of these discussions is grounded in my discussions with other women and my own research into the areas of discourse, power, and knowledge. I hope that as you read through them, you find things that you can incorporate into your own life.

We need to start small
We experience the bulk of our body dissatisfaction at an intimate, personal level. Even though we may hear the voices of others when we look in the mirror, we still face only ourselves in the reflection.

When Shirley and I discussed the future of body dissatisfaction, she shared some poignant thoughts on the issue:

> I think we have to deal with it on a personal level. We can't change reality and stuff because you can't change what other people are going to think. But if you keep it on a personal level and say, "This is who I am. This is who I will always be. I'm comfortable with it. I can accept myself. I'm good at what I do. I'm a smart person. I can do this." On a personal level, then you'll be fine.

Shirley's comments provide a solution for moving beyond the status quo: change the way you view and think about yourself. Recall that much of the cycle of dissatisfaction revolves around the constant disparaging and often distorted ways that we view our bodies. Instead of focusing on the positives, we tend to zero in on those areas that we think are most problematic. When I look at myself in the mirror, the first place I look is my midsection. My eyes then venture slightly south to my thighs. Only through a conscious effort do I remember that these two areas are only a small part of my body.

As I discussed in Chapters One through Three, the cycle of dissatisfaction involves three interrelated personal factors:

- A constant struggle with acceptance of one's body and hope for an ideal body,
- A fight to eat healthy foods,
- A fear of looking less than cute in clothes.

As individuals, we each experience these factors differently. I tend to struggle more with the clothing issue than the other two. To help you find the areas you particularly struggle with and to focus your thoughts, I've included a series of reflection questions in Appendix A. Working through these questions provides a way for you to start to gain a deeper understanding of the ways body dissatisfaction has manifested itself in your life. Thinking about these questions won't magically transport you to the point of saying, "This is what I am" and being happy with it. However, it will help you to begin to understand the kinds of changes you need to make to get to that point.

This is only the beginning. The lived experience of body dissatisfaction is more than a personal problem. It is also a social problem indicative of systemic discourses mandating appropriate appearance and behavior for women. Because the female body is a social body and we as individuals are social beings, long-term change must move beyond the merely personal. We need to work with each other.

Throughout this project I've noticed that my experiences with my personal feelings of body dissatisfaction have changed. The more I talk with other women, the better I feel. I still have those cringing moments when I catch a glimpse of my ass under the harsh lighting of a fitting room. In general, though, I find that I no longer obsess over my body. I will sometimes go for days without even thinking about it. I've also come to realize how much time I've wasted on my unnecessary and futile quest for the ideal tall and skinny body. With my short and stocky frame, this ideal is just physiologically impossible. Even though I still find it difficult to say that I am completely satisfied with my body, the simple act of talking with other women has made a significant change in my overall feelings.

Other women involved in this project have expressed similar feelings. Remember Isabelle who in the Introduction fretted over being a size two instead of a zero? During our discussions of competition, she had asserted that all women are her "enemy." At the time I made a notation of how destructive this line of thinking seemed. Yet toward the end of our conversation she began to change her viewpoint and said, "I feel like in talking about it, it gives it recognition. It makes me think that yeah that's what I've been thinking." She resolved to open similar conversations with her friends. Isabelle's vow to discuss body dissatisfaction issues with other women was especially surprising. Clearly her change is a drastic reversal of thinking and a perfect example of how the power of our interpersonal discourse can be used to reverse some of those larger body discourses.

Annette also advocated using the power of friendship:

> "I think one of the good things is friendships. I think it ties with body image because I think that friends can help each other individually to not worry so much about it."

Annette's remarks here provide a way to blend the personal with the interpersonal. While body dissatisfaction is a complex and deeply held way of experiencing life, it is not the only way. Instead of adding to the pressures by battling with other women, we can turn to them to help us battle the larger problems that precipitate the body dissatisfaction phenomenon. We can help each other to find other ways of experiencing our bodies and our lives in general.

Taking the idea of using friendships for our benefit in the body dissatisfaction war, Butterfly proposed a type of grassroots consciousness-raising based on the movie "Pay it Forward."[21] In the movie, a young boy is given an assignment to come up with an idea that will improve mankind. He decides to do good deeds for three people. If they then "pay it forward" to three other people, positive changes will occur. Using this model, Butterfly proposed the following:

> If you find three females and you just say you know what, they're your friends. I mean it could be three of your friends right now. And you do something nice for them and you all start to either have coffee or something like that where you can talk about yourself and say, "This is who I am." This isn't a bitch session where you talk about how you had a terrible week or this happened to me. Instead, you say, "This is what makes me, me." And then everybody found two more friends and did the same thing, I wonder if that would help us become stronger individuals?

Notice that Butterfly focuses on finding a way to say, "This is who I am," the exact same words that Shirley used in her proposal for change. I find it fascinating that both women locked onto the importance of saying these specific words. Not only had Butterfly and Shirley never met, but I met with each of them over a period of three years and they live over seven hundred miles apart. Perhaps these five words are the true key to eradicating body dissatisfaction.

Butterfly's pay it forward idea could be a way to get more of us to say, and believe, that this is who I am and how I look, and I like it. Although telling three friends may not result in widespread societal change, it is a tangible way to "help us become stronger." It is a start. In the words of Arlo Guthrie, "If three people do it, they may think it's an organization ... and if fifty people do it, it's a movement."[22] In the next section, I highlight the discussion questions and activities found in Appendix B. These provide one way with which to open a body dissatisfaction discussion with each other.

We need to teach others
In order to effect long term change, we need an approach that takes Butterfly's pay-it-forward idea and applies it in a more organized format. While researching social and cultural discourses for Chapter Eight, I became fascinated with the model presented by religious

discourse. One biblical mandate for religious femininity is that older women are to "train the younger women."[23] I think we can use the idea of training younger women to our benefit in the body dissatisfaction wars. Perhaps one of the most important, and arguably most difficult, things to do is to act as role models that young girls can emulate. Instead of involving young girls in our own body dissatisfaction battles or in crazy dieting schemes, we can help them develop healthy eating behaviors—no matter what their bodies look like. We can help them understand that it's fine to splurge once in awhile without feeling guilty. Yes, extra chocolate or cream cheese might cause you to gain weight, but eaten in moderation as part of an otherwise healthy diet, they're fine. I've spoken with a number of young women who have "adopted" younger girls to mentor. The women find that they often learn as much as their younger charges. They also find that they worry less about their own body dissatisfaction when they are faced with the distinct possibility that their actions may be emulated by a young girl who looks up to them. Though I see this as a small step, I like to envision the possibilities of armies of young women mentoring young girls. The progressive social change that could emanate from such a mass of positive body energy is unlimited.

In a related vein, we can, and should, model friendly behavior toward other women instead of the battling model we now tend to use. Instead of complaining about skinny models or stars, we can acknowledge that their beauty is just one of many ways to be beautiful. We can even acknowledge that despite all of the discourses saying otherwise, it may not even be the best type of beauty. I would caution against taking this to the extreme of saying that skinny girls are ugly or are bitches or using similar negative epithets.[24] While this type of bashing may provide a momentary emotional release, the long-term damage it creates is not worth it. This type of beauty bashing merely reinforces the methods used in creating the existing dichotomy that indicates skinny is beautiful and everything else is not.

An affirmative action that we can each take and implement immediately is to ban the skinny greeting with each other. Instead of commenting on how good our friend looks after losing weight, we should just tell her that she looks good and healthy. Many of my friends and I have started doing this, and it takes time to unlearn the emotional baggage of the skinny greeting. After losing much of the weight I had gained following my father's death, I found myself wanting that verbal acknowledgement of my change; I wanted to know that others noticed the change. But I had to remind myself that as a person, I am much more than my weight. This is yet another thing that we can help young girls understand. If we compliment them on things other than their beauty, we can help them understand that they are more, much more, than their bodies. We can help them understand that their destiny is theirs and is not wholly contingent on their looks.

As a teacher, I can attest first hand to the power of education in helping to open individuals' eyes to the various discourses that influence their lives. In my classroom, I try not to force feed my students but to guide them into discovery. For example, the media aversion project I mentioned in an earlier chapter allows students to see firsthand how many myriad ways media discourses impact them. I could just as easily make this point through a lecture with multiple examples; however, the experiential impact of the aversion project personalizes the point. Students have shared with me their conclusion that trying to avoid media for one week was not only the hardest assignment of their college career but the one that had the most lasting impact on their daily lives. Since I first created the assignment four years ago, I've heard from several students that they adapted it for their roommates or for their dorms.

Understanding the pervasiveness of media discourse is only one thing that we can do in the body dissatisfaction battle. We also need to address specific body discourses. In my classes, when I point out the disparity between the average model's size at five feet eleven inches, 117 pounds and the average woman's size at five feet four inches, 145 pounds, my students are stunned. As a future middle school teacher, Annette plans to incorporate this type of information into her classroom:

> I just like the idea of being able to educate students to realize that there is not one ideal body image and to disregard what advertising and the media shows us as ideal. I'd like to show the facts that these models are anorexic or have signs of anorexia because of how low they are from the normal weight or whatever.

Annette told me that when she used this information during her student teaching, her students enjoyed it and responded enthusiastically to it. Many of them began openly discussing the pressures they were already feeling.

In addition to teaching young girls, we can also teach each other. In Appendix B, I've included activities designed to be used in groups. While they will work in a classroom, they need not be limited to such a formal environment. Any group of women can get together and work with the activities and form a Bitchin' Bodies Bitch group—much like a Stitch 'n' Bitch group but with body dissatisfaction as the focus instead of knitting or crocheting. Opening and maintaining a body dissatisfaction dialogue in a group like this will work to create an alternative body discourse, one that resists the existing mandates.

In my experience, these types of group exchanges prove enlightening and enriching for all involved. The meeting usually begins as a traditional bitch session with complaints covering all of the issues affecting women's lives today. Generally there comes a moment when the feeling of the room changes, though, and bitching turns to questioning. People start asking why these situations exist. More importantly, they ask what we can do to change them. When this happens, a permanent shift occurs where women change from being passive bodies that have discourses inscribed on them to active bodies that inscribe. The possibilities for change with such a shift are limitless.

Maybe all this seems idealistic.
Maybe it seems unrealistic.
Maybe it is.
But it's time to do something other than bitch.
It's time to take back what a bitchin' body looks like.
It's time for each of us to revel in our bitchin' bodies.
And it's time for us to bitch about something else.

Appendix A:

Bitchin' back

Bitchin' back:
Personal reflection questions

Included in this appendix are a number of reflection questions that will help you to understand the various ways that you personally experience body dissatisfaction in your life. The goal with these questions is to get you to start bitchin' back. Instead of just being a bitchin' body, be a body that bitches about why we're still struggling with body dissatisfaction in the twenty-first century. There is no one way to start bitchin' back. My hope is that with these questions, you'll find a way to bitch back and take back your experiences of your body.

To get the most benefit out of these questions, I suggest that you start a Bitchin' Back journal. While you read through each chapter, you can record the various thoughts that come to mind, questions that the reading prompts, and areas where you disagree with me. Within each chapter I have incorporated numerous examples. For each one example that made the cut, there are at least ten that did not. In your journal, you can keep track of other examples that you see in your life. These will help you come to a deeper understanding of the material.

Additionally, I suggest that you record all of your reflections in the journal. As you progress through these questions you may find yourself wanting to return to previous reflections. You may also find yourself changing your thoughts from previous questions. This type of recursive process is normal. As you think about these issues more, you will probably find yourself questioning things that you thought were written in stone. Allow yourself the opportunity to grow with your thoughts. Even after spending years thinking about and working with this material, I still find myself rethinking earlier conclusions.

In answering each question, be as thorough as possible. Allow yourself plenty of time to reflect on the concepts. I find that my best insights occur when I don't dwell on the matter. If I take a walk, do yoga, or engage in some other unrelated activity, my mind works through the issue on its own. The slight physical distraction allows my mind to process through the material without my consciously attempting to direct or edit the thoughts. If you find that when you approach a reflection question your thoughts are jumbled or nothing comes to mind, allow yourself to take a break. Do something different. You'll probably be surprised at how quickly your jumbled thoughts crystallize.

To gain the most benefits from the reflections, be honest with yourself. Don't censor or edit your writing. Don't try to find the "right" answer. Don't worry about the style or way that you are recording your answers. Write whatever comes to mind. Just sit down and let yourself go. It takes conscious dedication to write like this, but in the end you'll find that it's worth the effort.

When I write, I use what I jokingly call the vomit/clean-up method. I sit down and write everything that comes to mind—the vomit. I then set the vomit aside and do something else. When I return to the vomit, I read through it and make changes—the clean-up. For example, numerous times while working on this book I found myself struggling with how to say something. I would make several attempts only to find that what I had written was boring, confusing, or just plain bad. After several futile and frustrating attempts, I would finally remember what I tell my students—just write. I would then sit down, vomit out everything in my mind, and put it aside. Time after time, I found that when I returned to clean up my vomit, my writings weren't as messy as I'd imagined. With very little clean-up, many of them were actually quite good. In fact, many of the best parts of the book are cleaned up vomit.

Just as there are no "right" answers to these questions, there is no "right" way to work through them. I have labeled each Reflection Goal so as to indicate the chapter that it coincides with. You may choose to work on each goal in this linear manner, or you may choose to jump around as you see fit. Do what works best for you. There is no set time limit to complete each Reflection Goal. Work at your own pace. More than anything else, remember that the purpose of completing these reflection goals is to help you find how you experience your body dissatisfaction.

Reflection Goal Introduction:
Establish a baseline of your current body dissatisfaction thoughts and practices.

- Do you feel dissatisfied with the size and/or shape of your body? On a scale of one to ten with one being very little and ten being all of the time, how often do you think about your body?
- Do you think that you live your life based on cultural norms and expectations? Why or why not?
- Do you think that you are influenced by the way women are presented in media? Why or why not?
- Do you think that you are influenced by the things other people say about your body? About the bodies of other women? Why do you think this is?
- Do you think that body dissatisfaction is just a natural part of women's existence that we're stuck with? Why or why not?
- As you continue to work through the remaining Reflection Goals, periodically return to the answers you've recorded so far. Keep track of how and when your feelings change.

Reflection Goal 1:
Determine the specific ways that you experience body dissatisfaction.

- Without thinking about it, quickly list the specific areas of your body that you are dissatisfied with. Why do you think these areas bother you?
- Look at yourself in a full-length mirror. Do you find yourself looking at your whole body or focusing on those areas you listed in the previous question?
- Think about the women in your family. How would you describe their bodies? Are there any similar traits? Now consider your body in light of this information, are the areas you focus on as problematic part of your genetic heritage?
- For at least one week, keep track of how you view and think about other women's bodies. Do you find yourself comparing yourself to them and/or determining where they would fall on the body continuum?

Reflection Goal 2:
Determine your eating habits and consider whether you might be experiencing disordered eating or an eating disorder.

- Do you find yourself monitoring what you eat and worrying that you've eaten too much?
- Do you find yourself making food bargains with yourself? For example, if I don't put butter on my baked potato and take a thirty-minute walk tonight, then I can have dessert?
- Do you and your friends practice the skinny greeting? Do you find yourself looking forward to or waiting for that verbal acknowledgement?
- Return to the list of behaviors associated with anorexia and bulimia; honestly evaluate if you find yourself participating in any of these. If you find yourself exhibiting more than a couple of these behaviors, please consider talking to someone. (I've provided a list of places you can turn to in order to find help in Appendix C.)
- Return to the list of physical indicators of anorexia and bulimia; honestly evaluate if you find any of these present in your body. If you find more than a couple of these symptoms, please consider talking to a doctor or other health professional soon. (I've provided a list of places you can turn to find help in Appendix C.)

Reflection Goal 3:
Determine how you feel about clothes and clothing sizes.

- When you get dressed in the morning, do you find yourself picking your clothes based on what you have to do for the day, how your clothes make you feel, or some combination of both?
- Make a list of all of the different sizes of clothes that fit and are currently in your closet. Do you notice a predominance of one size or are the numbers all over the board?
- Think about how you evaluate other women's clothing. Do you find yourself thinking they are sluts based on the fit and/or cut of their clothes?
- Do you find that you make clothing judgments based on the size

of the individual garment? For example, if you found a pair of jeans that you loved in terms of style and cut but found that you had to purchase them in a size two sizes larger than what you normally wear, would you immediately snap them up, hesitate, or forego purchasing them?

• The next time you try on new clothes, try to forget about the sizes—yes, it's hard to do this. When you look in the mirror, focus on the fit and appearance of the clothes. If a larger size would look better, try it on. Reflect on how this activity makes you feel.

Reflection Goal 4:
Determine how your opinion of your body is influenced by your parents and other relatives.

• Reflect upon the food practices in your childhood home. Were there any dominant practices or mandates? For example, were certain foods banned? Was there a back and forth practice of indulgence and moderation?

• For one week, keep track of your eating practices. It's less important to record what you eat than the ways you eat it and the things you think about when eating it. Consider these practices in light of those in your childhood home. Do you see any similarities?

• If you find that you are recreating negative practices from your past, formulate a plan of change. Think about things that you can do to break this cycle.

• Make a list of comments that relatives have made about your body. This may be emotionally difficult, but it is a necessary step in understanding your experiences of your body dissatisfaction.

• Compare this list to the one you made for Reflection Goal 2 about areas of your body you are dissatisfied with. How do your thoughts about your body reflect these comments?

• If you see overlap between the two lists, think of ways that you can change this cycle of influence and move beyond the limitations of the comments.

Reflection Goal 5:
Determine how your opinion of your body is influenced by other women.

- Think about how you feel about having other women as friends, trusting other women, etc. Make a list of all the words, phrases, and thoughts that come to mind. Don't limit or censor yourself.
- Objectively critique your list and add to it the reasons why you think these things.
- Think about the women in your life. Do they embody the traits you listed? If not, why do you still think these traits are important?
- For one week, track instances of Body Shape Discourse in your life. I recommend that you note the people with whom you are talking, the basic topic of the discourse, and the context within which it occurs, in addition to any other information you think will be important.
- Look for patterns in your practices of Body Shape Discourse. Do you see questions, statements or a mix of both? Do you find that certain topics are raised more frequently than others? Do you find that certain friends participate in Body Shape Discourse more frequently than others?
- The next time you find yourself participating in Body Shape Discourse, stop and think about how it makes you feel. Do you find that this is the most productive form of discourse you could be participating in at this moment? If not, change it. Instead of continuing to participate in Body Shape Discourse discuss the discourse itself. Create a "No Body Shape Discourse" with this friend in which you both promise to stop the cycle of discourse. Make a pact with the friend you are talking with to hold each other accountable for maintaining this promise.

Reflection Goal 6:
Determine how your opinion of your body is influenced by comments from guys.

- Think about the guys that you regularly interact with—friends, brothers, other relatives, etc. Reflect on how they view and discuss other women's bodies. Do you find that their comments tend to fall into certain categories or patterns?

- For one week, keep track of the comments that you hear guys make about women's bodies. Include comments that are made directly to you and those you may overhear. As part of your records, note how you feel upon hearing the comments. Reflect on the list of comments you made and look for patterns.
- Reflect on the notes you made about your feelings. Do you find any patterns? For example, do certain kinds of comments tend to evoke certain feelings? Look for connections between the ways that you perceive your body and your list of feelings.
- If you are involved in a romantic relationship with a guy, reflect on the things that your boyfriend says to you about your body, clothing, and eating habits. Be honest. Do you find that your boyfriend makes negative comments? Does he create an expectation for what your body should look like? If so, consider his comments in connection with the ways you feel about your body. Do you find that the two overlap?
- If you find that a guy is adding to your feelings of body dissatisfaction, reflect on the relationship itself. Is this a positive relationship? Consider discussing with the guy how his comments influence you and make you feel. If you find that he is unwilling to change his discourse, consider if this is a relationship worth continuing.

Reflection Goal 7:
Determine how your perception of your appearance is impacted by media ideals.

- Make a list of all of the media women who you think embody the ideal in appearance. For each woman on the list, explain the specific aspects of her appearance that are ideal. Put this list aside for now.
- Make a detailed list of all the things you like and dislike about your appearance. For each entry, include a brief explanation of why you like it or dislike it.
- Take your two lists and compare them. Where do you see the

ideals in your first list recreated in your list of your likes and
dislikes?

- Return to your list of dislikes and re-evaluate them. Are the
reasons you listed an accurate reflection of the way you look or
are they a reflection of how you think you should look?
- Train yourself to become a more critical consumer of media
messages. The next time you find yourself admiring a picture
of a media woman, think about all of the "work" that has gone
into creating her image. Try to remember that even most ideal
media women don't look the same in everyday life as they do
in their media world.

Reflection Goal 8:
*Find the "traditions" and other cultural norms that influence your
everyday life.*

- We often dismiss parts of our experiences by saying, "they're
just normal" or "that's just the way it is." What things about
women do you consider to be normal?
- For each item on your list, determine why you think it is normal.
Include specific reasons, not just general statements.
- Working from your list of specific reasons, try to determine
what cultural institutions, both formal and informal, influence
each reason.
- Think about every woman you've met in your life. Does each one
act in the "normal" ways you listed above? If not, why? (Saying
that she's abnormal or just weird doesn't count.)
- Why do you think these things have developed as cultural
norms? Are these norms good, bad, or both? Why?
- Divide the list into two columns—positive and negative. Are
there any common themes present in each list? Why do you
think these themes are so popular?
- Looking over your lists, do you think that these items are an
accurate reflection of the women you know? What traits are
missing from your lists?
- How and where do you see these items having an impact on
your life and identity?

Reflection Goal 9:
Formulate a plan of action for your life.

- Go back to your reflections from the Introduction and Chapter 1. Reread them and see if and how your thinking has changed since then. Why do you think this is?
- Review your collection of reflections and look for the patterns that are specific to your life.
- Question your interactions with cultural discourses. Using the patterns you identified above, find the cultural discourses that most influence your life. Determine the discourses that are exerting a constraining force on your life. How can you change your interactions with these discourses so that you have more control?
- Question your interactions with media discourses. Using the patterns you identified above, find the media discourses that most influence your life. Determine the discourses that are exerting a constraining force on your life. How can you change your interactions with these discourses so that you have more control?
- How can you change your interactions with other women so that you are not simply reproducing cultural norms?
- The next time that you find yourself dishing with a friend, take a few minutes and reflect on the situation. Why are you focusing on these issues? What are the underlying discourses influencing the situation?
- What affirmative steps can you take to help change the way other women experience body dissatisfaction in their lives?
- Find a group of friends or other women in your life and form a Bitchin' Back group. Together, work through the Reflection Activities in Appendix B.

Appendix B:

Bitchin' back together

Bitchin' back together:
Group activites and discussion questions

This appendix brings together a collection of activities and discussion questions for use in small groups. They are designed for use with other people—your friends, family members, book clubs, classes, or other groups you are a member of; however, they will also be helpful if you do the activities on your own. If you are working in a group and find that time is an issue, try dividing your group into smaller groups and assign each one a different activity. Each group can then summarize their findings to the larger group. If you are keeping a Bitchin' Back journal, I recommend that you use this to record your answers and thoughts on the questions. Additionally, your group may want to use some sort of white board or large tablet to help organize group responses.

It is not necessary that individual members complete the personal reflection questions and activities found in Appendix A before moving on to these questions and activities. You may find that working back and forth between the appendices works best for you. Or you may find that doing one set of activities before the others is a better approach. I encourage you to experiment and figure out what works best for you. Remember that the purpose of these questions and activities is to help you come to a great understanding of your personal experiences of body dissatisfaction and body discourses.

I've divided the activities by section of the book instead of individual chapters. Because so much of the way we experience body dissatisfaction is personal, there will be slight variances across individuals. I find that focusing on the larger issues covered in the sections creates more avenues of discussion for groups. However, if your group is particularly close to each other and comfortable with more personal disclosures, you may want to incorporate some or all of the personal reflection activities into your group discussion.

Introduction activities

- As a group, discuss the idea of cultural norms and media depictions of women and how they influence our everyday experiences. Discuss ways that cultural norms influence your lives. Discuss the predominant appearance and behavior traits of the women you see presented throughout media. Think about your activities with your friends and as a group; do you spend time bitchin' about your body, and/or the bodies and appearances of other women?
- Remember that this is merely an introduction to the rest of the book. You may want to ask someone to record the group's answers so that you can refer back to them in the future.
- Make a list of goals for the group. I recommend that you incorporate an element of socializing into each group meeting. Getting together to discuss these issues should not become a chore or a job; therefore, find a way to blend more serious discussion with more lighthearted issues.
- Many of the issues that you will be discussing may evoke strong feelings and emotions. Remember that a distinct component of body dissatisfaction discourses involves an element of competition and battling with other women. Some conflict is good and should be fostered. Through conflict we move forward to change. However, finding a balance between productive conflict and outright battling can be difficult to achieve. I suggest that the group establish a list of meeting rules or a code of conduct. Declare the space of your group meetings a friendly space and hold each other accountable for maintaining this friendly atmosphere.

Personal unit activities

- Of all the units in the book, this one probably presents the most difficult material to introduce into a group environment. One way to do this is to find a way to combine discussion with bonding. An interesting way to achieve this is through the creation of a group Dissatisfaction Dance.[1] Have each group member think about the specific parts of her body that she would like to change and how she would like them changed. Each member should then physically enact one change while walking around the room. For example, if you would like your breasts to have more cleavage you would use your hands to raise them and push them up and out. After a set amount of time, one or two minutes, have each member add in another physical change while maintaining the first. You can keep adding changes until it becomes physically impossible to function and move around the room.

Questions to Consider:
1. What are your first impressions of seeing body dissatisfaction enacted en masse?
2. Discuss the frustrations or problems that you experienced in trying to turn your desired changes into a dance.
3. As a group, generate a list of the body parts each member wanted to change. Include as part of this list the desired change. Discuss similarities between the desired changes. Why do you think it is that so many of you wish for the same thing? What does this mean in terms of body dissatisfaction discourse?

Interpersonal unit activities

• For one week before the meeting, keep track of all instances of Body Shape Discourse that you find yourself participating in. Record both declarative examples and questions. (Note: This task may prove to be quite cumbersome as Body Shape Discourse is much more prevalent than we realize. You may choose to do this exercise for a shorter length of time.) For each instance, record the context, the people speaking, and the circumstances of the conversation. At your meeting, have each member share her list with the group. If the lists are too lengthy, as they very well may be, have each member divide her individual items into categories. A summary of each category can then be shared with the group.

Questions to Consider:
1. Are there certain types of Body Shape Discourse that are more prevalent than others? Why do you think this is?

2.   Are there specific patterns in the context or circumstances of Body Shape Discourse? If so, what do you think it is about these things that foster Body Shape Discourse?
3.   What cultural and media discourses are being played out through Body Shape Discourse?
4.   Why do you think Body Shape Discourse is a common form of discourse in women's friendships?
5.   What are more productive ways to discuss these issues?

- Brainstorm the ways that body discourse from guys has influenced individual group members. You may want to work in groups of 2-3 to come up with a list of specific examples of comments that guys have made to individual members. As a group look for similarities across comments.

Questions to Consider:
1.   Are there certain comments or remarks that are more prevalent than others?
2.   Are there specific patterns in the context or circumstances of these comments?
3.   Why do you think that these comments are allowed to pass in society as an acceptable way of communicating?
4.   Generate a list of specific things that group members can say when confronted with comments like these.

- Repeat the previous activity focusing on comments from relatives.
- Generate a list of things you can do as an individual to educate other women about how their discourse controls themselves and other women. Generate a similar list of things you can do as a group.

Media/Culture unit activities
- As a group, view a recent film, television episode, or reality show together to examine how Body Shape Discourse in various forms is presented. Pay particular attention to how characters control each other and themselves through this discourse. Both kinds of dishing are depicted through media.

Questions to Consider:
(Note that you may want to divide into two groups and have one group focus on Body Shape Discourse and the other focus on control. You can work individually and then regroup to discuss your conclusions.)

1. Categorize the specific issues that are part of the discourse. Are certain issues more popular than others? Why do you think this is?
2. Are there specific patterns in the context or circumstances of how the discourse arises and is presented? If so, why do you think this is?
3. What cultural discourses are displayed through these representations of Body Shape Discourse?
4. How do you think media representations of Body Shape Discourse tacitly teach us to use it? Why do you think this is?
5. Categorize the types of control that are depicted. Are certain types more popular than others? Why do you think this is?
6. Are there specific patterns in the context or circumstances of how instances of control arise and are presented? If so, why do you think this is?
7. What cultural discourses are displayed and reinforced through these representations?
8. How do you think media representations of control tacitly teach us and encourage us to control each other? Why do you think this is?
9. What general conclusions about Body Shape Discourse and control discourses can you draw from this activity?

(Note that each of the following activities involve the use of magazines. They would, however, work equally well with films or television shows. They could also be done in one meeting by dividing into smaller groups.)

• Bring several recent women's magazines to the meeting (*Vogue, Redbook, Jane,* etc.). Divide into pairs and give each pair at least two magazines to work with. Have each pair look through the magazines for examples of ideal feminine beauty. Be sure and look at all parts of the magazines—fashion layouts, stories, ads, etc. Have each pair share their finds with the rest of the group.

Questions to Consider:
1. Make a list of all of the physical traits that are displayed by your examples. What traits are more prevalent than others? Why do you think this is?
2. Pick a few of the examples and analyze how they are presented on the page—clothing, hair, makeup, how they are posed individually and in connection with others on the page, etc. Are they depicted in a positive or negative manner? Why do you think this is?
3. How do these examples recreate cultural expectations for female beauty? How do they change these expectations?
4. Compare these examples to the members of your group and other women that you know. Are the examples an accurate reflection of the women you know? Why do you think this is?

•   Repeat the above activity but have each pair look through the magazines for examples of feminine beauty that differ from the ideal. Be sure and look at all parts of the magazines—fashion layouts, stories, ads, etc. Have each pair share their finds with the rest of the group.

Questions to Consider:
1. Make a list of all of the physical traits that are displayed by your examples. What traits are more prevalent than others? Why do you think this is?
2. Pick a few of the examples and analyze how they are presented on the page—clothing, hair, makeup, how they are posed individually and in connection with others on the page, etc. Are they depicted in a positive or negative manner? Why do you think this is?
3. How do these examples deviate from cultural expectations for female beauty? How do they recreate these expectations?
4. Compare these examples to the members of your group and other women that you know. Are the examples an accurate reflection of the women you know? Why do you think this is?

•   Repeat the above activity but have each partner look through the magazines to find examples of women who look like herself and like her partner. Be sure and look at all parts of the magazines—fashion layouts, stories, ads, etc. Have each woman share her examples with her partner. Discuss how the examples chosen for yourself compare with those chosen by your partner.

Questions to Consider:
1. Did you have any problems finding representative examples? Why do you think this is?
2. Discuss the perceptions you have of your body versus the reality of how your body looks to your partner. Why do you think this is?
3. How do our individual perceptions of ourselves reflect cultural and media discourses?
4. What specific things can we do to bring our perception closer to our reality?

- As a final "debriefing" activity, reflect on what can you do as an individual to educate others about the role and impact of media presentations of ideal beauty? As a group?

Reflection Goal: *Find the "traditions" and other cultural norms that influence your everyday life.*

- Make a list of the code words that we use to label something as a norm. For example, women are housewives because historically they always have been.

Questions to Consider:
1. How do these words work to sanction the norm in question?
2. What is the power in the use of these words? For example, if a wife is not a housewife, what do we think of her?

- For one week before your meeting, track all of the cultural norms you experience. Be alert as these norms can and do pop up anywhere—in everyday conversations, in magazines and newspapers, in the news and even in entertaining pastimes like sit-coms and movies. At your meeting, have each member share her list with the group. If the lists are too lengthy, as they very well may be, have each member divide her individual items into categories. A summary of each category can then be shared with the group.

Questions to Consider:
1. Are there certain norms that are more prevalent than others? If so, do they relate to a certain aspect of everyday life?
2. Why do you think these norms are important in today's society?
3. How is language used to communicate these norms?
4. Are these norms good, bad or both? Why?

*   What can you do as an individual to educate others about cultural norms? As a group?

Bitchin' Back activities
*   Develop an action plan for things that you can do to change the way that media and cultural discourses influence your group interactions. What specific things can you change about the way that you communicate with each other so as to avoid recreating cultural norms?
*   What specific things can you do as a group to help others learn about the influences of cultural, media, and personal discourses in their lives?

Appendix C:

Resources

Resources

There exists a wealth of information on body dissatisfaction, eating disorders, and other issues covered in this book. Instead of attempting to provide a comprehensive resource, I have compiled a selected list. Use these as a starting point to learn more about the particular aspects of body dissatisfaction discourse that interest or intrigue you.

Organizations

- **National Eating Disorders Association (NEDA)**
  603 Stewart St, Suite 803
  Seattle, WA 98101
  Business Office: (206) 382-3587
  Toll Free hotline: (800) 931-2237
  E-mail contact: info@NationalEatingDisorders.org
  Website: www.nationaleatingdisorders.org

- **National Association of Anorexia Nervosa and Associated Disorders (ANAD)**
  PO Box 7
  Highland Park, IL 60035
  Toll Free hotline (847) 831-3438
  E-mail contact: anad20@aol.com
  Website: www.anad.org

- **CampusBlues.com**
  328 Monomoscoy Rd., Suite 100
  Mashpee, MA 06249
  E-mail contact: connect@reconnectingu.com
  Website: www.campusblues.com

- **Finding Balance**
  PO Box 284
  Franklin, TN 37065
  E-mail contact: feedback@findingbalance.com
  Website: www.findingbalance.com

- **Eating Disorders Anonymous (EDA)**
  E-mail contact: info@eatingdisordersanonymous.org
  Website: www.eatingdisordersanonymous.org

- **Eating Disorders Shared Awareness (EDSA)**
  (Something fishy)
  E-mail contact: feedback@something-fishy.com
  Website: www.something-fishy.org

- **Fat!So?**
  PO Box 423464
  San Francisco, CA 94142
  E-mail contact: marilyn@fatso.com
  Website: www.fatso.com

- **National Association to Advance Fat Acceptance (NAAFA)**
  PO Box 22510
  Oakland, CA 94609
  (916) 558-6880
  E-mail contact: marilyn_wann@naafa.org
  Website: www.naafa.org

- **The Media Watchdog Program**
  603 Stewart St., Suite 803
  Seattle, WA 98101
  Business office: (206) 382-3587
  Toll Free hotline: (800) 931-2237
  E-mail contact: watchdog@NationalEatingDisorders.org
  Website: www.nationaleatingdisorders.org/programs-events
  media-watchdog.php

- **Body Image and Health Task Force**
  E-mail contact: rudd.1@osu.edu
  Website: www.hec.osu.edu/bitf

- **Eating Disorder Referral and Information Center**
    E-mail contact: edreferral@aol.com
    Website: www.edreferral.com

- **Media Awareness Network**
    1500 Merivale Rd., 3rd Floor
    Ottawa, Ontario Canada K2E 6Z5
    E-mail contact: info@media-awareness.ca
    Website: www.media-awareness.ca

Selected Media

(Note this is nowhere close to an exhaustive list of print resources available. This should be enough to get you started, though.)

Books

- Alison Abner, and Linda Vilarosa, *Finding Our Way: The Teen Girls' Survival Guide,* (New York: Harper, Collins, 1995).

- Sandra Lee Bartky, *Femininity and Domination: Studies in the Phenomenology of Oppression,* (New York: Routledge, 1990).

- Boston Women's Health Book Collective, *Our Bodies, Ourselves: A New Edition for a New Era,* (New York: W. W. Norton, 2005).

- Susan Bordo, *Unbearable Weight: Feminism, Western Culture, and the Body,* (Berkeley: University of California Press, 1993, 2004).

- Laura S. Brown and Esther Rothblum, *Overcoming Fear of Fat,* (Binghamton: Harrington Park Press, 1989).

- Joan Jacobs Brumberg, *The Body Project: An Intimate History of American Girls,* (New York: Vintage, 1997).

- Thomas F. Cash, Ph.D., *The Body Image Workbook: An 8-Step Program for Learning to Like Your Looks,* (Oakland, CA: New Harbinger Publications, 1997, 2008).

- Wendy Chapkis, *Beauty Secrets: Women and the Politics of Appearance,* (London: The Women's Press, 1986).
- Mary Anne Cohen, *French Toast for Breakfast,* (Carlsbad, CA: Gurze Books, 1995).

- Kaz Cooke, *Real Gorgeous: The Truth about Body and Beauty,* (New York: W. W. Norton, 1996).

- Linda W. Craighead, *The Appetite Awareness Workbook: How to Listen to Your Body and Overcome Bingeing, Overeating, and Obsession with Food,* (Oakland, CA: New Harbinger Publications, 2006).

- Susan J. Douglas, *Where the Girls Are: Growing Up Female with the Mass Media,* (New York: Times Books, 1994).

- Ophira Edut, ed., *Body Outlaws: Young Women Write about Body Image and Identity,* (Seattle: Seal Press, 1998).

- Barbara Ehrenreich and Deidre English, *For Her Own Good: 150 years of the Experts' Advice to Women,* (New York: Anchor, 1978, 1989, 2005).

- Viola Fodor, *Desperately Seeking Self,* (Carlsbad, CA: Gurze Books, 1997).

- Rita Freedman, *Bodylove: Learning to Like our Looks—and Ourselves,* (New York: Harper & Row, 1990, 2002).

- Debra L. Gimlin, *Body Work: Beauty and Self Image in American Culture,* (Berkeley: University of California Press, 2002).

- Sarah Grogan, *Body Image: Understanding Body Dissatisfaction in Men, Women, and Children,* (London: Routledge, 1998, 2007).

- Sharelene Hesse-Biber, *Am I Thin Enough Yet?* (New York: Oxford University Press USA, 1997).

- Jean Kilbourne, *Can't Buy My Love: How Advertising Changes the Way We Think and Feel,* (New York: Touchstone, 1999).

- Andrea LoBue and Masea Marcus, *The Don't Diet, Live-It! Workbook: Healing Food, Weight, and Body Issues,* (Carlsbad, CA: Gurze Books, 1999).

- Valerie Rainon McManus, *A Look in the Mirror: Freeing Yourself from the Body Image Blues,* (Washington, D.C.: Child & Family Press, 2004).

- Rebecca Ruggles Radcliffe, *Dance Naked in Your Living Room: Handling Stress and Finding Joy,* (Minneapolis: Eaze, 1997).

- Marilyn Wann, *Fat!So?,* (Berkeley, CA: Ten Speed Press, 1998).

- Naomi Wolf, *The Beauty Myth: How Images of Beauty are Used Against Women,* (New York: Anchor, 1991, 2002).

Notes

Introduction: Bitchin' bodies bitchin'

1   Though not specifically limited to college age women, an interesting study in this area can be found at: Marlene B. Schwartz, Lenny R. Vartanian, Brian A. Nosek, and Kelly D. Brownell, "The Influence of One's Own Body Weight on Implicit and Explicit Anti-fat Bias" *Obesity* 14 (2006): 440–448. In the study the researchers surveyed over 4,000 people to determine what they would be willing to do in order to avoid being obese. 46% of the respondents said that they would give up a year of their life, 445.

2   Candace Kurth, Dean D. Krahn, Karen Nairn, Adam Drewnowski, "The Severity of Dieting and Bingeing Behaviors in College Women: Interview Validation of Survey Data". *The Journal of Psychiatric Research* 29 (1995): 211–225.

3   For a more detailed discussion of this phenomenon see L. Smolak, *National Eating Disorders Association/Next door Neighbors Puppet Guide Book* (1996).

4   In her 1989 book, *Composing a Life,* Mary Catherine Bateson explores the pivotal role of stories in helping us "compose" our lives. Through examining the life stories of herself and five friends, she illustrates how "storytelling is fundamental to the human search for meaning" (34).

5   Art Bochner, "Perspectives on Inquiry II: Theories and Stories," in M.L. Knapp & G. R. Miller, eds., *The Handbook of Interpersonal Communication,* 2d. ed. (Thousand Oaks, CA: Sage, 1994) 21–44, p. 30.

6   One of the questions I am frequently asked is what about body dissatisfaction in men? I honestly don't know the answer to that question. My research interests for the last several years have

focused on women. It does seem that with increasing attention given to men's appearance, the phenomenon of body dissatisfaction will sadly become an increasing presence in men's lives. Statistics from the Renfrew Center indicate that approximately 1 million boys suffer from eating disorders, suggesting that the phenomenon is already in progress. Renfrew Center Foundation for Eating Disorders, "Eating Disorders 101 Guide: A Summary of Issues, Statistics and Resources," published September 2002, revised October 2003, available at www.renfrew.org.

7   This concept has been discussed by a number of feminist scholars: Judith Butler, *Gender Trouble: Feminism and the Subversion of Identity* (New York: Routledge, 1990); Gloria Anzaldua, Introduction. In Gloria Anzaldua, ed., *Making Face, Making Soul: Creative and Critical Perspectives by Women of Color,* (San Francisco: Aunt Lute Foundation, 1990) xv–xxviii; Chandra Mohanty, "Cartographies of Struggle: Third World Women and the Politics of Feminism", in Chandra Mohanty, A. Russo and L. Torres, *Third World Women and the Politics of Feminism,* (Bloomington: Indiana University Press, 1991) 1–47; bell hooks, *Feminist Theory: From Margin to Center,* (Boston: South End Press, 1984); Angela Davis, *Women, Race and Class,* (New York: Vintage, 1981). As these readings strongly suggest, the crux of the problem is that women who do not fit the white, middleclass, heterosexual norm are devalued when their experiences are devalued.

8   Becky Thompson has written extensively on this topic in *A Hunger So Wide and So Deep: A Mutliracial View of Women's Eating Problems* (Minneapolis: University of Minnesota Press, 1997). See also her interview with Ophira Edut on the Adios Barbie website: www.adiosbarbie.com/features/features_becky.html.

9   I base these assumptions on the premises of Mikhail Bakhtin as interpreted by Todorov: "meaning (communication) implies community ... human existence is originally social, and cannot be reduced to its biological dimension without being deprived of those characteristics that make it human," Tzevtan Todorov, *Mikhail Bakhtin: The Dialogical Principle,* (W. Godzich, trans.) (Minneapolis: University of Minnesota Press, 1984), 30. In other words we are physical beings living within the social realm. While we are different biologically, we are similar linguistically.

10 I base my three categories on Bakhtin's three categories: primordial, social, and national. Mikhail M. Bakhtin, "Discourse in the Novel," In M. Holquist, ed., C. Emerson and M. Holquist (Trans.), *The Dialogic Imagination,* (Austin: University of Texas Press, 1981), 259–422, 275. Primordial discourses are those "amid others' utterances inside a single language." Social discourses are those "amid other social languages with a single national language." National discourses are those "amid different national discourses" within the same culture. I have changed the labels of each type to make them easier to understand.

11 This premise is based on Herbert Blumer's theory of Symbolic Interactionism, which states that all meaning is learned through interaction with others. For more information see: Herbert Blumer, "Symbolic Interaction," in *Interdisciplinary Approaches to Human Communication*, Richard D. Worth, Richard W. Budd, Brent D. Ruben, (Rochelle Park, NY: Hayden 2003), 135-153.

12 See Chapter Seven, Note 2.

13 In order to understand these connections between discourse and power, it helps to consider Foucault's discussion of the panoptic gaze. Foucault turns to the concept of the panoptic prison to help illustrate the physical and social uses of power. The panopticon is a tall tower surrounded by prison cells at its base. Inmates can see the tower but not who or if anyone is occupying it. The result is that prisoners know that they could possibly be under continual surveillance. Based on this possibility of surveillance, the prisoners learn to constantly monitor themselves and change their behavior accordingly. In other words, they internalize a surveillant gaze that may not even be there. Michel Foucault, *Discipline and Punish: The Birth of the Prison,* (New York: Vintage, 1995).

14 Angela McRobbie, *Postmodernism and Popular Culture,* (London: Routledge, 1994), 71.

Chapter One: Just look at my stomach

1 A more detailed discussion of media influences such as these can be found in "Chapter 6: She's got big boobs and she's tiny." This chapter presents an in-depth analysis of the way female bodies are portrayed in media and the impact these portrayals have on young women's body dissatisfaction.

2 Angela Trethewey, "Revisioning Control: A Feminist Critique of Disciplined Bodies," in *Rethinking Organizational and*

Managerial Communication from Feminist Perspectives, Patrice
Buzzanell, ed., (Thousand Oaks, CA: Sage, 2000),107–127.

3   Roberta Seid, *Never Too Thin: Why Women are at War with Their
Bodies* (New York: Prentice-Hall, 1989.) I would argue that Seid's
5% is even lower today, perhaps as low as 2%. Since its publication in 1989, we have seen a disturbing trend in which the thin,
ideal images of media women are becoming even thinner.

4   At 5'7" and approximately 120 pounds, Daisy is probably considered skinny by most standards.

5   This is not to say that all young women would agree. Throughout
my interviews, I have spoken to two women who felt that their
bodies were too thin. Both of them were tall and skinny. They
compared their bodies to Olive Oyl from the Popeye cartoons.
While neither of them wanted to necessarily gain weight, they
did both wish that they had more curves.

6   In this way, they negotiate meaning, a social product from
interaction with others, according to Herbert Blumer and the
Symbolic Interactionists. They take the surrounding physical
world and turn it into a symbolic world of words in order to
communicate and make sense of the world around them. For a
brief introduction to Blumer's theory of Symbolic Interactionism,
I recommend Herbert Blumer, "Symbolic Interaction," in
Interdisciplinary Approaches to Human Communication, Richard
D. Worth, Richard W. Budd, Brent D. Ruben, (Rochelle Park,
NY: Hayden 2003), 135-153. A more extended discussion can be
found in: Herbert Blumer, *Symbolic Interactionism: Perspective
and Method* (New York: Prentice Hall, 1969).

7   Marya Hornbacher, *Wasted: A Memoir of Anorexia and Bulimia*
(Harper Collins: 1999), 47.

8   A detailed discussion of anorexia and bulimia can be found in
"Chapter 2: The food is awful here."

9   I saw this same phenomenon in a number of the women I interviewed. They would start out the interview proclaiming that they
were happy in their bodies and didn't feel the need to change,
lose weight, workout, etc. However, as we continued to talk, they
slowly began sharing stories of dissatisfaction, diets, exercise,
etc. After the first few times this happened, I began asking them
why the change. The typical response was that coming into the
interview they were convinced that they were stupid or alone
in their feelings and that I would judge them harshly or think

negative thoughts about them. Once they realized that none of these things would happen, they felt comfortable enough to be fully honest about their feelings.

10 In this discussion I am focusing on the internal personal dimensions of body battles. However, often these internal struggles are turned outward into actual battles between women. This aspect of body battles will be discussed in Chapter Five: You've got to impress the girl.

11 Alexandra Robbins, *Pledged: The Secret of Sororities* (New York: Hyperion, 2005).

Chapter Two: *The food is awful here*

1 Candace Kurth, Dean D. Krahn, Karen Nairn, Adam Drewnowski, "The Severity of Dieting and Bingeing Behaviors in College Women: Interview Validation of Survey Data," *The Journal of Psychiatric Research* 29 (1995), 211–225.

2 This information is taken from the Renfrew Center Foundation for Eating Disorders, "Eating Disorders 101 Guide: A Summary of Issues, Statistics and Resources," published September 2002, revised October 2003, available at www.renfrew.org. The more common figure cited is that 8 to 10 million people suffer from eating disorders. However, this figure is an underestimate and does not account for all types of individuals and all types of eating disorders. The Renfrew Center arrived at the 24 million figure by using US Census numbers and statistics from the National Institute of Mental Health. This figure combines anorexia, bulimia, and binge eating disorders for all ages and genders.

3 This figure is derived from information gathered by the Substance Abuse and Mental Health Services Administration (SAMHSA), The Center for Mental Health Services (CMHS), offices of the US Department of Health and Human Services.

4 *Glamour,* July 2005.

5 *Cosmopolitan,* July 2005.

6 *Cosmogirl,* August 2005.

7 Information compiled from the *Publisher's Weekly* list of Bestsellers as reprinted in The Writer's Yearbook Extra (2005).

8 Leptoprin and its generic counterpart Leptopril are advertised as an "acute metabolic regulator for the significantly

overweight." According to the ads, the "casual dieter wishing to lose 5 or 10 vanity pounds" should not use them; however, since the drugs are sold through mail order there is no control over who orders them. Information compiled from A.G. Waterhouse, the manufacturer of Leptoprin. More information can be found on their website: www.leptoprin. com.

9   The CDC defines an overweight individual as an adult within a Body Mass Index (BMI) between 25 and 29.9. An obese individual is an adult with a BMI of 30 or higher.

10   The full text of the guidelines is contained with a brochure produced by the Department of Agriculture. The full text of this brochure can be accessed online at: www.health.gov/ dietaryguidelines/dga2005/document.

11   Fast food options are not exclusive to larger campuses, though. For instance, King College in Bristol, TN, a liberal arts campus of approximately 800 students hosts a Starbucks among its cafeteria offerings.

12   Mandi is referring to a McDonald's double cheeseburger value meal that includes a medium order of French fries and a soda. At the time, these meals were selling for $2.99.

13   More information can found online at: www.renfrew.org.

14   More information can be found at the ANAD website: www. anad.org.

15   This information is compiled from both the ANAD website and from the Eating Disorders Coalition, www.eatingdisorderscoalition.org.

16   It is with grave caution and care that I include these examples. One of the dangers in writing about eating disorder related behavior is that your words can be read as an instruction manual on how to be a bulimic. Knowing this, I have struggled with how much information to include so as to provide a thorough discussion. Erring on the side of caution, I have decided to include fewer details and only the most commonly known methods used to induce vomiting.

17   Hornbacher, *Wasted* (1998), 91.

18   More information can be found at Anorexia Nervosa and Associated Disorders web site, www.anad.org.

19   Lean Cuisine entrees vary in their specific nutritional content; however, most have fewer than 500 calories and fewer than 10

grams of fat. For example, the Balsamic Glazed Chicken dinner has 400 calories and 8 grams of fat. The Steak Tips Dijon
dinner has 320 calories and 8 grams of fat.

Chapter Three: I look cute today

1 From the Bureau of Economic Analysis, US Department of
   Commerce, Gross Domestic Product final report for the first
   quarter of 2005. For fiscal year 2004, clothing sales totaled
   $326.5 billion. The total GDP for the year was $11,735 billion
   with $8,229.9 in personal consumption expenditures.
2 As will become clear in the following pages, there is no uniform
   definition of what "too large" is. For some women, too large is
   a size 2, while for others it is anything in the double digits, and
   for others still it's anything designated plus size.
3 By flimsy, Diva means loose and not tight.
4 If you are the size indicated in your clothing and that size is a
   zero, then it would seem that you are saying you are nothing.
   While this proposition may seem a stretch, on another level
   it doesn't seem all that far from what is happening. For many
   women, they do feel as if they are nothing if they do not fit the
   parameters of the ideal. It would be interesting to explore this
   rhetorical flourish in greater depth.
5 For an interesting and more in-depth discussion of this phenomenon, see Joan Jacobs Brumberg's *Fasting Girls: The History of
   Anorexia Nervosa,* (New York: Vintage Books, 1988), 237–238.
6 In recent years, some manufacturers have implemented an even
   smaller size 00.
7 In addition to having a range of clothing sizes, many women
   also keep a supply of "fat clothes" for days when they are bloated
   and "skinny clothes" for times that they are a few pounds lighter.
   Many women also specifically keep clothes that are several
   smaller sizes than what they currently wear as motivation to
   lose weight.
8 Our "experiment" was not a scientific study and the "results"
   I discuss herein are not intended to present generalizable
   information.
9 For an interesting insider's look at this trend, see "Why Models
   Got so Thin," by Megan Turner, *Cosmopolitan,* August 2001,
   172–175.
10 Ladybug accentuated this remark by pushing her breasts up and

out to demonstrate the amount and type of cleavage created by the dress.

11   From the descriptions given to me by Butterfly and Angel, the suit in question was a bikini in a somewhat modest cut, similar to wearing a bra and panties.

12   *Oxford American Desk Dictionary and Thesaurus Second Edition* (New York: Berkley Books, 2001).

13   More in-depth discussions of how the term slut is attributed to women have been recently compiled by Leora Tanenbaum and Emily White. *Slut: Growing up Female with a Bad Reputation,* by Leora Tanenbaum (New York: Harper Collins, 2000) and *Fast Girls: Teenage Tribes and the Myth of the Slut,* by Emily White (New York: Penguin, 2003).

14   Lane Bryant is a popular plus-size retailer.

15   Manufacturers are arranged alphabetically.

16   Information found online at www.ashro.com, Sizing chart. Ashro sells Misses sizes up to 26. Their plus size line is called "Women's Sizes" and include the addition of a "W" after the number.

17   Information found online at www.avenue.com, Avenue Service Desk, Size charts and product guides.

18   Information found online at www.eddiebauer.com, 16W–26W Woman page. Like Ashro, Eddie Bauer distinguishes between Misses and Woman's clothes. Misses are sold up to size 22. Woman's sizes run from 16–26 with the addition of a "W" after the number.

19   Information found online at www.elisabeth.com, Elisabeth size charts.

20   Information found online at www.lanebryant.com, Frequently Asked Questions.

21   Information found online at www.llbean.com, How to Measure, Women's. L.L. Bean also distinguishes between Misses and Women's with a W. Misses sizes go up to size 20.

22   Information found online at www.roamans.com.

23   Information found online at www.sillhouettes.com, Sizing chart. In addition to adding the W designation, Silhouettes distinguishes between plus sizes and "extended sizes". Clothing sized 28 and up is in the extended category.

24   Information found online at www.sydneyscloset.com, homepage.

25 Information found online at www.ullapopken.com, Smart Fit Guide Size Chart.
26 Information found online at www.walmart.com, Women's Plus Sizes.
27 Information found online at www.chicos.com, Unique Sizing.
28 Information found online at www.junonia.com, Junonia Size Chart.
29 Information found online at www.torrid.com, Size Chart.

Chapter Four: You've gotten a little bigger
1   This phenomenon has been discussed in-depth by a number of feminist scholars. For more information see, Jean Kilbourne, *Can't Buy My Love: How Advertising Changes the Way We Think and Feel* (New York: Simon and Schuster, 2000); Susan Bordo, *Unbearable Weight: Feminism, Western Culture, and the Body* (Berkeley, CA: University of California Press, 1995); Susan Douglas, *Where the Girls Are: Growing up Female with the Mass Media* (New York: Random House, 1994). Up to date media monitoring is available through *Bitch* magazine's "Love it/Shove it" and "The Bitch List" sections.
2   An even more extreme variation of this phenomenon occurs with pregnant women whose swelling bellies are often viewed and treated as public property upon which any random stranger can place her/his hand.
3   Charles Horton Cooley, *Human Nature and the Social Order,* (New Brunswick, NJ: Transaction Publishers, 1983).
4   Sandra Lee Bartky, *Femininity and Domination: Studies in the Phenomenology of Oppression,* (New York: Routledge, 1990), 38.
5   John Bowlby, *Attachment and Loss: Vol. 1 Attachment,* (New York: Basic Books, 1969). Bowlby's theory that early attachment styles continue to influence us well into old age has been further developed by Victor Cicirelli's Life-Span Attachment Theory. A summary of this discussion can be found at; Victor Cicirelli, "Attachment Theory in Old Age: Protection of the Attached Figure," in Karl Pillemer and Kathleen McCartney, eds.,*Parent-Child Relations Throughout Life,* (Hillsdale, New Jersey: Earlbaum, 1991), 2–42.
6   For an interesting recent study of this part of the body dissatisfaction phenomenon, see; Gordon B. Forbes, Leah Adams-

Curtis, Rebecca L. Jobe, Kay B. White, Jessica Revak, Ivanka Zivcic-Becirevic, & Alessandra Pokrajac-Bulian, "Body Dissatisfaction in College Women and Their Mothers: Cohort Effects, Developmental Effects, and the Influence of Body Size, Sexism, and the Thin Body Ideal," in *Sex Roles: A Journal of Research* 53 (2005), 281–263.

7   Christine Northrup, M. D., *Mother-Daughter Wisdom: Understanding the Crucial Link Between Mothers, Daughters, and Health* (New York: Bantam, 2005).

8   Northrup, 3. Northrup also argues that childhood food experiences "set the tone for daughter's relationships to food and heath for a lifetime" (357).

9   In Chapter Nine, I explore the future of body dissatisfaction in greater depth. Included in this discussion are suggestions for ways that we can make this better future a more distinct possibility.

10   Each time that Annette made this statement, she emphasized the fact of the girl's age.

11   I later learned that Marie wore between a size 3 and a size 5.

12   In Chapter Six, the comments of college age guys will be discussed in length.

13   Marie pointed to her waist and hips while saying this.

Chapter Five: You've got to impress the girl

1   Katie clarified that her "acting" would involve dressing up as some type of animal character and entertaining the guests.

2   The movie revolves around Cady Heron who moves to a suburban Chicago school after being raised in Africa. In her new school she is confronted with psychological torture and a series of unwritten rules enforced by a group of popular girls. *Mean Girls,* Mark Waters, Director, 2004: Paramount Pictures.

3   Susan Douglas, *Where the Girls Are,* p. 17.

4   Terri L. Russ, "Body Shape(ing) Discourse: Bakhtinian Intertextuality as a Tool for Studying Discourse and Relationships. Gendered approaches to applied communication," Patrice Buzzanell, Helen Sterk, Lynn H. Turner, eds., *Gender in Applied Communication Contexts,* (Thousand Oaks, CA: Sage, 2004).

5   See page 13 of this text's introduction for further information about a surveillant social gaze. Also see Michel Foucault, *Discipline and Punish: The Birth of the Prison,* (New York:

Vintage, 1995) for discussion of the surveillant gaze via the prison model of Jeremy Bentham's panopticon.

6   This is not to imply that comments from guys are without power. Chapter Six delves into the destructive nature of such comments and how women experience them.

Chapter Six: *I like a girl with a little meat on her*

1   For many young women, being considered a lesbian is in the same category as being considered fat—something to be avoided at all costs. Even though same sex relationships are now seen in numerous pop culture venues, they are still taboo in many college environments. For example, in the Greek system—both fraternities and sororities—being gay is often considered cause to be kicked out of the organization (see Alexandra Robbins, *Pledged*, 2003).

2   Even though the majority of women I interviewed identified as heterosexual, the things that they discuss concerning guys, comments, and body dissatisfaction are not limited to the heterosexual community. A woman who struggles with body dissatisfaction and is the recipient of a negative comment like those discussed throughout this chapter will still tend to internalize the specifics of the comment. The sexual orientation of the speaker is only one factor affecting the impact of the comment.

3   Madeleine was 19 at the time of our interview. She divulged that most of her friends were 19 or 20. One friend from high school was 18 and planning on marrying one week after the end of the spring semester.

4   *Mona Lisa Smile,* Mike Newell, Director, 2003, Sony pictures.

5   Alice and her boyfriend were planning on spending spring break in Florida as part of their involvement in a campus ministry group.

6   A year or so later I heard from Claire that Alice's boyfriend did indeed propose and that they were planning on marrying before the year was over.

7   According to the National Committee on Pay Equity, the median earnings for women in 2004 were 77 cents on the dollar for the year. This represents a one cent increase from 2003. More information can be found on the National Committee of Pay Equity's website at: www.pay-equity.org/index.html.

8   Gloria Y. Gadsen, "The Male Voice in Women's Magazines,"

Gender Issues (Spring 2000), 49–57.

9   Gadsen, 56.

10   Laura Mulvey "Visual Pleasures and Narrative Cinema," *Screen 16*, no. 3 (1975): 6–18.

11   According to Freud, scopophilia is the sexual pleasure that we get from looking at others. Scopophilia involves taking other people as objects and subjecting them to a controlling gaze. Most people are scopophilic to some degree. Scopophilia should not be confused with voyeurism, in which the sole method of sexual arousal is from illicit viewing of others. Sigmund Freud, *Three Essays on Sexuality,* (New York: Basic Books Classics, 1905, 2000).

12   Mulvey, "Visual Pleasures," 11.

13   Naomi Wolf, *The Beauty Myth: How Images of Beauty are Used against Women* (New York: Harper Collin, 1991), 157.

14   Based on my discussions with women, I would argue that most, if not all, women use media images as a point of comparison to some degree . However, I don't have any statistical evidence to back this assertion up.

15   The ideal is also seen in other media venues—film, television, music videos—just about anywhere we see women, we see examples of the ideal.

16   A brief discussion of the historical development of the discourses surrounding ladyhood can be found in Chapter Eight.

17   "Ladies First: Race, Class, and the Contradictions of a Powerful Femininity," Kristen Myers, *Sociological Spectrum* 24 (2004). In this article Myers discusses the various ways that being a lady is enacted today. She additionally points out the inherently racist and sexist aspects of the way we define ladyhood.

18   Myers, 13.

19   I have heard from both men and women that many of them consider anything other than vaginal penetration to not be sex. Oral sex, anal sex, manual manipulation, mutual masturbation, and related acts are thought to be just another form of foreplay. The dangers inherent in this line of thinking are obvious. Since such behaviors are not considered to be sex, they usually occur without the safety of condoms, making the threat of pregnancy and the spread of STDs a growing concern on campuses.

20   Marie's friend was referring to the *Miss America* contest, not just the currently reigning Miss America.

21 During our conversation, Roxy mentioned that she thought the model her boyfriend was referring to was named Adrianna, possibly Adrianna Lima. However, Adrianna has brown eyes, not blue. Ana Hickmann, also Brazilian, more closely resembles Roxy's description.

22 The activities I describe in this section represent a telling example of the lived experience of the male gaze. For a more in-depth discussion of the theoretical underpinnings of the male gaze phenomenon, see Chapter Seven: She's got big boobs and she's tiny.

23 Unfortunately, as will become quickly clear in Chapter Seven, the prevalence and saturation of media ideal women makes any such dismissal temporary at best.

Chapter Seven: She's got big boobs and she's tiny

1 Karen was out of town at the time Stacie and I spoke, so I wasn't able to verify Stacie's comments with her.

2 This number is based on figures from the 2000 census. According to these census figures, each home has on average 2.4 televisions. More information can be found in the 50th Anniversary of *Wonderful World of Television* press release, March 11, 2004, reference number: CB04-FFSE.04.

3 At the end of 2005, personal computer prices had dropped dramatically. An entry level Dell desktop computer could be purchased for under $300. The Dimension B110, Dell's basic desktop computer was going for $299.00. Dell is just one of many companies that offer affordable entry level computers.

4 In my Gender and the Media class, I require students to avoid all forms of media for one week. None of them successfully make it through the entire week, and many of them experience physical signs of withdrawal during the process. On average, I lose 4-5 students who choose to drop the class rather than complete the assignment.

5 Susan Bordo, *Unbearable Weight: Feminism, Western Culture, and the Body*, (Berkeley: University of California Press, 1993, 2004).

6 Joan Jacobs Brumberg, *Fasting Girls: The History of Anorexia Nervosa*, (New York: Vintage, 1988), 35.

7 Bordo, *Unbearable Weight*, 25.

8 Kim Chernin, *The Obsession: Reflections on the Tyranny of Slenderness*, (New York: Harper Collins, 1981), 88.

9   Most studies use the phrase "body image."
10 For example see Kristen Harrison, "Television viewing, fat stereotyping, body shape standards, and eating disorder symptomatology in grade school children," *Communication Research,* 27, no. 5 (2000): 617–640. Kristen Harrison & Joanne Cantor, "The relationship between media exposure and eating disorders," *Journal of Communication,* 47, no. 1 (1997): 40–67. Sharlene Hesse-Biber, "Women, weight and eating disorders," *Women's Studies International Forum* 14, no. (1991): 173-191. Sherry L. Turner, Heather Hamilton, Meija Jacobs, Laurie M. Angood, & Deanne Hovde Dwyer, " The influence of fashion magazines on the body image satisfaction of college women: An exploratory analysis," *Adolescence,* 32, no. 127 (1997) : 603–615. All of these studies show that there does appear to be some link between exposure to media and feelings of negative body image.
11 Because of the prevalence and complexity of media in society today, I can only scratch the proverbial surface cliché of media influence in this chapter. What I highlight in the following pages are the issues and concerns that emerged from my interviews; however, they by no means represent all of the potential issues and concerns. For more detailed discussions of media influence see; Susan Bordo, *Unbearable Weight: Feminism, Western Culture, and the Body* (Berkeley: University of California. 1993, 2004), Jean Kilbourne Douglas, *Can't Buy my Love: How Advertising Changes the Way we Think and Feel* (New York: Touchstone, 1999), Naomi Wolf, *The Beauty Myth: How Images of Beauty are Used against Women* (New York: Harper Collin, 1991).
12 This concept is another variation of the women as meat concept that was discussed in Chapter Six.
13 At the time, Daisy wasn't sure which magazine cover this was. After a bit more research, it appears that the cover in question was the January 31, 2002 edition featuring No Doubt with Gwen Stefani.
14 *S1m0ne,* directed by Andrew Niccol (2002: New Line Home Video, 2003).
15 There are numerous versions of Barbie's creation. Early creation stories have Barbie modeled after the two dimensional women of paper dolls. This version is still promoted by Mattel. However, the Lili story appears to be more accurate and has never been officially denied by Mattel. According to Erica Rand, *Barbie's*

Queer Accessories, (Durham, NC: Duke University Press, 1995), 33, since the 1970s Mattel appears to have downplayed Handler's role in Barbie's creation by "obliterating her image, past and future, from the public domain."

16 An interesting example of this is found on the "Adios Barbie" website accessible at www.adiosbarbie.com. The site features a blend of Barbie trivia with healthy body image messages.

17 Kamy Cunningham, "Barbie Doll Culture and the American Waistland," *Symbolic Interaction,* 16, no. 1 (1993): 79–83. Cunningham described how at age 10, while gazing at her first Barbie, she decided that "this pneumatic creature…was what I was supposed to grow up to look like."

18 Jackson's full story can be found in her memoir, *Living Doll* (London: Trafalgar Square, 2002). Additional information about recent surgeries can be found on Jackson's website: www.cindyjackson.com.

19 Sophie Blyth, *Covershots.* This and the following descriptions are all collected from Jackson's website.

20 Katrina Tweedie, *Daily Record.*

21 Cathy Stapells, *Toronto Sun.*

22 Vicky Davidson, *Sunday Mail.*

23 Based on my discussions with women, I would argue that most, if not all, women use media images as a point of comparison to some degree. However, I don't have any statistical evidence to back this assertion up.

24 The ideal is also seen in other media venues—film, television, music videos—just about anywhere we see women, we see examples of the ideal.

25 *US Weekly,* March 19, 2001.

26 *People,* March 27, 2002.

27 *In Touch Weekly,* November 18, 2002

28 *In Touch Weekly,* January 20, 2003.

29 *Life & Style,* January 9, 2006

30 *Life & Style,* May 29, 2006

31 *Life & Style,* November 5, 2007

32 *In Touch Weekly,* January 14, 2008

33 *US Weekly,* January 14, 2008

34 *Star,* September 27, 2004

35 *Star,* May 17, 2004

36 *Star,* November 15, 2004

37   *US Weekly,* May 27, 2007
38   *In Touch Weekly,* January 7, 2008
39   *Life & Style,* November 21, 2005
40   "Jessica gains 30 pounds in 3 months!" *Life & Style,* November 21, 2005, 34-39, p. 35.
41   *Us Weekly,* May 30, 2005
42   *In Touch Weekly,* May 30, 2005
43   In the February 2006 edition of *Vanity Fair,* Lohan admitted to bulimic episodes in which she would make herself sick. ("Confessions of a Teenage Movie Queen" by Andrew Richardson). Likewise, in the June 2006 edition of *Vanity Fair,* Richie admitted to being "too thin right now" and that she is "not happy with the way I look right now." ("Nicole Weighs In" by Leslie Bennetts).
44   *Life & Style Weekly,* May 30, 2005
45   *In Touch Weekly,* August 15, 2005
46   Shows like this often present both men and women losing weight.
47   Although no longer on air, one of the most onerous plastic surgery shows was *The Swan.* The premise of the show was to take a group of "ugly duckling" women and through extreme plastic surgeries turn them into "swans." The woman judged to have undergone the greatest transformation was deemed the winning swan. According to a 2004 cover story in *People* magazine, in the show 16 women underwent a total of 151 medical procedures. ("Beautiful Dreamers" by Michelle Green and Michael A. Lipton, *People,* June, 2004).
48   *Life & Style,* March 27, 2006
49   More information about the magazine can be found on its website: www.newbeauty.com
50   Shirley is referencing the Gazelle exercise machine advertised in numerous commercials.
51   *Elle,* September, 2005 pp. 414-416

Chapter Eight: Am I really fat?

1   Barbara Ehrenreich and Deirdre English, *For Her Own Good: 150 Years of the Experts' Advice to Women,* (New York: Doubleday, 1978), 8.
2   Ehrenreich and English, *For Her Own Good,* 102.
3   The phrase "Angel in the House" has its origins in the title of Coventry Patmore's 1854 poem extolling the virtues of his ideal,

self-sacrificing Victorian wife. The phrase has since appeared extensively in work by feminist authors critiquing docile domesticity, most notably Virginia Woolf, *Professions for Women,* 1966; Sandra Gilbert and Susan Gubar, *The Madwoman in the Attic: The Woman Writer and the Nineteenth-Century Literary Imagination,* 1979; and Nel Noddings, *Women and Evil,* 1984.

4   For more information about the public/private divide and of the demands placed on working class women, see: Mary P. Ryan, *Womanhood in America: From Colonial Times to the Present.* (New York: New Viewpoints, 1975); and Carol Hymowitz and Michaele Weissman, *A History of Women in America,* (Toronto: Bantam, 1978).

5   Ehrenreich & English, *For Her Own Good,* 50.

6   Ehrenreich & English, *For Her Own Good,* 3.

7   Ehrenreich & English, *For Her Own Good,* 4.

8   Laverne is referencing the numerous exercise programs and equipment advertised by Tony Little. For more information about these items, see www.tonylittle.com

9   This is a pseudonym for Diva's teacher.

10 For more information about this phenomenon, see: Richard J. Ilkka, "Applicant Appearance and Selection Decision Making: Revitalizing Employment Interview Education," *Business Communication Quarterly,* 58, no. 3 (1995): 11-18.

11 Title VII says in part that "it shall be an unlawful employment practice for an employer to fail or refuse to hire or to discharge any individual, or otherwise to discriminate against any individual with respect to his compensation, terms, conditions, or privileges of employment, because of such individual's race, color, religion, sex, or national origin." Title VII of the Civil Rights Act of 1964, Vol. 42, section 2000e.

12 According to Jose A. Pagan and Alberto Davila in "Obesity, Occupational Attainment, and Earnings" *Social Science Quarterly* 78, no.3 (1997): 756–770, "overweight females are penalized for their obesity in the wage sector." See also, Susan S. Lang, "Overweight White Working Women Make Less Money" *Human Ecology,* March 2002, 23.

13 Ladybug's comments were made before Brittney married and started having children.

14 The film that Ladybug is referencing here is *About Schmidt,* (2002). The movie revolves around Warren Schmidt and his journey to find fulfillment after retiring and losing his wife of

42 years. The scene in question occurs while Warren is visiting his future in-laws. During the scene, Warren is resting in their hot tub when the character played by Kathy Bates gets into the tub naked. The controversy revolved around the fact that Bates is a plus-size woman doing a nude scene.

15   This statement was made by Daisy.

16   For more information see: Christiane Klapsich-Zuber, ed., *A History of Women: Silences of the Middle Ages* (Cambridge: Berkeley Press, 1992).

17   A specific example is seen in the historical case of "Emma," a poor white woman who in 1872 sued the Reverend Wood for seducing her by promise of marriage. In deciding against Emma, the court noted that "virtue in a woman was a function of gender roles and class status." Mary Francis Berry, *The Pig Farmer's Daughter and Other Tales of American Justice: Episodes of Racism and Sexism in the Courts from 1865 to the present* (New York: Alfred A. Knopf, 1999), 215.

18   This was the era of Southwest Airline's ad: Remember what it was like before Southwest Airlines? You didn't have hostesses with hotpants.

19   According to the National Committee on Pay Equity, in 2002 women earned on average 77 cents for every dollar earned by men. Over their prime working years, women will earn 38% less than men. The disparity is even greater for women of color. Black women earn on average 64 cents for every dollar, while Hispanic women earn on average 52 cents for every dollar. More information can be found at www.pay-equity.com

20   According to the 2006 annual report of the American Association of University Professors, women make up 39% of all faculty members. However, they make up only 31% of all tenured faculty and 24 % of all full professors. Martha S. West and Joan W. Curtis, *AAUP Faculty Gender Equity Indicators 2006*. The full text of the report can be found online at: www.aaup.org/AAUP/pubsres/research/geneq2006.htm.

Chapter Nine: Body image is the biggest issue women have

1   Naomi Wolf, *The Beauty Myth: How Image of Beauty are Used Against Women* (New York: Doubleday, 1991), 157.

2   For more information about these pressures see Jean Kilbourne, *Can't Buy my Love: How Advertising Changes the Way We Think*

and Feel (New York: Touchstone, 1999); Levina Clark and Marika Tiggemann, "Appearance culture in nine- to 12-year-old girls: Media and peer influences on body dissatisfaction," *Social Development* 15, no. 4, November 2006: 628-643; Helga Dittmar, Emma Halliwell, Suzanne Ive, "Does Barbie make girls want to be thin? The effect of experimental exposure to images of dolls on the body image of 5- to 8-year-old girls," *Developmental Psychology* 42, no. 3, March 2006: 283–292.

3 For more information about these pressures see Jean Kilbourne, *Can't Buy my Love: How Advertising Changes the Way We Think and Feel* (New York: Touchstone, 1999); Levina Clark and Marika Tiggemann, "Appearance culture in nine- to 12-year-old girls: Media and peer influences on body dissatisfaction," *Social Development* 15, no. 4, November 2006: 628–643; Helga Dittmar, Emma Halliwell, Suzanne Ive, "Does Barbie make girls want to be thin? The effect of experimental exposure to images of dolls on the body image of 5- to 8-year-old girls," *Developmental Psychology* 42, no. 3, March 2006: 283–292.

4 Although called "Barbie.com" the actual web address is: www.barbie.everythinggirl.com.

5 www.BarbieStyleByMe.com.

6 From what I can determine, the number is merely another decorative touch that can be used to personalize the shirt. The accompanying text simply informs you to "pick your favorite number" up to four digits.

7 Kristen Harrison, "The body electric: Thin-ideal media and eating disorders in adolescents," *Journal of Communication* 50, no. 3, 2000: 119–143, 121.

8 The likelihood of media exposure leading to an eating disorder and the type of eating disorder shows slight variations based on age and media content. What I present here is a very brief overview of Harrison's findings. Related information can also be found at: Kristen Harrison (2000), "Television viewing, fat stereotyping, body shape standards, and eating disorder symptomtology in grade school children" *Communication Research* 27, no. 5, 2000: 617–640.

9 Dianne Newmark-Sztainer, *"I'm, Like, SO Fat!": Helping Your Teen Make Healthy Choices about Eating and Exercise in a Weight-Obsessed World* (New York: Guilford Press, 2005), 5.

10 "Girls are abusing steroids too, experts say," April 26, 2005. The full text of this article can be found online at: www.msnbc.msn.

com/id/7633384/print/1/displaymode/1098.

11   Rachel Simmons, *Odd Girl Out: The Hidden Culture of Aggression in Young Girls* (New York: Harcourt, 2002).

12   Simmons, *Odd Girl Out,* 156.

13   57-year-old Carrie said this to me during an informal interview.

14   Christy Smith, "Britney Spears: Post-Baby Diet or Tummy Tuck?" *Star,* November 21, 2005, 34.

15   "The Best Post-baby Slim-Downs," *In Touch Weekly,* January 23, 2006, 40–45.

16   As reported on Cnn.com, "Americans: 60's are the new middle age."

17   For more information on the show, the official *Desperate Housewives* webpage can be found at: www.abc.go.com/primetime/desperate/index?pn=about.

18   In its most recent season, the show has added a seventh woman to the roster of regular characters.

19   Barbara Mangweth-Matzek, Claudia Ines Rupp, Armand Hausmann, Karin Assmayr, Edith Mariacher, George Kemmler, Alexandra B. Whitworth, Wilfried Biebe, "Never too old for eating disorders or body dissatisfaction: A community study of elderly women" *International Journal of Eating Disorders* 39, no. 7, November 2006.

20   I couldn't bring myself to divulge the number in the main text, but for those of you diligent enough to check the footnotes, the magic number—as of today—is most often 14 with just a smidge of 12 and 16 thrown in for good measure.

21   *Pay it Forward,* directed by Mimi Leder, (2000: Warner Brothers Pictures).

22   This is paraphrased from the lyrics of "Alice's Restaurant" as found in *The Arlo Guthrie Songbook* (New York: Amsco Music Publishing Co, 1969), 91-95.

23   Titus 2:4-5 (New King James Version)

24   There seems to be a trend in recent years to perpetuate this type of behavior. For example, actress Mo'Nique's memoir is entitled: *Skinny Women are Evil: Notes of a Big Girl in a Small-Minded World,* (2003, New York: Atria). Throughout the book, she refers to skinny women as bitches. While the behavior of many of the skinny women she knows may indeed be bitchy or otherwise mean, I hate to see this behavior extrapolated to all women of the skinny persuasion. The fact is that bitchiness tends to have

less to do with body size than with general personality. Instead of perpetuating this us versus them mentality, it seems that our time might be better spent fighting more important battles such as decreasing the pay gap between men and women.

Appendix B: Bitchin' back together
1   I am indebted to the eminent wisdom of Jaclyn Thompson, MFA for the inspiration for this activity. She graciously agreed to allow me to include it in the book.

Index

About the author and artist

Terri L. Russ is intimately familiar with the phenomenon of body dissatisfaction from years of personal experience and professional study. Terri earned a PhD at Purdue University in Communication Studies, as well as a JD from DePaul University. A former practicing attorney, she has worked with a number of community organizations involving issues pertaining to girls and women. She is an Assistant Professor in the department of Communication Studies, Dance, and Theatre at Saint Mary's College in Notre Dame, Indiana, where she continues to explore expectations for female beauty in her teaching and scholarship. Learn about Terri's writing process and upcoming projects on her blog at www.bitchinbodies.blogspot.com.

Karin E. Lekan is the visual artist responsible for the strangely empowered young women who appear throughout Bitchin' Bodies. She grew up outside of Chicago and received her BFA in Illustration from the Kansas City Art Institute in 2002. Karin's images have appeared in *Venus* magazine, and she has exhibited with the Chicago Art Brigade, Sweet N' Slow at the Elbo Room, and Monkey Business in Chicago, at the Yacko Gallery in Kansas City, Missouri, and at the Moreau Art Galleries at Saint Mary's College in Notre Dame, Indiana. Karin created her first animation *We got a brand new ocean. We got a friend inside.* as part of the exhibit *Moving through medium* at the Moreau Art Galleries. She lives and works in San Francisco, California.

Bitchin' Back: Call for Submissions

- Are you tired of bitchin' about your body?
- Are you fed up with all the stupid comments people make about women's bodies?
- Are you exasperated with always feeling the need to count calories, carbs, fat grams, sugars, and all other things food-related?
- Are you ready to change the current culture of discontent?

This is your chance to break out of the bitchin' body mold and take back your experience of your body.

In the Introduction to *Bitchin' Bodies* I discuss the story of body dissatisfaction as it is currently lived by many women. *Bitchin' Bodies* interrupts that story and opens the possibility of sending the narrative trajectory in another direction—where we are more than bodies that bitch about our bodies. There are many different ways to write this new story. **Bitchin' Back is one form of this story—a form determined and written by you.**

Bitchin' Back will comprise your stories, thoughts, and reflections. If you read *Bitchin' Bodies* and found yourself filled with thoughts and emotions that deserve to be aired, this is your opportunity. Challenge the discourses that say you have to be tall, tan, and thin to be beautiful. Let others know that you are more than your body. Stop the cycle of dissatisfaction and embrace who you are—no matter what your size. While *Bitchin' Bodies* focused on the lived experiences of young women, *Bitchin' Back* opens the discussion to men and women of all ages.

I am looking for your essays, stories, and poems about living with body dissatisfaction—good, bad, happy, sad, whatever you have to say. They can be in any format that best serves your voice—personal narrative, story, fairy tale, etc. Your essay should be no more than 2500 words and include all of your contact information—name, address, phone number, e-mail. Please send your submission to the mailing address below. If you would like your submission returned, please include a self-addressed, stamped envelope. I am also looking for original artwork related to living with body dissatisfaction. Your artwork should be submitted as a print-out, 8.5 x 11 inches, and as a digital image on CD in jpeg, tiff, or psd format, at least 8.5 x 11 inches at 300 dpi. Please send only documentation of artwork, no originals, as I cannot guarantee the safety of your materials. While I promise to carefully review and consider each submission I receive, I can't promise that all of them will be included in the final collection.

Start Takin' Back Your Bitchin' Body and send your submission to:

Terri L. Russ
Saint Mary's College
Department of Communication Studies, Dance, and Theatre
102 Moreau
Notre Dame, IN 46556

If you have questions, feel free to e-mail me at terrilruss@gmail.com.

For additional copies of
Bitchin' Bodies: young women talk about body dissatisfaction,
please order online at StepSisterPress.com. Please contact us if you would like to schedule bitchin' author appearances.
Thank you for your support.